THE NAKED IMAGE

BOOKS BY HAROLD CLURMAN

The Fervent Years
Lies Like Truth
The Naked Image

The Naked Image

OBSERVATIONS ON
THE MODERN THEATRE

by HAROLD CLURMAN

"Don't blame the mirror if your mug is crooked."
—*Russian proverb quoted by Chekhov*

"Every art contributes to the greatest art of all:
the art of living."—BERTOLT BRECHT

THE MACMILLAN COMPANY · NEW YORK
COLLIER-MACMILLAN LIMITED · LONDON

For Juleen Compton

FIRST PRINTING

The Macmillan Company, New York

Collier-Macmillan Canada Ltd., Toronto, Ontario

Library of Congress catalog card number: 66–15658

Printed in the United States of America

ACKNOWLEDGMENTS

Many of the reviews and essays included in this book
were originally published in *The Nation, The New York
Times, Texas Quarterly, Partisan Review, Show.* The
article "One Hundred Years In The American Theatre"
first appeared in *The State of The Nation,* edited by
David Boroff © Prentice-Hall, 1966 and is printed here
by permission of the publisher.

Foreword

THE reviews and essays included in this volume appeared first during the past seven years in the pages of *The Nation, Show, Partisan Review, The Texas Quarterly* and *The New York Times*. I wish to thank the editors of these periodicals for permitting me to use these pieces here.

The title of this book is indicative of its purpose. I conceive of the theatre, to quote a revered, though not sufficiently heeded, practitioner of the art, as a "mirror . . . to show the very age and body of the time his form and pressure."

This is not to be construed as a dodge for propaganda or literal realism—though neither of these terms offends or scares me. Propaganda has occasionally performed admirable services in the theatre. Everything depends on how, whose and what!

I am more concerned with principles and prejudices than with opinions—"opinions" in the sense of measuring the degree of pleasure or pain a play has caused me at the moment of my seeing it or on recollection a few hours or days later. I may change my opinion—"good," "bad," "terrible," "great" or "lousy"—on a second or third viewing or on reading the play's text. I have sometimes modified my opinions in the course of time and on further reflection. For example, my opinion of Beckett's *Endgame* (slighted in my earlier book *Lies Like Truth*) is no longer that which I held when I saw it for the first time in Paris.

What interests me most in theatre commentary of contemporary performances is the critic's attitude toward the theatre, the quality of his perception, the kind of interest he seeks to arouse, the feeling about life he communicates, the light he may shed on the world around him—his spirit. . . . But I anticipate . . .

H. C.

January, 1966

Contents

Introduction

CRITICISM IS, has been and eternally will be as bad as it possibly can be." Thus spake George Bernard Shaw, the best theatre critic in the English language in at least the past hundred years. What he meant was that critics will never satisfy everyone concerned, that they will always make horrendous "mistakes," that they are bound occasionally to cause damage, and that the degree of their benefactions will always fall under the shadow of serious doubt.

What is a critic anyway? For the reader of the daily newspaper he is one who issues bulletins in the manner of a consumers' report. He is a sort of advance man, a freeloading publicity agent charged with the duty of instructing the prospective theatregoer as to what he should or should not buy. He is to tell his readers in no uncertain terms, "I like it" or "I don't like it."

If the reader were as careful in his perusal of printed matter as he is admonished to be about his diet, he would realize that in most cases the inference contained in the declaration "I like it" is of little value, in fact, is nearly meaningless. All three words are vague!

First: who is the "I" that speaks? Why should his assertion carry any particular weight? For him to exercise any decisive influence over me, should I not take the measure of the man, learn something of his intrinsic qualifications, his human disposition, his beliefs, his personal complexion? There are critics whose most emphatic encomia fill me with misgivings.

1

Second: what does the critic mean by the word "like"? In what way does he like it? I like pretty girls and I do not particularly "like" Samuel Beckett's work; yet I do not rush to a show which boasts a cast of pretty girls (I can meet them elsewhere) but I hope never to miss a Beckett play.

Above all: what is the "it" which the critic likes or dislikes? I like candy and I like meat, but before consuming either I should be able to distinguish between the two. The primary obligation of the critic is *to define* the character of the object he is called upon to judge. The definition itself may constitute a judgment, but insofar as they are distinct from each other the definition should precede the judgment. It is perfectly proper to rave about *Barefoot in the Park* as candy, and I can well understand the critic who damns Wedekind's *The Awakening of Spring,* but I can have little respect for him if he does not recognize that it is meat. It is certainly true that one man's meat is another man's poison, but the manner and reason for the choice may characterize the man.

To put what I have said another way: the reviewer whose reaction to a play is contained in some such ejaculations as "electrifying," "inspired," "a thunderbolt," "a mighty work," "a dismal bore," may in each instance be right, but his being right does not by itself make him a critic. For these epithets only indicate effects: pleasure or displeasure. The true critic is concerned with causes, with the composition of human, social, formal substances which have produced the effect. Strictly speaking, it is not even necessary that the critic name the effect; it is imperative that he take into account the sources from which it springs. In doing this the critic is faithful to the work he treats of, while at the same time he affords the reader some idea of what manner of man the critic himself is—which is a crucial consideration.

In estimating Shaw as a critic it does not upset me that he was captious about Wilde's *The Importance of Being Earnest*—he was wrong—and that he was much more receptive to the same author's *An Ideal Husband,* a play for which I have less regard. In both cases he said things of great interest and moment; I am more impressed by him in my disagreement than I am by the critic who pronounces *Any Wednesday* a "wow"—a statement which brooks no denial.

Theatre having become a luxury commodity with us, the person in quest of entertainment demands instantaneous guidance, and the daily critic is there to supply it with the necessary dispatch. His columns tend to make the pronouncement of opinion a substitute for criticism, so that very few of his readers have any idea of what criticism really is.

Newspaper editors are not especially interested in the theatre. Their views are generally similar to that of the ordinary playgoer. There is, thus, little inquiry into the qualifications of the person who is to occupy the post of theatre critic. If he is a competent journalist, is not so eccentric in his tastes that his recommendations are likely to disappoint or offend readers, the editor is satisfied. If, in addition, the critic can wisecrack and shape his opinions into formulas as efficient as an advertising slogan, the editor is delighted. What concerns him is circulation.

The daily critic is actually responsible to no one but his newspaper. In the context of our present theatre situation the critics of at least three or four of our dailies (the columns themselves even more than the people who write them) exercise far more power than anyone desires them to—power, that is, which affects sales. The critic may himself be embarrassed by the commercial influence he exerts. He will even go so far on occasion as to disclaim that he is a critic, protesting that he is simply a reviewer, that his word is hardly more important than the next fellow's. After all, as has often been remarked, he is usually constrained to write his review immediately after the performance in less than an hour. While such defenses are largely sincere, they contain some unconscious hypocrisy. The fact remains that most of the daily reviewers mistake their opinions for criticism. They are as much in the dark on the subject as their readers.

Criticism, to paraphrase Anatole France, is the adventure of a soul (or a mind) among presumed works of art. Just as the artist seeks to communicate his experience of life through the use of its raw materials and the specific means of his art, so the critic, confronting the resultant creation, sheds a new light on it, enhances our understanding of it, and finally ends by making his own sense of life significant to his readers. At best, the critic is an artist whose point of departure is another artist's work. If he is a truly fine critic, he will make his reader something of an artist as well. It is not essential that he also make him a customer!

Let us agree that the daily reviewer is rarely a critic of this kind because, for one thing, he has no time to be. One notices, however, that he infrequently has more to say about a play after a week's reflection than he said immediately after the performance. Some reviewers do not even desire more time. They trust that the rush from playhouse to typewriter will furnish them with the impetus to convey hot-off-the-griddle reaction.

For my part, I often do not know what I really think about a play as I leave the performance. Momentary satisfactions and immediate irritations frequently warp my judgment. My thoughts and feeling become clear to me only when I read what I have written! And then, I must confess, I sometimes alter my view, in the sense that I see plays—as I do people—in many different perspectives according to time and circumstance. The critic ought to proclaim the right to change his mind, just as an art work itself changes even for its own creator. Our relation to art ought not be static; it is a very human business.

To be candid, however, let us assert that most daily reviewers are not critics because they are not richly enough endowed with sensibility, thoughtfulness, personality, knowledge of art and life or literary skill to hold our attention for much longer than it takes to read their reviews.

It should not surprise us that great theatre critics—Lessing, Hazlitt, Lewes, Shaw—and even lesser ones of the same line are rarely employed as daily reviewers because men of this rank have prejudices about which they are as explicit as possible—prejudices, moreover, which are rarely those of the casual reader. And one of the authentic critic's main purposes is to enunciate or construct an attitude toward life—if you will, a "philosophy"— and to make it as cogently relevant as possible. This must necessarily scare a newspaper editor whose publication is designed to please "everybody," that is, from 400,000 to a million readers daily.

Criticism can never be wholly objective—though the critic should keep the "object" well in view—but our basic complaint is not that certain daily reviewers are too subjective but that too often they are themselves such puny subjects.

Critics of the mass-circulation weeklies are usually men who write in the vein of the daily reviewer except in that they employ a more specialized or more "pointed" vocabulary. The men who write for the smaller (usually liberal) weeklies aim to fulfill the requirements of true criticism, though too often—as sometimes in the case of George Jean Nathan—they believe they will attain this goal by defiantly reversing the daily reviewers' coin. To thumb one's nose at Broadway values is not in itself an artistic gesture. Still there is a value in upsetting settled and stupid habits of mind.

In the monthlies and the scholarly quarterlies, criticism generally becomes aesthetic debate or exposition, frequently valuable instruments in criticism. (Aristotle's *Poetics* is the classic model for this sort of criticism.) Often this proves to be drama, rather than theatre, criticism. It is necessary to make the distinction because criticism of drama is a branch of literary criticism (though to be sure drama, like poetry and the novel, has its own laws), while the theatre critic, who must be thoroughly aware of literary values, looks upon drama as it historically came into being—as a part of, but not the whole of, the theatre, which is an art in itself. There are men of sound literary judgment who are unattuned to the theatre, just as there are cultivated folk who have little real feeling for music or the visual media. One has only to compare Max Beerbohm's essay on Duse with Shaw's corresponding piece to become aware of the difference between a brilliant commentator on the drama and a complete theatre critic.

In the introduction to my earlier collected volume of theatre reviews and essays, *Lies Like Truth* (Macmillan, 1958), I said: "My notices in the weeklies tended to be milder than those I wrote for the monthly, and I suspect that I should be more careful to be kind if I wrote for a daily."

One may well ask how this statement can be reconciled with "honesty" and high standards. "My years of work as a producer and as a director," I went on to say, "taught me many lessons about snap judgments and the dangers of a too proud or rigid dogmatism . . . I would conduct myself in criticism . . . with due regard for immediate contingencies without ever losing sight of the larger issues and aims. Do not, I tell myself, squash the small deeds of the theatre's workers, trials and errors with an Absolute."

Can a person professionally engaged in the theatre also be a reliable critic? The simplest answer is to cite—I have already indirectly done so above—the names of some of the best critics of the past who have been craftsmen and critics in their respective artistic areas—a list I might extend further to include poets, musicians and painters. But I shall once again call upon Shaw to speak for me: "I do my best to be partial, to hit out at remediable abuses rather than at accidental shortcomings, and at strong and responsible rather than at weak and helpless ones . . . A man is either a critic or not a critic . . . He cannot help himself."

I shall go further. The fact that I am engaged in active stage work does not render me either timid and indulgent or resentful, malicious and vindictive. It makes me scrupulous and responsible. I am convinced that a critic of contemporary effort owes it to his job to be responsible to everyone in the theatre: the audience, to begin with, as well as to the dramatists, actors, directors, designers. In doing this he becomes responsible to the Theatre as a whole.

George Jean Nathan once cavalierly said that he did not care if every box office in the country closed. I do care. For the closing of the box office bespeaks closing of the theatre, and this would mean that we would end by being more culturally maimed than we are with the theatre in its present deplorable state. There can be no "masterpieces" where there is no production, no routine theatre activity. Even in Elizabethan times, without a box office, no theatre; without a theatre (and inevitably many bad plays), no Shakespeare to write for it.

I would encourage playgoing. (Do not lift your brows too high; it makes you look idiotic.) I would encourage it not by rave reviews of mediocre plays, not by discovering "genius" in every promising talent, but by being wholly committed to saying, with due regard to all the complexity of the elements involved, what I feel at each theatrical occasion I am called on to attend. Such treatment, which arises from a devotion to talent howsoever modest, will arouse interest in the theatre. Making extravagant claims for entertainment which one knows will prove remunerative, with or without critical ballyhoo, depresses such interest as much as does the neglect of promising, but not yet wholly ripe, efforts. I regard the writer to whom the practical economic, social and professional aspects of the theatre are totally alien as at best a curator of the drama, not as a true critic.

As to my own "philosophy" of life and the theatre: it must become apparent with the continuity of my progress as man and critic. It is for that rather than for my incidental recommendations—when I take the trouble to make them—that I write. Just as opinions, yours are as good as mine.

Recently I was introduced to a gentleman as a person about to stage a new play. "What do you think of it?" I was asked. "It's a good play," I answered. "Ah, I notice you are careful not to say it's *great*," he remarked.

I then explained that in the history of the theatre from Aeschylus to Axelrod there were probably less than a hundred plays I would call indisputably great. Not all of Euripides, Shakespeare, Molière, Ibsen or Chekhov is great. Shaw, Pirandello, O'Neill, Brecht, Beckett, Genet are important but I hesitate to call them great.

The use of the designation, needless to say, depends on one's frame of reference. If one believes a play may retain its efficacy for, let us say, fifty years, one may reasonably call it great—though that is not the yardstick by which I measure. In contemporary American theatre criticism the word has come to signify gushing enthusiasm, similarly indicated by such a phrase as "the best play of several seasons." With us, the superlative is largely an implement of first aid to the box office.

Our theatre and its status among us are in such a sorry plight that when a reviewer labels a play "good" or "interesting," we take it to mean mediocre—hardly worth the expense of seeing it. Only a "money notice" is considered a favorable review—something having at least the force of a full-page newspaper ad. Criticism in such an atmosphere is perilously difficult. Theatre managers who complain about the reviewers do not want criticism; they want praise verging on hysterics. This generally holds true for playwrights and actors as well.

The reaction on the part of some critics to this journalistic inflation is to reverse the process: to preserve their critical chastity they assume an attitude of absolute severity. They will have nothing but the "best"; they insist on "the highest standards." One cannot be too extreme, they feel, in defense of Excellence.

Such a posture strikes me as no less false than the promiscuity of those addicted to raving about any presentation that can decently be commended at all. For while some absolute standard must be latent in the critic's mind if he is to give any play its proper place, it is not at all necessary or desirable to judge every new play on the basis of that ideal. There is even something inimical to art in such a practice.

"Masterpieces," says the poet W. H. Auden, "should be kept for High Holidays of the Spirit." That is certainly not to deny that we need organizations to keep masterpieces perennially in view. But what we must demand above all in plays is that they *speak* to us, stir us in ways which most intimately and powerfully stir our senses and our souls, penetrate to the core what is most truly alive in us. To do so plays do not have to have the stamp of universality or impeccable inspiration, or signs of top-flight genius. They have to be the consistent and persuasive expression of genuine perception, individual in origin, social in application. If Aeschylus, Shakespeare, Molière are prototypes of dramatic greatness, it must be evident that many second-third-fourth- and fifth-rate plays may also fulfill the function of usable art.

It is no special feat to determine greatness retrospectively. The critic who implies that nothing less than the absolutely first-rate will do is usually more pedant than artist. Immortality awards are best conferred by our descendants. "A 'high standard,' " said Henry James, "is an excellent thing, but we fancy it sometimes takes away more than it gives." We live more fully on what we create now than on what was created for us in the past. That is as true for audiences as for the makers and doers.

Since we are speaking of the total phenomenon of the theatre, rather than of drama alone, we must remind ourselves that masterpieces badly produced or produced at the wrong time and place cease to occupy their exalted position; in fact, they no longer serve the purposes of art. Under the proper circumstances, on the stage and in the auditorium, plays of more modest literary pretentions may excel them. I am often given to understand that Sophocles was a greater dramatist than O'Neill. I need no such instruction. It is nonetheless true that most productions of Sophocles (and of other Greek masters) have struck me as singularly empty, while certain O'Neill staged plays have impressed me deeply. To make this crushingly clear, on a recent radio program I informed the manager who sponsored both the 1964 Broadway *Hamlet* and *Beyond the Fringe* that I believed the latter contained the greater artistic value.

We have also learned that some dramatists of unquestioned stature—Goethe, Kleist, Racine, Strindberg—do not have the same impact in one country as in another, or make the impression they presumably should, even upon their own people at all times.

Talent of every kind, even small talent, must always be credited. That is particularly so of talent close to us in time and place. I do not suggest that we follow Herman Melville's injunction "Let America first praise mediocrity in her children before she praises . . . the best excellence in children of other lands." I submit, however, that a sense of the present and of presence are factors which it is unwise to overlook or underestimate. But the critical faculty does not consist only in recognizing talent; there must be also an ability to evaluate it. The American theatre is richly supplied (I almost said lousy) with talent, but too often talent not worthy enough to put to the best uses.

This raises an aspect of theatre criticism in which we are decidedly at fault. Our praise is usually the response to an effect, a register of stimulation. We applaud the person who produces the effect in an acclaim which ranges from a compliment to cleverness to the proclamation of genius. But what counts in talent is its specific gravity, its meaning, how and in what way it affects us, the human nourishment it offers us. Cyanide of potassium is tremendously effective, but it is not food.

Everything—even the damnable—must be expressed in the theatre. I cannot hold anything to be true unless tested by its opposite. I need Beckett's negations if for no other reason than that they fortify me in my affirmations. I need Genet's "decadence" to sustain my health. I embrace the madness in certain modern dramatists to find my balance. To be sure, there is authentic "far-out" writing and there is its fashionable simulacrum; it is the critic's task to distinguish between them. He must sift the stuff which composes each particular talent in relation to himself as a person representative of a certain public. "Entertainment," "good theatre," "beauty" are not enough. We must know what these virtues actually do, how they work. The critic's main job, I repeat, is not to speak of his likes or dislikes as pleasure or distaste alone, but to define as exactly as possible the nature of what he examines. It were best to do this without the use of tags intended for quotes to be read on the run.

What I have said about the judgment of texts applies equally to acting and to those other ingredients which go into the making of a play in the theatre. ("To see sad sights," Shakespeare tells us, "moves more than to hear them told/For the eye interprets to the ear . . .") Most criticism nowadays is even more meager in regard to acting, direction and design than in evaluation of the texts themselves. Merit in acting is weighed chiefly by the degree of personal appeal it exercises. The actor is rarely judged for his relevance to the play as a whole since the play's meaning to begin with is frequently unspecified. To speak to the point about acting, the critic must judge the texture and composition of the role as the player shapes it through his natural endowment and through the authority of his craft.

Perhaps critics should not be held to too-strict account for neglect or oversight in the matter of acting, direction, etc., since most acting and direction on our stage today is rarely better than competent. In such cases a consideration "in depth" becomes supererogatory when it is not pretentious. Still, even with actors as eminent as Laurence Olivier, Alfred Lunt, Paul Scofield, Jean-Louis Barrault, or with directors as accomplished as Tyrone Guthrie, Peter Brook, Orson Welles, what our critics have to say usually comes down to little more than catchphrases, a bleat of unreserved enthusiasm or regretted disapproval. In this connection I must cite a fact first called to my attention by Jacques Copeau, the actor-director who strongly influenced Louis Jouvet, Charles Dullin and a whole generation of European theatre folk from 1913 to 1941: there have been fewer *great* actors in the history of the theatre than great dramatists.

No doubt I have often made hash in my reviews and essays of many of my own prescriptions. In extenuation I can only urge that while I am not sure I agree with an admirable literary critic I heard lecture many years ago in Paris who said, "The artist has every right; a critic only obligations," I always bear it in mind.

The Playwrights

Edward Albee

The Zoo Story and Beckett's
Krapp's Last Tape, 1960

SAMUEL Beckett's *Krapp's Last Tape* and Edward Albee's *The Zoo Story* have this in common: both are studies in loneliness. Beckett's play is a sort of marginal sketch in the body of his more ambitious work; Albee's play is the introduction to what could prove to be an important talent on the American stage.

Some may consider it ironic that, whereas Beckett's far more accomplished plays—*Waiting for Godot* and *Endgame*—were generally received here with skepticism, indifference or hostility, this new, rather slight piece has been greeted with considerable sympathy. One reason for this is that Beckett's reputation and the respect shown him by many European and several American critics have grown. It is no longer easy to shrug him off. A more immediate reason for the cordiality toward *Krapp's Last Tape* is that a thread of sentimentality runs through its dismal fabric. The play's "story," moreover, is simple, realistic, unelusive.

A solitary old man sits in abject poverty doing nothing but feeding himself bananas that are hoarded in drawers like precious possessions; periodically he washes the fruit down with deep draughts of alcohol. This old man was once an author. He has among the few miserable relics of his past some copies of a book he wrote, a book which sold eighteen copies at the trade rate. "Getting popular!" he mutters.

In the half-light the old man listens to tapes upon which he once recorded events now long past. One of these tapes is a memory of love—set down when he was thirty-nine—an appar-

13

ently sincere love which for some unexplained reason never resolved itself into anything beyond its fugitive existence. The old man, absorbed and yet impatient with himself, listens to the tape, curses and mocks himself—we are not certain why—broods, possibly regrets, suppresses a sob and subsides into what is probably an endless silence.

The atmosphere of the play is grotesque, deeply bitter and yet tender. Beckett is here with something of his sardonic mutism, his mastery of concentrated dramatic image, the determination to wring the neck of his passion. The play is well acted by a young newcomer from Canada, Donald Davis.

The Zoo Story is flawed by improbabilities and perhaps needless notes to provoke, shock or outrage—comic and horrifying by turn. Yet the play gives ample evidence of genuine feeling and an intimate knowledge of certain aspects of the contemporary scene, especially of our metropolitan area. If there were not some danger of being taken too superficially, I should say that in *The Zoo Story* certain tragic and crucial factors which have contributed to produce the "beat" generation have been brilliantly dramatized.

The young man in *The Zoo Story*, who intrudes on a respectable and modest citizen sitting on a Central Park bench, is isolated in his poverty, his self-educated ignorance, his lack of background or roots, his total estrangement from society. He has no connection with anybody, but he seeks it—in vain. When he succeeds in approaching an animal or a person, it is always through a barrier of mistrust and in a tension of disgust, fear, despair. When he breaks out of the emotional insulation of his life, it is only by a violent intrusion into the complacent quiet of the mediocre citizen on the park bench; and that unoffending bystander is then forced into effecting the mad young man's suicide. To put it another way: the derelict finally achieves a consummation of connection only through death at the unwitting and horrified hands of society's "average" representative.

This story is conveyed with rude humor—very New York—a kind of squalid eloquence and a keen intuition of the humanity in people who live among us in unnoticed or shunned wretchedness. We come not only to know the pathetic and arresting central figure as well as the astonished stranger he "victimizes," but through them both we also meet the unseen but still vivid characters of a lady janitor, a Negro homosexual neighbor, a dog and other denizens in the vicinity of both the West and East Seventies of Manhattan.

The Zoo Story interested me more than any other new American play thus far this season. I hope its author has the stuff to cope with the various impediments that usually face our promising dramatists.

The play is perfectly cast. George Maharis and William Daniels give admirable performances. Maharis, as the play's interlocutor, is truthful as well as intense. His acting is both economical and gripping. He seems possessed by all the hurts, resentment and compressed hysteria of the bewildered youth we hear so much about, but who is rarely made this real in newspaper reports, editorials, sermons or fictions.

The American Dream, 1961

The importance of *The American Dream* is that it's Edward Albee's. A young playwright of genuine talent—that is, one who is not merely clever—is rare nowadays. (I hope I am wrong about this scarcity.) So everything that Albee writes should be given special attention. This should not be adulatory: it is dangerous to make "stars" of playwrights while they are in the process of growth; nor should our attention consist of slaughtering the playwright's second or third play in behalf of the hallowed first one.

The American Dream is a one-act abstract vaudeville sketch. It purports to typify the well-to-do American middle-class home in this age of automation and mechanized men and women. The excellent little set is hung with frames without pictures; the room itself has expensive furniture hideously gilded, blank prefabricated walls and above them all the Stars and Stripes—in short, no intimacy, no personality, no vibrations. Daddy, who earns the money, has had part of his gut removed and of sex there is no question. The family is childless. Grandma, who has a remnant of spunk left in her dry bones, is at once a protected and abandoned bit of household crockery—a sort of skeleton in the closet. She says all the right things at the wrong time and the wrong things at the right time. No one listens to anyone else or cares about what is said when they do listen. There is total spiritual, intellectual stasis. The child—called a "bumble" rather than a baby—once adopted by this juiceless family was smashed and dismembered by them.

Into this vacuum enters the "American dream" in the person of a tall, good-looking boy, a perfect juvenile specimen. He has no feelings, no active desires, no real ambition. Passively waiting, he is a prettily furbished shell. He is adopted by Mommy and Daddy—to undergo the same treatment as the earlier "bumble."

The play is funny and horrid, a poker-faced grotesque. It reminds one of Ionesco's one-act plays *The Bald Soprano* and *Jack* (page 83), although the Frenchman's plays are freer in their extravagance and more devastating. There is no harm in a young writer's being influenced—it is inevitable; besides, one chooses one's influence in the direction of one's sympathies. But there is a certain literalness in *The American Dream*—even at moments a flatness of writing—which makes me suspect that the French influence on Albee (Genet, Beckett, Ionesco and others) is not altogether helpful.

I mean by this that Albee's talent—as with most Americans—lies closer to realism than perhaps he knows. *The Zoo Story* (page 14) had its "symbolic" side too and was also terrifyingly humorous—as well as obliquely tender—but what abstraction there was in it arose from true observation of specific people in specific environments.

Abstraction becomes decoration when it loses touch with its roots in concrete individual experience; and the word "decoration" is just as appropriate where the abstraction is satirically fierce as where it is beguiling. So while I appreciate the comment and the bitter barbs which *The American Dream* contains, I would caution the author to stick closer to the facts of life so that his plays may remain humanly and socially relevant. For it is as easy to make a stereotype from a critical and rebellious abstraction as from a conformist one.

The cast of *The American Dream* is well chosen and ably directed by Alan Schneider.

The Death of Bessie Smith, 1961

The Death of Bessie Smith is a notably sharp piece of dramatic writing.

Bessie Smith, a famous Negro blues singer of the twenties and thirties, bled to death after a car accident in Memphis, Tennessee, because she was denied medical assistance in all of the city's white hospitals. Albee has dramatized the incident in an unusual manner. Instead of emphasizing the shameful shock of the episode he helps us understand its human sources.

One never sees Bessie. The play is focused on a nurse who is a receptionist in one of the Memphis hospitals. Her life is a tissue of fear, frustration and sadistic compensations. She loathes her semi-invalid father, whose family was once (long ago) imperiously prosperous in Dixie fashion. He is an idle, shriveled, mean man—disfigured by impotent venom and the ludicrous grimaces of racist superiority. In her own way the nurse continues the paternal pattern, for though her job is ill paid and almost menial, she cracks the whip of her "position" over a colored orderly at the hospital, a young fellow with pretentions to self-betterment. She also teases an intern at the hospital who wants her—even offers to marry her—teases him with calculated provocation without satisfying her own or his needs. In addition, she warns him against any aspirations beyond the bounds of their town's horizon. From her inner constriction and the spite that this begets she mocks and terrorizes the two men; and she does this because she is too weak to fight her way out of the impasse of her life. She insists on accepting the constraints the community imposes. Her dominance over the men embodies the environment's stranglehold on all of them. But just this power maims her as well as her victims; underneath the grinning grimness of her will she is consumed by self-abomination. It must be clear from all of this that the nurse and the others, even the death of Bessie Smith herself, are peripheral symbols pointing to a tragedy wider than that of one county or segment of our society.

The writing of the play is biting, tensely risible, euphonious— making for heightened speech which approaches stylization. It marks Albee once again as a new American playwright from whom much is to be expected.

The most aptly cast actor in the production is Harold Scott as the orderly, but Rae Allen and the others who are of a softer natural disposition play with professional authority and intelligence, though they are directed a little too "psychologically" for a play in which psychology is implicit in the incisive slashes of the dramatist's "drawing" rather than in an internal probing of mental processes. But perhaps this is only a refined quibble: the production is eminently proficient.

Who's Afraid of Virginia Woolf?, 1962

Edward Albee's *Who's Afraid of Virginia Woolf?* is packed with talent. Its significance extends beyond the moment. In its faults as well as in its merits it deserves our close attention.

It has four characters: two couples. There is hardly a plot, little so-called "action," but it moves—or rather whirls—on its own special axis. At first it seems to be a play about marital relations; as it proceeds one realizes that it aims to encompass much more. The author wants to "tell all," to say everything.

The middle-aged wife, Martha, torments her somewhat younger husband because he has failed to live up to her expectations. Her father, whom she worships, is president of a small college. Her husband might have become the head of the history department and ultimately perhaps her father's heir. But husband George is a nonconformist. He has gone no further than associate professor, which makes him a flop. She demeans him in every possible way. George hits back, and the play is structured on this mutually sadistic basis. The first cause of their conflict is the man's "business" (or career) failure.

Because they are both attracted to what may be vibrant in each other, theirs is a love-hate dance of death which they enact in typical American fashion by fun and games swamped in a sauce of strong drink. They bubble and fester with poisonous quips.

The first time we meet them they are about to entertain a new biology instructor who, at twenty-eight, has just been introduced to the academic rat race. The new instructor is a rather ordinary fellow with a forever effaced wife. We learn that he married her for her money and because of what turned out to be "hysterical pregnancy." The truth is that she is afraid of bearing a child though she wants one. Her husband treats her with conventional regard (a sort of reflexive tenderness) while he contemplates widespread adultery for gratification and advancement in college circles. George scorns his young colleague for being "functional" in his behavior, his ambition, his attitudes.

So it goes: we are in the midst of inanity, jokes and insidious mayhem. Martha rationalizes her cruelty to George on the ground that he masochistically enjoys her beatings.

Everyone is fundamentally impotent, despite persistent "sexualizing." The younger wife is constantly throwing up through gutless fear. Her light-headedness is a flight from reality. The older couple has invented a son because of an unaccountable sterility. They quarrel over the nature of the imaginary son because each pictures him as a foil against the other. There is also a hint that as a boy George at different times accidentally killed both his father and mother. Is this so? Illusion is real; "reality" may only be symbolic—either a wish or a specter of anxiety. It does not matter: these people, the author implies, represent our environment; indeed, they may even represent Western civilization!

The inferno is made very funny. The audience at any rate laughs long and loud—partly because the writing is sharp with surprise, partly because an element of recognition is involved: in laughter it hides from itself while obliquely acknowledging its resemblance to the couples on the stage. When the play turns earnestly savage or pathetic the audience feels either shattered or embarrassed—shattered because it can no longer evade the play's expression of the audience's afflictions, sins and guilts; embarrassed because there is something in the play—particularly toward the end—that is unbelievable, soft without cause. At its best, the play is comedy.

Albee is prodigiously shrewd and skillful. His dialogue is superbly virile and pliant; it also *sounds*. It is not "realistic" dialogue but a highly literate and full-bodied distillation of common American speech. Still better, Albee knows how to keep his audience almost continuously interested (despite the play's inordinate length). He can also ring changes on his theme, so that the play rarely seems static. Albee is a master craftsman.

Strangely enough, though there is no question of his sincerity, it is Albee's skill which at this point most troubles me. It is as if his already practiced hand had learned too soon to make an artful package of venom. For the overriding passion of the play is venomous. There is no reason why anger should not be dramatized. I do not object to Albee's being "morbid," for as the conspicuously healthy William James once said, "morbid-mindedness ranges over a wider scale of experience than healthy-mindedness." What I do object to in his play is that its disease has become something of a brilliant formula, as slick and automatic as a happy entertainment for the trade. The right to pessimism has to be earned within the artistic terms one sets up; the pessimism and rage of *Who's Afraid of Virginia Woolf?* are immature. Immaturity coupled with a commanding deftness is dangerous.

What justifies this criticism? The characters have no life (or texture) apart from the immediate virulence of their confined action or speech. George is intended to represent the humanist principle in the play. But what does he concretely want? What traits, aside from his cursing the life he leads, does he have? Almost none. Martha and George, we are told, love each other after all. How? That she cannot bear being loved is a psychological aside in the play, but how is her love for anything, except for her "father fixation" and some sexual dependence on George, actually embodied? What interests—even petty—do they have or share? Vividly as each personage is drawn, they all nevertheless remain flat—caricatures rather than people. Each stroke of dazzling color is superimposed on another, but no further substance accumulates. We do not actually identify with anyone except editorially. Even the nonnaturalistic figures of Beckett's plays have more extension and therefore more stature and meaning. The characters in Albee's *The Zoo Story* (page 14) and *Bessie Smith* (page 17) are more particularized.

If we see Albee, as I do, as an emerging artist, young in the sense of a seriously prolonged career, the play marks an auspicious beginning and, despite its success, not an end. In our depleted theatre it has real importance because Albee desperately wishes to cry out—manifest—his life. The end of his play—which seeks to introduce "hope" by suggesting that if his people should rid themselves of illusion (more exactly, falsity) they might achieve ripeness—is unconvincing in view of what has preceded it. Still, this ending is a gesture, one that indicates Albee's will to break through the agonizing narrowness of the play's compass.

Albee knows all he needs to know about play-making; he has still to learn something other than rejection and more than tearfulness. His play should be seen by everyone interested in our world at home, for as Albee's George says, "I can admire things I don't admire."

The production—under Alan Schneider's painstaking direction —is excellent, as is the cast. Uta Hagen, with her robust and sensuously potent *élan*, her fierce will to expression and histrionic facility, gives as Martha her most vital performance since her appearance as Blanche in *A Streetcar Named Desire*. She is an actress who should always be before us. George Grizzard is perfect in conveying the normal amusements and jitters of the mediocre man. Melinda Dillon as his debilitated spouse is appallingly as well as hilariously effective, and though I have some difficultly in accepting Arthur Hill, in the role of Martha's husband, as a tortured and malicious personality he does very well with a taxing part.

A final note: though I believe the play to be a minor work within the prospect of Albee's further development, it must for some time occupy a major position in our scene. It will therefore be done many times in different productions in many places, including Europe. Though I do not know how it is to be effected, I feel that a less naturalistic production might be envisaged. *Who's Afraid of Virginia Woolf?* verges on a certain expressionism, and a production with a touch of that sort of poetry, something not so furiously insistent on the "honesty" of the materials, might give the play some of the qualities I feel it now lacks; it might alleviate the impression of, in the author's pithy phrase, "an ugly talent."

Tiny Alice, 1965

When Edward Albee's *American Dream* (page 15) was first produced I presumed to "advise" him. Though the play was specifically American in its humor, I suggested that he eschew the abstract. After the deserved success of *Who's Afraid of Virginia Woolf?* (page 18), Albee in his latest play, *Tiny Alice,* has relapsed into abstraction.

Thirty-seven in March, Albee is still the best of our younger playwrights. Since Shaw was forty-five when Max Beerbohm chose to speak of him as "young," I do not feel it improper to refer to Albee as young and to persist in "advice." The kindest way to view *Tiny Alice* is as an honorable experiment. To be candid, the play struck me as the sort of thing a highly endowed college student might write by way of offering us a Faustian drama.

Its locale is generalized (neither England nor America), its action unreal, its speech a mixture of literate vernacular and stilted literacy. The settings (designed by William Ritman) are expensively and toweringly monumental, with a touch of the vulgarly chic. Except for the first scene, they represent the habitat of "the richest woman of the world."

I shall not discuss the plot because that might lead you to believe that I complain of its being too extravagantly symbolic or too obscure. The significance of certain details may elude one—and no harm done—but the play's intention is clear enough. It tells us that the pure person in our world is betrayed by all parties. The Church is venal, the "capitalist" heartlessly base, the "proletarian" cynical and, for all the good he may do, powerless and subservient. There remains Woman: enticing mother image and never-perfectly-to-be-possessed mate. (She may also embody the universal "Establishment.") The crisis in the pure man's life arises when, having found himself uncertain of his faith, he commits himself to a home for the mentally disturbed. Suffering from the need for tenderness and from religious anguish, he dwells in this womb of conscience to emerge after six years as a lay brother determined above all "to serve." But those who rule us—Church, the Economic Forces and Woman—bid him accept the world as it is. Being pure he cannot do so. Isolated and bereft of every hope, he must die—murdered.*

Like Picasso, who said that his pictures do not have to be "un-

---

* Mr. Albee disagrees with this interpretation. The play, he maintains, is about the confusion of illusion with reality.

derstood," only seen and felt, Albee has suggested that people need not puzzle over his symbols; they have only to relax enough to be affected by them. There is this difference, however: Picasso paintings, whatever their "meaning," are fascinating on the surface. So too are Beckett's plays, Genet's and the best of Pinter's. Their images hold us; their complexities are compact with material in which we sense substantial value even when we are unable to name the exact nature of their composition. In art, Braque once observed, "It is not the ultimate goal which is interesting but the means by which we arrive there."

The surface or fabric of *Tiny Alice* is specious. The first scene (between "capitalist" and Cardinal) has some of the comic venom of *Virginia Woolf* but—except for those exhilarated by insults aimed at the clergy—it is by no means as apt. There is a certain cunning of suspense in the play, but the clearer it becomes the less convincing it seems. Its artistic method is too generalized to wound or even to touch us. Its pathos is weak, its scorn jejune, its diction lacking in most of its author's personal flair.

I do not ask Albee to stick to realism. *The Zoo Story* (page 14) and *The Death of Bessie Smith* (page 17) are not, strictly speaking, realistic plays—nor, in fact, does *Virginia Woolf* belong in that category. But in those plays Albee's dialogue had a true eloquence, a refreshingly dry and agile muscularity because it issued from the concrete. Their vocabulary was grounded in a life Albee had intimately experienced in his environment and in his senses. In *Tiny Alice* all his artful devices leave one impassive. The only moment my interest was piqued, I confess, was in the ambiguously sexual scene when the pure one succumbs to the millionairess' naked body.

Even though the play's terms rather than their meaning are what disconcert me, something more should be said about the content. Though Albee's spirit and gifts are entirely distinct from those of such recent masters of European drama as Beckett and Genet (each of whom in turn is different from the other), there is evidence of a similar "defeatist" strain. I do not share their view of life, but I recognize the aesthetic potency of Beckett's and Genet's work. They speak with genuine originality. They are, moreover, voices revealing of our day. That is their justification and their merit. (It is also to be noted once again that their work, though divorced from realism, is composed of indelibly memorable theatre metaphors.)

We often speak of their work as "negative" or "pessimistic." In a way, however, the pessimism of *Tiny Alice* has an even greater coherence, a more thoroughgoing finality than that of the Europeans. But though it is always easier to adduce evidence for a black view of life, that is, to prove the world an intolerably damned place, than to urge us in any contrary sense, one soon discovers that the conclusions of pessimism have only a minor value. For logic and proof bear little relation to the processes and conduct of reality. The more tightly one argues the futility of our life's struggle, the more futile the point becomes. It is much too simple. Thus the importance of *Tiny Alice* diminishes as our understanding of it increases.

The play is directed by Alan Schneider, and has been cast with such admirable actors as John Gielgud, Irene Worth, William Hutt, Eric Berry and John Heffernan.

Jean Anouilh

~~~~~~~~~~~~~

The Fighting Cock, 1959

I WAS ENTERTAINED by Anouilh's *The Fighting Cock* when I saw it in Paris, but thought it rather too locally French for popular consumption in New York. As I said then, it was clever and on the whole a good evening, though it seemed disjointed.

My reaction on seeing the Broadway production is peculiar. Though my mind or *ear* convinced me that it was a play superior to anything else presented here this season—except *Heartbreak House*—I took little pleasure in it as a spectator. The production —highly praised even by those reviewers who were cool to it as a play—is bad. This surprised me because its director, Peter Brook, is perhaps the most talented of the regularly functioning English directors (Tyrone Guthrie's work is rarely to be seen in London) and did a superb job with Anouilh's *Ring Around the Moon* in London some years ago.

The Fighting Cock is Anouilh's *apologia pro vita sua*. It is an unusual apology in that Anouilh kids and admonishes himself shrewdly even more than he defends himself. The General, who is "the fighting cock" of the title—he was a "scatterbrain" in French—is a romantic, a roaring individualist, an idealist and an ass. He is explosive in denunciation of everything now happening in France (and to a Frenchman that is tantamount to saying the world). He has no faith in progress, in equalitarianism, in science as a key to wisdom. "Man has never changed," he says, "and he never will change despite what the liberal journals say. He may blow up our planet or reorganize it as he wishes, the real problems will remain as they were. One is handsome or ugly, intelligent or stupid, one has 'it' or one hasn't."

25

The General believes in true love, in fidelity, in honor, in honest work; his conduct is a long, rude protest against everything that sullies his vision of these virtues. His bitterness, he explains, is not hate, but pain. What he does not see, but what Anouilh in his dialogue with himself confesses for him, is that he has no sense of reality, that his inflexibility bores his wife, that he has little understanding of his children, that he is out of touch with everything—including the army, the Church and the conservative institutions of his day.

All this is conveyed with considerable humor of an acrid sort and with occasional moments of tenderness. Anouilh feels, as T. S. Eliot once wrote, that "there is no such thing as a lost cause. . . . We fight for lost causes so that our defeat and dismay may be the preface to our successor's victory . . . ; we fight to keep something alive rather than in the expectation that anything will triumph."

Politically speaking, Anouilh is an anarchist of the Right, which is hardly any kind of politics. His dogged romanticism is breached. His misgivings and hurt create cynicism, sentimentality, laughter and cunning. Most French intellectuals hold him in contempt; he is, nonetheless, one of the ablest dramatists alive.

The type represented by the General is almost nonexistent in our country. Our reactionaries believe in exactly the kind of mechanical progress the General despises. The little "underground" movement he tries vainly to form to rid the world of its "maggots" does not resemble any of the subversive leagues we know. The absurdity of the French breed Anouilh depicts is almost charming in its parochialism. I do not believe our audience can identify itself (even in opposition) with this aspect of the play.

The worst of *The Fighting Cock* is that its production has been meaninglessly stylized. The cast—including such a persuasive actor as Rex Harrison—is made to disport itself with little relation to any concrete reality, so that the actors are prevented from striking a recognizable chord even in terms of caricature. There is shouting and some cute stage business, but no atmosphere or idea is established. It is as if a group of separate masks were strung on a cord and we had only the vaguest notion how or why they all came to be hanging there.

Anouilh is not a realistic playwright, but one can still make a coherent whole out of his world with its own truth and its own communicative values. Most of the actors in this production are English, but they do not seem English and they are certainly not convincing as Frenchmen. They remain actors—impelled by the whim of a willful director who did not see the play as something to be said but as a series of scenes that were to be displayed as tricks. Very few of them come off, so that this play of quality ends as more or less a dud.

Becket, 1960

When I saw Jean Anouilh's *Becket* in Paris last spring and was asked by a French friend my opinion of it, I ruffled him by saying I thought it amusing. What? "Amusing!" This play which some Parisian critics called "a tragedy of friendship," while others emphasized the exalted note in Becket's defense of the "honor of God" against the demands of Henry II, who argues reasons of state. In its New York version I should say of *Becket,* being kind, that it is a virtuous play for adults.

The explanation for these adjectives and description is that the play has little real intellectual, historical or moral substance, but is rather a sometimes clever recounting of events loosely culled from popular biographies. Henry II is shown as a lusty, good-natured oaf who is learning "things"; Becket as a worldling who, given the job of protecting the interests of the Church, finds it his gentlemanly duty to fight his former friend, who wishes nothing to stand in the way of his selfish desires. In other words, Becket's acts are prompted by a high sense of courtesy rather than by motives of religious faith. And there is no hint that Henry II laid the foundations of the basic English legal system. One perceives no real conflict of principle, no true definition of issues.

There are, however, quite a number of bright lines that reveal Anouilh's sophistication—quips and sallies on a variety of topics relating to politics, the Church, saintliness, that constitute the coin of conversation among intelligent grown-ups. But nothing is truly probed or revealed; no single creative idea or sentiment emerges. What is displayed is a shrewd employment of adult subject matter for purposes of facile entertainment on the educated level of the French theatregoer.

The Paris production—perhaps because it was more modest—was more fluent and more fun than this one. If Laurence Olivier were not the very famous actor he is, I should not notice his portrayal of Becket, apart from listing the actor's permanent attributes: a fine voice, an impressive presence—both debonair and sad—a capacity to read lines beautifully. Anthony Quinn, also a good actor, serves honorably as Henry II without contributing to any style or meaning the play might have. Generally speaking, the production never seems to get off the ground.

Becket, 1961

Readers may have noticed that I frequently omit discussion or appraisal of actors from my notices. In view of my belief that acting is the crucial ingredient of the theatre as theatre, my failure to comment on the acting of many of the plays I see must seem peculiar.

The reason for this contradiction is that in most productions the acting is reasonably competent rather than creative. The actors—usually chosen because they physically approximate the characters the dramatists may have had in mind and because they have formerly proved some ability—illustrate the play acceptably, lend it body. In these circumstances the play presents the actors instead of the actors making the play.

It is not always the actors' fault that they commonly serve chiefly as attractive mouthpieces and models for the dramatist's text. The conditions of theatrical production on Broadway and in the commercial theatre generally are not conducive to creation. The director—even when he is an artist—also is burdened by limitations which make it difficult for him to lead the actor toward creative goals.

There can be little pleasure or gain to the reader of a review to be told that an actor is "O.K." or "will do"—which is how one feels about most performances. Nor does it serve any purpose to make the actor bear the brunt of sharp criticism when he is an actor of middling stamp, chosen for the wrong reasons, directed by a harassed gentleman who is required to deliver a "smash" within three and a half weeks for an audience with few considered standards.

We may learn something about acting, and the critic may usefully spend time discussing it, when the performance is very fine or when a splendid actor fails to act well. This latter is the case of Laurence Olivier as Henry II in Anouilh's *Becket*.

In the first place, the return engagement of this play is something to be studied. Despite a generally enthusiastic press and more or less packed houses, the original (New York) production —with Anthony Quinn as Henry II and Olivier as Becket—lost an estimated $100,000. Olivier generously undertook to do the play on the road to help the producer recoup some of his losses. The actor would also have the opportunity to play Henry, the more colorful of the two leading roles. On the road the show did enormous business; Sir Laurence won great acclaim. The second batch of notices in New York have been ecstatic and the three-week engagement is a sellout.

The first thing which must strike the most casual eye is that the production now seems shopworn: even the scenery looks shabby. The original director, Peter Glenville, could not have supervised the present proceedings—or if he did, he must have been listless or powerless. I suspect that a stage manager was nominally in charge while the star "arranged" his own interpretation.

Arrangement is the proper word, because Olivier's Henry is a congeries of characteristics or playing points rather than a unified portrayal. Leaving aside the harsh fact that Olivier may be too old for the role—the play is in some measure the story of two young comrades—Olivier has no conception of Henry as a person because he sees him only as a fat part, a series of acting opportunities. Because he is brilliantly endowed, because he speaks beautifully, moves beautifully and has a thorough command of the stage, Olivier enacts some of the part's "moments" with impressive power; but, for lack of direction or thought, he enacts them without much finesse. Here he is coy, there he is fierce, now he is devilish, again he is hysterical. None of these turns are genuine (they are often transparent tricks) because they are not related to a center of meaning.

Anouilh's Henry is a naïve, healthy, natural, instinctive "peasant" with the capacity to grow in understanding. He loves Becket, in whom he beholds the perfection of his own best qualities—a high liver with the education and sophistication of an intelligent and disciplined worldling. Henry's personality is deeply rooted in what we think of as normal. He is innocently and savagely sensuous, he is trusting though wary, he is not at all stupid, he is curious and he is brave. He wants to rule, and despite the impediments of his average selfishness he will become a man of considerable stature. There is no element of caricature in him, for all Anouilh's temptation in the direction of buffoonery, and when he cries out in anger, frustration or pain, his agony is never that of a neurotic.

From all this, Olivier selects the elements of the most conventional comedy and outbursts of emotion (indicated through bold muscular violence and neurasthenic outcries copied from previously praised performances), all of them irrelevant to the composition and intent of the whole play. The result may make the groundlings applaud but must "make the judicious grieve."

I shall say little of Arthur Kennedy's Becket. He is a sensitive actor, but has had scant preparation (or careful guidance) for this part. His long soliloquy proves how little effect sincerity alone can have in such a play without careful training in simple dramatic *reading*.

As to the play itself, now that I have seen it three times, I cannot agree with those who maintain that it is one of Anouilh's best plays. It has many of Anouilh's virtues, as well as some of his worst faults: the Roman scene between Pope and Cardinal is atrociously vulgar.

Those who are respectful of the play on intellectual, moral or religious grounds are fooling themselves. It is intellectually (as well as historically) skimpy; of true religious sentiment there is barely a trace, and its morality is without real commitment. Instead of speaking of the "honor of God," Anouilh might more fittingly have spoken of the honor of one's job. Becket, as Chancellor, had defended Henry (that is what the head of a state is supposed to do); so, as Archbishop, Becket fights for the Church (or God) against the state, since that is what is demanded of a prince of the Church. If the play espouses a precept it is: stand for *some* principle. Perhaps even this is helpful at a time when no principles beyond success and self-interest seem to obtain.

Traveller Without Luggage, 1964

Since Jean Anouilh's *Traveller Without Luggage* has suffered, as have many other French plays in the past, in being transferred from the boulevards to Broadway, I shall not dwell on its production here. The cast includes several talented actors—Ben Gazzara, Mildred Dunnock, Rae Allen, to name only three—and there are some well-played passages, notably in the second scene, but the right tone is never found. This is largely due to the very real difficulty that confronts American actors and directors who try to realize the exact nature of French behavior. They are removed from the cultural environment of such plays, and even their earnest efforts to suggest it therefore seem like affectation in moments of comedy and ungainly "emotionalism" in more dramatic exchanges.

The text itself is interesting in several respects. Written in 1937, when its author was twenty-seven, it was his first success. Though by no means his best play, *Traveller Without Luggage* shows some of the salient features of Anouilh's personality and an attitude which were to place him in the front rank of French playwrights between the late thirties and the fifties.

Anouilh despises the world that bred him—the "wondrous time" before the First World War (1900–14), the last period of bourgeois security in France. The war was to explode many of the myths about the proverbial worth and refinement of its civilization. If there was truth in any of these myths, it could be substantiated after the war only by an acknowledgment of the moral and spiritual bankruptcy of the old bourgeoisie. And that class became the particular object of Anouilh's hatred.

The war-injured amnesiac of *Traveller Without Luggage*, attempting to recall the conditions of life from which the shock of his wound cut him off, slowly discovers the rottenness of a life that contributed in no small measure to his own wretched character. He sees himself the product of a world that was mean, egotistic, snobbish, frivolous, cruel, sex-obsessed and loveless. Venomous scorn for the wealthy French middle class (as well as for the still lingering remnants of a well-heeled aristocracy) permeates most of Anouilh's work like an acid. The only redemption for a man born of that world is to reject it utterly. In *Traveller Without Luggage,* anathematizing his past, Anouilh became a typical voice of a whole generation in a similar state of revulsion.

Anouilh—fortunately and unfortunately—has been unable to discard the luggage of the past. There is a good deal of a particular kind of French sentimentality in Anouilh's disillusionment; it has the taste of a rancid romanticism. There are also traces of a nobility whose antecedents are in an older (seventeenth-century) tradition mixed with a certain stored national experience. This produces a striking canniness (healthy in a Montaigne), which in Anouilh sometimes expresses itself as worldly wisdom and peppery humor, and sometimes as rather petty cynicism. All this is significant because the dramatist shares these traits with a very large segment of his compatriots.

Among the still serviceable things that Anouilh has inherited from the past is a sure sense of the stage. He is a consummate craftsman. Part of Anouilh's superb theatrical equipment is his ability to borrow and make new use of the staples of classic comedy—the oldest devices from Plautus through Molière to vaudeville. The surprise ending of *Traveller Without Luggage*— in which the man who in horror wishes to escape his newly recovered family, and seizes upon a new family found by "poetic" license in a little boy—is a case in point. This is in itself a telling image and it turns an acrid and not very plausible tale into something beguiling.

The most genuine facet of Anouilh is his gift for artifice. All his plays are basically fables, contrivances of brilliantly imaginative showmanship, full of surprises and fascinating sleight of hand. Whatever his intentions, they often serve fundamentally serious ends.

The critical pendulum has swung from revering Anouilh as one of the "great" dramatists of our day to dismissing him as a highly skilled cheap-Jack (Anouilh has recently taken to disclaiming any exalted artistic aim). I myself veer from admiration to distrust. There is something meretricious in Anouilh's soulfulness and aching idealism. His unmistakable adroitness, his adult shrewdness, independence, rebelliousness and corruption, mixed with the rich humanistic substance bequeathed by his country and which he seems to love with considerable resentment, make him representative of his time and place and give him an individual *face*. All this will finally be found to have value and will surely count when the overestimation of his excellence becomes as obsolete as are the too drastic denunciations of his defects.

Poor Bitos, 1964

The early career of Jean Anouilh's *Poor Bitos* is worth summarizing. When the play was first produced in Paris in 1957 it was received by a completely hostile press. Yet it was a box-office success. All Paris flocked to *hate* it. Was there an unavowed assent in this? Or had the audience come bravely prepared to face its accuser?

Apart from appreciation of Donald Pleasence in the title role (which he also plays here), the London reviewers were grudging but impressed. It is interesting to speculate as to what elements in the play caused the ambiguity of these reactions.

André Bitos occupies an important post in the public prosecutor's office of a provincial French town ten years after the last war. He is politically "Left," and had fought in the Resistance. The son of a perennially impoverished laundress, he had used his keen mind for persistent study, had been granted a scholarship and had always been first in every class. But he is physically unprepossessing and is detested by almost everyone in town—particularly by the well-to-do collaborationists, many of whom had been his schoolmates. As assistant to the public prosecutor Bitos has proved himself ruthlessly rigid in pursuit of justice. He appears obsessed by a punitive passion.

Maxime, the handsomest, most elegant, most affluent of his old-time schoolmates—a man Bitos once worshiped for the qualities he himself lacked—arranges a "wig party" to humiliate Bitos beyond healing. At this party each of the guests—Bitos' enemies and their wives—is asked to assume the role of one of the famous personages of the French Revolution: Mirabeau, Danton, Desmoulins, Louis XVI, Marie Antoinette, *et al*. They are to vent

their spleen on Bitos, who has been invited to come as Robespierre.

The guests manage to scare Bitos into insensibility. He passes
out and during his coma is riddled by images of anxiety in which
personal memories merge with distorted incidents from Robespierre's life. By the time the final curtain has come down, a parallel has been established between Bitos and his "incorruptible"
antecedent.

It is probably unimportant that Anouilh's "Robespierre" is not
in accord with the conclusions of modern French historians who
maintain the real person to have been much maligned by the
nineteenth-century image of him as a cold-hearted monster. Some
of these historians (professors in French universities) believe
Robespierre to have been politically and morally superior to
Danton and other national heroes. The point is that Anouilh has
made Bitos-Robespierre the prototype of all political tyrants—
puritanical, bigoted, filled with venomous envy, murderously
vindictive. These attributes spring from the hurt inflicted upon
him by his poverty, his gracelessness, the scorn the socially privi-
leged have heaped upon him.

In one brief instance Anouilh tries to absolve himself of animus
toward the "Red" contingent in the Resistance by having another
guest at the gathering say that he shares Bitos' political views and
despises him only because of his wretched character. Still, the
inescapable implication of Anouilh's portrait is that most Left-
oriented leaders are impelled by base motives, often kindled by
frustration and the crippling of their humane instincts.

Anouilh, however, is "impartial" in his vilifications. If he is
relentless in respect to the radicals, he is almost equally harsh
with the wealthy of the Right. They are heartless with less cause.
Those of the "Center" are more or less neglected. Anouilh probably regards them as featureless conformists who bend or turn
with every wind. Besides a kindly woman there is only one sympathetically drawn character in the play—presumably a scion of
the old nobility and therefore almost totally apolitical. One such
man Anouilh later affectionately ridiculed for his lack of realism
in *The Fighting Cock* (page 25), but in *Poor Bitos* he takes
him at his own value.

In a brief but striking passage, Bitos-Robespierre says to this
character, Vulturne-Mirabeau, something to this effect: "You are

a genius; I am second rate. I am on the side of the second rate because we are more numerous. We are France." To which the other replies: "The millions you speak of merely inhabit the country. Six hundred great men *created* France." These—the "larks," as Anouilh has called them—are the only ones who truly matter; it is they who make France (the world itself) supportable.

This is majestically false. Genius does not rise out of nothing; it represents the flower of a folk. One cannot take Anouilh seriously on this point, or believe that he takes himself seriously. But the attitude bespeaks a tendency, the subjective impulse of Anouilh's baffled spirit, which resorts, when challenged, to a disclaiming grin that signifies, "I am only a man of the theatre." About this one must remark two things: first, such men are nearly always inclined to romanticize a halcyon past and in a crisis do their utmost to avoid any kind of partisanship. Second, the pessimism to which their tension leads them is echoed by thousands of philosophically and politically frightened men everywhere who finally take refuge in some posture of comfort which usually includes this pessimism itself. This in part explains the play's fascination for so many people both in France and beyond.

Do I therefore condemn Anouilh? Not altogether. To begin with, his message is conveyed with arresting craftsmanship, and as I have often repeated, every position must find its formal expression. Then, too, this play, like almost everything Anouilh has written, is the product of a subjective urge responsive to certain objective situations. Anouilh's plays reveal an individual: they have a face—something more than his considerable theatrical guile. Anouilh does not wholly despise Bitos as a warped creature; he shares some of Bitos' suffering, though little of his courage.

Anouilh would have us pity Bitos. He hardly succeeds in this. But at least in France, where after the war the audience experienced guilt, anger, self-contempt, torn as it was by all manner of internecine conflict according to class, conviction and prior behavior, the play gripped as well as discomfited the public. The French looked bad to themselves between 1945 and 1960 and *Poor Bitos* showed them their own lesions, inspiring them with both loathing and awe.

Standing apart from all this, I find the play brilliantly despicable. I dislike and admire it! It is not only extremely skillful in construction and writing; it is, as plays go nowadays, thoroughly adult. It is worth support and attack. But I fear the greater Broadway audience will find itself indifferent.

The production, directed (as in London) by Shirley Butler, is scrupulous. I find the setting burdensomely literal. The acting though authoritative and lucid—the dialogue well spoken by generally fine voices—tends to limit itself to the verbal. C. K. Alexander brings warmth to the role of Vulturne-Mirabeau. Charles D. Gray, as Maxime, scores by his presence. Donald Pleasence should be applauded for a performance leaning heavily on details of voice, speech, idiosyncrasy of gesture, etc.—knowingly executed—all of which makes us take more interest in the actor than in poor Bitos.

James Baldwin

~~~~~~~~~~~~~~~~~~~~~~~

Blues for Mister Charlie, 1964

U NLIKE MANY reviewers and readers, I do not believe it to
be the function of criticism (even theatre criticism) to
issue stop-go orders. The critic hopes to elucidate the subject of
his discussion so that some light may be shed on the work itself
and indirectly on himself. It is the reader's business to decide
what "practical" use he will make of this process. Nevertheless, I
say that you should see James Baldwin's *Blues for Mister Charlie*.

My injunction has a special significance in this instance, for I
intend to dwell on the play's flaws even more than on its merits.
The reader usually gathers from such critical treatment that a
play need not be seen, an inference arising from the commercially
induced habit of supposing that recommended plays are more or
less "perfect" and that nothing less than perfection is worth the
price of a ticket. I recommend *Blues for Mister Charlie*, peculiarly enough, for some of its defects as much as for its positive
attributes.

The play, based on an actual event, tells of a young Southern
Negro, a minister's son, sent North to study to be a jazz musician,
but more especially sent because his father hopes that in New
York his son will be spared the terrible indignity of the colored
man's life in the South. But the boy, Richard Henry, finds New
York less liberating than loose, its freedom sufficient only to dig
pockets of corruption in the city's nameless concentration camp.
He finds release in vengeful sex bouts with white girls and ultimately in drugs.

When Richard returns to his home town he is all savage resentment. The persistent object of his rancor is Lyle Britten, a poor

white man who everyone is certain murdered a Negro whose wife Lyle had pressed into adultery. He has been tried for the crime and acquitted. (Richard Henry's mother was also presumed killed by another white man whose advances she had repulsed.) Richard Henry seeks to provoke, humiliate and possibly kill Lyle. He succeeds in the first two aims but desists from the fatal temptation of the last only to have Lyle shoot him to death. A trial follows and once again the murderer is pronounced "not guilty."

This plot, presented in somewhat novelistic or "Faulknerian" fashion, is the frame for thematic material composing a texture broad enough to suggest many of the author's thoughts on this country's interracial problems. Among the play's characters is a religious Negro who hopes to repay evil with righteous endurance, thus to alleviate the sufferings of his people. This man comes to recognize his failure. Then there is a white editor, liberal through intellectual conviction and a profound sympathy for the colored townsfolk he has befriended and among whom he once found the one true but frustrated love of his life. He wants to help all concerned but falters and satisfies neither side. There are, in addition, the town bigots, a disemboweled white clergyman, the dehydrated middle-class (white) wives and their semicastrate husbands. Standing apart from these is Lyle Britten's wife, who—though she knows herself unloved by her husband, whom she suspects of being a killer as well as a lecher with an appetite for colored flesh—cannot emerge from the morass of ignorance, fear and lies in which she and her kind are sunk.

The first act introduces the situation with furious power and narrative sweep. The second act offers details of crime-story fascination, though tension and interest tend to diminish here since we not only foresee the story's outcome and anticipate its point but have already experienced the impact of Baldwin's message. He tries to enrich the trial scene (of which the conclusion is never in doubt) through a series of interpolated soliloquies that reveal aspects of the various characters' psychic drives which he has not been able to convey through the unfolding of the plot itself. Here, for all its occasional bursts of feeling and eloquence, Mr. Baldwin's rhetoric becomes naked preachment.

The last statement must be qualified. Since we in the New York theatre audience are already convinced of the play's thesis, we demand new insights, a deeper probing than Baldwin supplies. Yet to dismiss the play on these grounds is an evasion. The fact remains that, though benevolent, perplexed and disturbed, most of us are not yet burningly aware not only of "the fire next time," but that the conflagration has already begun. It is no longer just the colored who must raise a hue and cry, but more irrepressibly, the whites. In this regard we are culpable through our sloth, timidity and in many instances through our "aestheticism." So while *Blues for Mister Charlie* may be artistically faulty, so much of its being "crude propaganda," perhaps it is just as well—since we are provided with so little "art" in the theatre and since our relation to politics is at best tenuous and flaccid—that our ears and heads be buffeted by just such propaganda.

There is an even subtler fault in the play, but it is to some degree mitigated by Baldwin's moral personality. One suspects that Baldwin's use of the present story material is in a sense perfunctory: any similar incident might have suited him as well. Subject and object have not become organic. The author's intimate self is not integral with the body of the play.

Still a Baldwin "touch" is there: Richard Henry is not a "good boy." Not only is he filled with hatred; to a considerable degree he is hateful. The whites in the trial scene all lie; so do most of the blacks. Baldwin saves his play from the special pleading which relates such stories as a conflict between vicious oppressors and innocent victims, the sort of plea for "justice" and "tolerance" that makes me want to claim in moments of exasperation the privilege of disliking the Negro as much as I do the white man! Baldwin's play never quite achieves its own poetry, but through his badly blemished characters he manages to sound a voice of some force and originality to which we are obliged, indeed compelled, to listen.

The value of the text is greatly enhanced by the excellence of the acting. Under Burgess Meredith's direction the entire cast deserves praise. This is especially true of Al Freeman, Jr., Rosetta LeNoire, Pat Hingle and Diana Sands, whose final outburst is rendered in a mighty flow with which Shakespeare should be but rarely is acted. Miss Sands' passion came close to making me accept the content of her speech, which struck me as a lyricism more forced than found.

Samuel Beckett

~~~~~~~~~~~~~

Happy Days, 1961

SAMUEL BECKETT'S *Happy Days* is a poem for the stage—a poem of despair and forbearance. It is to be seen and suffered. It is painfully lucid. But because it is a work of art, its lucidity is manifold in meaning.

There are only two characters in the play: a woman of fifty and her husband of sixty. We discover the woman sunk up to her waist in a mound of scorched grass. Her husband lives out of sight behind her in his own hole in the ground. At rare moments he emerges to read an old newspaper, a recurrent item of which he mumbles: "Wanted bright boy." At the close of the play he crawls in full evening dress toward his wife; we do not know whether he has come to visit her in "the old style"—a phrase which runs through the play like a refrain—to pay tribute to her long years of married isolation, or to put her (or himself) out of misery. They look at each other in terrible silence: she with a quizzical look of amused compassion and contempt, he with a heartrending stare of impotence, regret, bafflement. Her name is Winnie, his Willie—and one guesses that either one might have been the other, by which I mean that both add up to the idea of Mankind.

What has their life been? A kind of blank; literally, stasis. They are sustained by nothing except the ground in which they are stuck. (In Act Two the woman has sunk to her neck in the earth. "Oh earth you old extinguisher," she cries, reminding me somehow of Joyce.) Man and wife have no beliefs, faith, passion, aim or great appetite.

Winnie's life is a matter of toilet preparations and taking patent

40

medicines, the names of which she does not understand, the purpose of which is unclear. She is nevertheless an irrepressible optimist. (The play might well have been called "The Optimist.") For as she wakes to the bell which heralds the morning, she exclaims, "Another heavenly day." She looks on the bright side of everything. She dimly remembers and usually misquotes the consoling and "unforgettable" lines of old-time classics. She enjoys listening to a music box tinkling "The Merry Widow" waltz (the "old style" again), and at the very end of the play she hums the same song, with its wistful-gay plea for love. The bag in which she keeps all her treasured possessions contains, along with toothbrush, comb, scent and a little mirror, a revolver—just in case— but she never avails herself of its service.

Her husband sleeps most of the time: "marvelous gift that," she reflects. She has "no pain, hardly any pain—great thing that." When she learns the meaning of a single word ("hog"), she observes cheerily, "Hardly a day without addition to one's knowledge." A hearty soul, she asserts, "That is what I find so wonderful, that not a day goes by . . . without some blessing—in disguise."

Most of the time she takes comfort in the thought "That is what I find so wonderful . . . the way man adapts himself." Only once does she break, crying out in ringing anguish, "No, something must happen in the world, some change." But nothing does change—except that night follows day. "One can do nothing." One prays the old prayers. One still clings to the hope that there may be a meaning to life. "Someone is looking at me still. Caring for me still." One senses one's aliveness because one does not always speak to oneself. The "other" therefore exists. And for all the bleakness and waste there is the inextinguishable sense that "There always remains something. Of Everything."

The most pitiable thing in the play is its pity. Behind the irony of its grimace there is a sort of repressed tenderness. It is this tenderness that makes Beckett's defenders (he needs no defense) deny that his message is all negation. To wait and suffer, perhaps to hope and pray in the empty world, is to evince a trait of nobility, even of heroism. Beckett, it is suggested, is a religious playwright. And it is true that many religious teachers have spoken in accents similar to his.

I am inclined to believe that this line of defense does Beckett a certain disservice. It is precisely through his particular kind of pessimism that Beckett has made his special contribution—indispensable for an understanding of our time. We require solace and remedies hereafter (I do not refer to the "next world"), but at present it is right, just, proper, necessary and helpful that brave men cry bloody murder.

Beckett is the poet of a morally stagnant society. In this society fear, dismay and a sort of a stunned absentmindedness prevail in the dark of our consciousness, while a flashy, noisy, bumptious thick-headed complacency flourishes in the open. Nearly all the finer artists of our day are saying this (very few are capable of saying more than this convincingly), and in the theatre Beckett's voice has been the sharpest, the most penetrating, the most symbolic.

Do I believe that life is what Beckett says it ("perhaps") is or seems to be? Not at all. Even the bag which holds all that remains of Winnie's existence contains much more than Beckett has put there. Do I prefer Beckett's black report to Chekhov's (or even Strindberg's) sorrow? Certainly not. The agony of the old plays was dense with human experience. Why then does Beckett write as he does? Apart from the facts of individuality and personal environment, the answer may possibly be found in this notation in Paul Klee's diary of 1915: "The more horrifying this world proves (as it is these days), the more art becomes abstract."

Must we accept Beckett wholly? No; his work represents an impasse. But we must understand him. For he feels strongly and writes unerringly. Despite their bareness, his plays are not barren, and if the stage is to be a true chronicle of the times, they belong in the theatre. *Happy Days* grows on one.

Ruth White's performance is extraordinary in its concentration, variety, nuance and endurance. (The play is almost a monologue and almost an hour and a half long.) The director—Alan Schneider—has helped her model the great mass of the verbal material so that it rises to poignancy instead of degenerating to monotony.

Brendan Behan

~~~~~~~~~~~~~~~~

The Hostage, 1960

THE HOSTAGE is an improvisation in beat time. Some may see in it a comedy in a semi-Brechtian manner: songs interrupt the dramatic action, actors address the audience and comment on the proceedings. It has already been called a vaudeville, a jig, a romp and a Rabelaisian prank. The audience which is not offended by its "bad taste" (a minority, I would judge) find it grand fun. I myself enjoyed it.

In its exuberance—its blarney—*The Hostage* smacks a little of certain characteristics we find in O'Casey—or in almost any raffishly bright Irishman. It is a product of that state of mind which makes for beatniks the world over. One might say that just as America speaks through plays like *The Connection* or *The Zoo Story* (page 14), England through Harold Pinter and John Osborne, France through Ionesco, Beckett and Genet, Ireland now jibes and jokes through Brendan Behan. That is why *The Hostage* strikes a responsive chord in London, Paris and New York.

What is at bottom of nearly all this work—of different artistic nature and merit—is a sense that society today (menaced by annihilation) has no firm values, that though we may despair we actually take very little seriously. Affirmatively the motto of this "school" might well be "Be kind to little animals."

You, I and our neighbors are the little animals—some friendly and pleasant, others mischievous and noisome. There is compassion—for all these writers are good fellows—but there is little belief in man: he stands for nothing. What he claims to stand for is mostly the bunk. Hip folk know it and find great satisfaction in saying or braying it.

This in itself is not without value. In a time of confusion, double-talk, hypocrisy, thickheadness, it may be useful to cry havoc—to laugh at ourselves, to curse, to give ourselves and the world at large the raspberry. The self-mockery does not hide the hurt and disarray. *The Hostage* in its oblique, cock-eyed, drunken eloquence—"Don't muck about, don't muck about, don't muck about with the moon"—is finally a social play in the dizzy mode of 1960. It is the peeling that is coming off the walls of our decaying fortress.

Behan is a talented writer—his *Quare Fellow*, not to mention *Borstal Boy*, in the realistic vein certainly gives evidence of this. But *The Hostage* is a special kind of work. It represents the collaboration of a playwright who furnished a thin thread of plot, some dialogue, a sense of milieu (locally Irish on the one hand and "universal" spirit of the times on the other) with an acting company whose determined and gifted leader, Joan Littlewood, believes that "theatre should be crude, vulgar, simple, pathetic . . . but not genteel, not poetical"—in other words *popular*. Most of us are now spiritually dispossessed—out on the streets—so that we must be harangued from the gutter in the voice of a brashly shrewd hawker. This is not Behan's play alone, nor has Littlewood "directed" it in the ordinary sense; they have made it together. It is specifically a theatre creation.

Joan Littlewood's London Theatre Workshop troupe was born for this play, as the play was born for it. The actors make an important contribution: improvisation and the "realism" of the music hall and the hustings are successfully combined. This is true ensemble. Everyone is right; outstanding are Maxwell Shaw, Avis Bunnage, Glynn Edwards, Aubrey Morris, Patience Collier, Alfred Lynch.

Saul Bellow

~~~~~~~~~~~~~~~~~~~~~~~~

The Last Analysis, 1964

To do justice to Saul Bellow as a writer we should have to view his first play, *The Last Analysis,* in the context of his other work. One can only suggest this here, both to give the play the credit which is its due and to help explain its intrinsic shortcomings.

It is called a farce. It is more exactly an extravaganza of the unconscious. It is "serious nonsense," a crazy parable.

Its central figure, Bummidge, is an immensely popular television comic (symbol for the American artist) surrounded by parasites—family, friends, fans, colleagues, agents, touts and whores—who are both the support and destroyers of such men. Born of poor Jewish (immigrant) parents, Bummidge senses his corruption and acknowledges his guilt. He is besmirched by the slime of success and knows that he has both invited it and wallowed in it. He yearns to recover his proper being. He plans to expose himself shamelessly in a televised self-analysis before a select audience of medical men, for which he alone must pay all the expense.

The program in which Bummidge acts as both patient and doctor is conducted in the same madly incoherent manner as everything else in his professional and personal life. But he is now possessed by an unswerving determination to examine himself in every detail, no matter how soiled or ridiculous. This enacted confession and its contemplation will, he believes, lead him and those who witness it to greater understanding and to the path of self-renewal.

He renounces the profits promised him as a result of his sensa-

45

tional telecast and rids himself of everyone who will not rally to his new "cause." For he now proposes to reopen an old theatre he once appeared in (it has since been converted into a meat market —another symbol), and there to conduct a Socratic academy for other "comics" who, having given themselves in bondage to "false needs, false thoughts, false sex," seek to rediscover their better selves.

"Suppose all we fumblers and bumblers," he says, "we cranks and creeps and cripples, we proud, sniffing, ragged-assed paupers of heart and soul, sick with spite, sick with every vice, spoiled by laziness and money, suppose we look again for the manhood we were born to inherit."

That is Bellow's major theme, one to which I am most sympathetic. It is no crime that the picture of abject vulgarity and cruel filth is made so much more convincing than the moment of redemption. What is dismaying is not that the analytic minutiae of Bummidge's psyche are sordid but that they are so commonplace —even in the play's most inventive scene, where Bummidge portrays his prenatal life and his emergence from his mother's womb.

Bellow is more proficient in depicting Bummidge as a gigantic effigy than in arranging stage action so that his puppet can move in a consistently sustained manner. Even figures of fancy must be endowed with a credible identity outside the author's consciousness. But Bummidge is a figment of verbiage. His progress through the world imagined for him does not have its own logic, a truly dramatic existence. It is chiefly in this respect that *The Last Analysis* is not a fulfilled play.

Still, there are passages that attain a horrendously hilarious eloquence, that proclaim the genuine writer and the promise of a playwright. The eloquence is a language of sophisticated literacy blended with a parody of the gibberish of our most potent media of publicity. As spoken prose—if not as true dialogue—*The Last Analysis* occasionally takes on a vigor that buzzes our nerves and assumes even more meaning than the play's ostensible message. It provides the creative vein of the evening.

All might have been saved if the production had a style. Granted that a stage style for such a play is not readily achieved, what we see is a hodgepodge that shifts from an attempt at vaudeville exaggeration—badly accomplished—to a prosaic "sincerity." This includes a setting of cluttered and unsightly realism with hardly anything of the boisterous imagination indicated by the speech and idea of the text. Did Joseph Anthony, the director, and David Hays, the designer—both gifted men—suppose that *The Last Analysis* takes place anywhere but in the realm of the dramatist's fancy?

A concomitant damage to the production is the lack of the right Bummidge—a role possibly more taxing than any in present-day theatre. Sam Levene is an excellent actor, a brilliantly sour comedian. But his talent is essentially down to earth. The play requires an out-of-this-world comic, a Rabelaisian monster. There are only two or three such beings extant—and they are rarely available on order.

Robert Bolt

~~~~~~~~~~~

A Man for All Seasons, 1961

ROBERT BOLT's *A Man for All Seasons* is civilized entertainment. "Entertainment" in our theatre is usually associated
with frivolity. Bolt's play, a London success, is not without humor
but it is not at all frivolous. It is entertainment in the sense that it
engages our interest if we are adult enough to appreciate solid
literacy, seriousness of intent, pertinence of theme and sound
theatrical performance.

What I am saying may strike many readers as redundant. The
attributes I ascribe to Bolt's play are normally qualities which
should have wide appeal. That is unfortunately not precisely so in
our theatre nowadays. To begin with, very few such plays are
being produced. For success, our serious plays require a touch of
sensationalism, a sadistic stress, a bite in which pain induces ex-
citation. *A Man for All Seasons* is an upright and eminently substantial play. At the moment, that is saying much.

It recounts the "life" of Sir Thomas More, the lawyer, writer
and for three years Lord Chancellor to Henry VIII of England.
Henry wants to rid himself of his Queen Katharine: first, because
she has not borne an heir to the throne; second, because he is
attracted to Anne Boleyn. As the Pope will not grant an annul-
ment of his marriage, which Henry demands on the grounds that
Katharine was his brother's widow, Henry sets up a new Church
of which he, as sovereign of the land, will be the supreme head.
This Church of England will grant a divorce and permit him to
marry Anne. Henry desires More's approval because More is
known to be devout as well as honest and many of the King's
subjects have misgivings about what Henry has done and may

prove rebellious. More does not challenge the King's action; neither will he approve it.

Henry forces his administration and his clergy to consent to his command in this matter, and he presses More, whom he values, to do the same. More resists, although he never declares his reason for doing so until he is brought to the point of trial for treason. More will not betray his conscience. Inwardly he holds to the Catholic view of divorce; he does not believe that the will of King or Parliament can legally be imposed on the Church. He stands for the separation of Church and State, though in this affair it is the State which is intruding itself on the Church. He upholds the law as set forth and guaranteed by the Magna Carta. At his "fixed" trial he is pronounced guilty and condemned to death.

Bolt accomplishes two things with this historical material. He dramatizes the heroism of the man who refuses to yield to the dictates of expediency, and he exposes the common man (most of us) who fails to fight in defense of such a person as More. We avoid trouble; we want to go about our business in mediocre pursuit of our ordinary interests.

The play emphasizes the importance of the law; without it, anarchy sets in and chaos must ensue. Bolt's argument may seem weak here because law may be changed as Henry changes it. What Bolt really wishes to convey is that we must hold to moral principles despite the temptation to abandon them when they prove personally inconvenient.

It is altogether probable that Bolt does not give a fig about the play's specific dilemma but has used this instance as a means of fashioning a parable for our time—a time when men are far too frequently made to suffer for opposing official opinion and authority, and most of us remain silent because we fear reprisal. Bolt has chosen a presently noncontroversial example to raise an issue that would be highly controversial were it applied to certain contemporary problems. This makes his play at once suggestive and safe.

He employs a technique of narration and presentation influenced by Brecht. The Common Man, a character in the play, addresses the audience as an ironic commentator (or chorus) while serving as a property man—helping to set each of the scenes —and playing various subsidiary roles: More's servant, a boatman, a jailer, chairman of the jury—all typical of a common man's employment. The part is both an amusing character and a useful device admirably rendered by George Rose.

What emerges from all this, artistically speaking, is a certain probity—spare, sober, honorable. The play is a thoroughly impressive demonstration and plea.

The production under Noel Williams' direction corresponds to the play's merits. The setting is stylized for function. (It has no special pictorial distinction, only a modicum of novelty.) The acting is clear, direct, well spoken, meticulously illustrative. One is reminded of a well-established English household in which everything looks dependable, comfortable and happily stable.

Almost the entire cast—notably Leo McKern as a stubby, forceful and abrasively practical Thomas Cromwell, David Stewart as an oily and slightly fatuous Spanish Ambassador, Albert Dekker as a massively honest Duke—is altogether competent.

Exemplary of the occasion's worth is Paul Scofield's More. Scofield is the outstanding figure in the middle generation of English actors. His voice is vinegar and velvet—a certain nasal resonance giving sharp edge to a rich smoothness of tone. His face is austerely handsome, thoughtful and even in levity troubled by some secret concern. He reaches us by the force of his mental processes and purpose, the efficiency of his simple means and an ever-abiding loftiness of sentiment. He rarely flashes, he is always arresting. One feels ennobled by his presence, for it combines intelligence, humility, humane stature, without cant or pose. If there were nothing else in the production of *A Man for All Seasons*, Scofield's acting would warrant our seeing it.

Bertolt Brecht

His Achievement

THE TROUBLE with theoretical discussion in the arts—most emphatically in the theatre—is that it often turns our attention away from the work itself and leads us into a semantic maze. A flagrant example of this is much of the writing which has accompanied or preceded the production of Bertolt Brecht's plays. Many more people have discussed Brecht and his theories than have seen his plays or read his poems.

There are several reasons for this. Brecht's plays are in German and are not easily translatable. Though Brecht himself has said that his plays do not necessarily have to be produced in the manner he himself employed as a director, I have yet to see a production in any other manner which does his plays justice.

Yet these plays, whether their language is understood or not, cannot fail to make an impression. They are "different"; they look "new." Without being in the least obscure, they strike the eye as being much more "modern" than the plays by the innovators of the contemporary French theatre. Brecht's plays lend themselves to controversy of all sorts—literary, theatrical, political.

The point so admirably made and elaborated in John Willett's very useful and thoroughly sensible introduction to Brecht's work* is that the only proper way to know Brecht is to see the production of his plays in the theatre he founded (the Berliner Ensemble) or at least to read them—if possible in the original. Brecht's theoretical writing—stimulating and instructive though it be—does not convey the "feel" of what he has created.

* John Willett, *The Theatre of Bertolt Brecht: A Study From Eight Aspects* (New York, New Directions, 1959).

It was inevitable that Brecht should become the subject of every type of exegesis. For his is the only manifestation of a total theatre style (text and presentation in organic relationship) since the emergence of the Moscow Art Theatre with its climactic peak in the plays of Chekhov and the corresponding development of the so-called Stanislavsky system or Method.

The modern theatre has known such influences as those of symbolism, expressionism, constructivism—impulses and tendencies which characterize certain writers, scene designers, directors, but hardly any of which shaped themselves into a complete body of work with any permanent organ to institutionalize them on every level of stagecraft. That is why no one today speaks of an opposition between Stanislavsky and symbolism or expressionism, while there is much talk of Brecht's practice as anti-Stanislavsky.

I mention this aspect of the Brechtian phenomenon for historical reasons only; it is not really fundamental. To approach Brecht as a stage director in "opposition" to the teachings of Stanislavsky is as critically bright as to point out that Brecht wrote plays that do not resemble Chekhov's. The Stanislavsky method—as distinguished from the nature of his productions—is not a style and does not by itself lead to a particular style. It is a craft technique of instruction for actors. Brecht's style is intimately related to what he had to say and is the mark of his contribution as an artist.

Brecht's plays are picaresque, poetic narrations for the stage. They are based on brief episodes of concentrated action—most of them almost complete in themselves—each of which makes a simple sharp point essential to the understanding of the play's idea as a whole. The intellectual approach is tersely factual, the tone ironic, crisp and detached. Songs in a similar vein embody the ideological point as in an epigram. The aim is frankly didactic. One play tells us that war debases everything and everyone, even those who seem to be outside its antagonisms. Another play tells us that it is virtually impossible to "do good" in a corrupt society. These are morality plays as certainly as anything ever written in the Middle Ages in behalf of the Church.

If you read Brechtian manuals you will learn that Brecht espoused the aesthetics of the Chinese and Japanese theatres rather than the Aristotelian aesthetic. You will learn that Brecht eschews "suspense," that his dramatic goal is not excitement but understanding. He wants his audience, it is said, to recognize its place in society and how it (the audience) can help change that society. He tries to induce in the spectator the attitude of an alert observer rather than that of a hypnotized person who seeks to be swept away by the show. He wants his public to use its critical judgment and ultimately its capacity to act, rather than to be drugged or overwhelmed by a suffused emotionalism which can have no effect on its thought patterns and social behavior.

All this may be interesting, but if not perceived through the plays themselves it is actually misleading. For the fact is that these plays with their somewhat ribald humor—part folk canniness and part twentieth-century sophistication—their starkly naïve "stories," their rude simplicity, their dry, yet poignant songs —witty homilies or grave and austere preachments—inspire a sense of nobility, a kind of humane asceticism which is cleansing and elevating. The spareness of the plays is sinewy; their slightly astringent timbre which might easily be mistaken for cynicism is invigorating; their pathos—and they have a pathos at times bordering on sentimentality—is classically serene.

What about the antiemotionalism of Brecht's *esthetique?* It exists chiefly there. Emphasis on it was made by Brecht himself both to purify the hysterical atmosphere which choked the German expressionist theatre and to counteract the orotundity and stomachic stress of "traditional" German acting. Just as there is as much "emotion" in the Parthenon as in Chartres Cathedral, as much in Stravinsky as in Tschaikowsky, so there are very few contemporary plays which provoke as much "emotion" as Brecht's masterpiece *Mother Courage*. To define the difference of "emotion" in each case is to discover the true nature of each particular work.

The artist does what he is, he makes what he can. Brecht's productions are what they are because they constitute the visible, palpable form of what he has written. Because he found the appropriate delivery, lighting, stage design for what he had to say, he was a great master, just as the Moscow Art Theatre in its day achieved mastery by finding the right stage form for the Russian realists.

How confused and confusing most explanations of Brecht's

work are (including at times his own—unless they are read
chronologically and in continuity) may be judged by a quote in
John Willett's book. In criticizing the German classical stage
Brecht said, "There is little chance of hearing any genuine human
voice, and one gets the impression that life must be exactly like a
theater instead of the theater being just like life." Was Brecht
then a realist—for it is presumably the realist school which aimed
to make the theatre "just like life." In Brecht's productions we are
constantly reminded that we are in the theatre—the electrical
apparatus is exposed, the actors often address themselves directly
to the audience, mottoes are flashed on a screen, etc.—all purely
theatrical devices and certainly nonrealistic.

Such confusion arises, I repeat, when we substitute argument
over artistic terminology for actual contact with the work of art.
Brecht's theatre is theatrical theatre *and* is very real. He endeavors to avoid ecstatic, stentorian, sweating, tremulous emotionalism, *and* at the same time his work communicates an emotion as
lofty as any we know in the theatre today.

Another provocation to controversy—particularly among people barely familiar with his writing—is Brecht's politics and his
relation to Marxism, the East-West struggle, etc. For the study of
Brecht as a man this may be an indispensable vein of inquiry. For
an understanding of his plays and poems the subject is much less
significant than it is presumed to be. But before entering such a
discussion we should ask what corruption demands that an artist
be politically "correct" in his work.

There is a duality or ambivalence in Brecht's writing, a dialectic process rooted in a deep-seated skepticism—which Brecht frequently referred to as the mainspring of knowledge. Together
with this we find shrewd common sense which counterbalances
his persistent moralism. This explains why Brecht changed the
ending of his *Galileo* several times to resolve the struggle in the
protagonist's (and author's) spirit between his conviction and his
"comfort."

Telling too are the lines from one of his poems: "Oh we who
wanted to prepare the ground for friendliness cannot ourselves be
friendly." Or examine the colloquy between Galileo and his disciple who says to the master, "I have recanted but I am going to
live. Your hands are dirty, we said. You said: Better dirty than
void." And finally this:

> *You have two rival spirits*
> *Lodged in you.*
> *You have got to have two.*
> *Stay disputed, undecided!*
> *Stay a unit, stay divided!*
> *Hold to the crude one, hold to the cleaner one!*
> *Hold to the good one, hold to the obscener one!*
> *Hold them united!*[*]

No doubt Brecht was deeply influenced by Marx and was often close to (though never a member of) the Party. As with many artists of our time, "what attracted Brecht above all was the humanism of Marxist theories." Their humanism and, I would add, their activism. He could neither remain alien to these impulses nor could he accept all that their votaries did. He would not shun them entirely, for much of what the votaries did was necessary and desirable. Thus Brecht's political "indecisiveness" lends his work a good deal of its universal relevance and value. For who today is not troubled by the society we live in and, if not a coward, is anxious to take steps to alter the course of its destructive march without always being sure of the right means? If Brecht was unorthodox both from the standpoint of the communist and the anticommunist, yet deeply involved in the tension which gave rise to the Marxist movement in general, he was, as far as I am concerned, in one of the healthiest of modern traditions. That is one of the reasons I find his work more central to our times than that of T. S. Eliot, Camus, Genet, Beckett, Ionesco, *et al.*

Brecht's work has already exerted a beneficent influence on the European theatre. And even such partial and not genuinely assimilated influence as may be observed at The Theatre East and The Royal Court Theatre in London, not to speak of Charles Laughton's production of Shaw's *Major Barbara* in New York, is useful in broadening the scope of our theatre concepts and practice.

In fine, Bertolt Brecht (1898–1956) is one of the outstanding figures of the contemporary theatre and with equal certainty one of the twentieth century's most notable poets.

In the Jungle of the Cities, 1961

You should remember if you see *In the Jungle of the Cities* by Bertolt Brecht that it was written and first produced in 1923, when its author was twenty-five. The play is not a didactic piece nor an example of "epic theatre." I mention these catchwords because Brecht has been so much discussed in this country and so little seen that the easiest thing for a reviewer to do is relate whatever Brecht play is presented—especially when it is so "peculiar" a piece as *In the Jungle*—to the labels with which the German dramatist has been frequently associated.

When he wrote this (his third) play Brecht's "political knowledge," he himself has said, "was disgracefully slight." Intellectually speaking, the play might be categorized as pessimistic anarchism, but it is not really proper to speak of this play ideologically. Pessimistic anarchism is not so much a philosophy as a state of mind, a mood. In fact, it hardly bears thought: one can make poetry with it—theatre, art or music—but one cannot reason with or live by it.

Still, it would not be altogether accurate to say that the play has no social significance. What Brecht probably meant by the statement quoted above—and it is important to keep this in mind in view of his reputation—was that in the early days of his career he was not yet a Marxist nor allied with any political group or theory. But there had been a Spartacist (leftist) uprising in Germany in 1919 and everyone—particularly the young intellectuals—dwelt in its atmosphere.

In the Jungle reflects the kind of fevered and desperate climate that was lived in between 1919 and 1926 by young Germans who survived the First World War. It was an inferno of inflation, unemployment, profiteering, degradation, misery, vice and morbid ferment. (The emblem of this era is to be found in George Grosz's caricatures.) And just as someone said that, after writing *Against the Grain*, Huysmans would have had either to commit suicide or seek the grace of the Church, so a sensitive German artist at the time of Brecht's beginning seemed to have little choice except that of flight in the direction of the extreme Left or toward the abyss on the Right. The Center was weak and had little support from the masses, who suffered in depressed confusion while the European democracies wallowed in treacherous ignorance, harboring the hope that the German national abscess which produced Nazism would infect the Soviet Union only.

One of the characteristic artistic movements after the war of 1914–18 (together with expressionism in the theatre) was Dada. It was a sort of spiritual stink bomb hurled by exasperated youth at the heads of the sluggish bourgeoisie. *In the Jungle,* which quotes verbatim several passages from Rimbaud's *A Season in Hell* (a romantic forebear of the postwar rebels), is sprung on many of the impulses which motivated Dadaism.

It is useful to refer to all this in order to understand Brecht's play, which is clearly a product of its time. But the play is not to be understood literally. We must feel it as we feel (and interpret) certain "difficult" modern poems.

The plot of *In the Jungle* is strangely violent. Though it has a seemingly logical progression, it resembles a montage of disparate images and speeches which add up to nightmare. The author tells us that we are in Chicago in 1912—a wholly "mythical" Chicago —and that we are to observe an inexplicable combat between two men whose motives will never be clearly explained. One of the men, the wealthy "Mr. Schlink of Yokohama," begins by attempting to buy an opinion from a young man "from the prairie" who works in a bookshop. When the young man refuses to sell his opinion, the bookshop is wrecked by the Asiatic's criminal henchmen: "Chicago gangsters." The young man vows vengeance, but the Asiatic retaliates by bribing the young man with the gift of a prosperous lumber business! The boy takes over the enterprise and runs it in the most ruinously fraudulent manner. We are off now to a series of madly extravagant events—each of which is "simple" enough in itself, but the total meaning of which is somehow elusive.

It appears that the young man and his tormentor (who makes himself into the boy's "slave") are bound together in a sort of homosexual love-hate relationship. I am inclined to understand the play as symbolizing the struggle between capital and labor, ruler and ruled, master and vassal—seen as a hysterical poet, attracted even by what he loathes (as Brecht in those days was spellbound by the evil that permeated everything in his world), might view it. I may be entirely mistaken about this; it does not matter. What matters—apart from Schlink's suicide and the young man's "escape"—is the sense of agony the play communicates. Its world is a place of mutual and universal torture, of aloneness for each individual. Its catechism reads: "It will get worse; it will get worse; it will get worse." There are moments of Teutonic bathos, but for the most part the writing is mordantly eloquent as well as grotesquely witty.

For Brecht to become Brecht—the classicist who espoused common sense and faith in human reason—it was necessary for him to pass through this phase. The last lines of the play—"To be alone is a good thing. The chaos is used up now. It was the best time."—suggests that there was a certain purification in the poet's struggle within his own and his society's corruption. Having gone through it, he may move forward to some less damaging experience and arrive at some saner knowledge. But the chaos comes first.

To articulate such a play satisfactorily on the stage demands not only consummate craft but a cast—even an audience—attuned to the deep inner and outer turmoil the play represents. It is not to be expected that the producers and actors of The Living Theatre should possess these qualifications. Their virtue is in their ambition. And there are people in our town—more numerous than we suppose—who will be fascinated by In the Jungle, or at least happier to puzzle over it than to be lucid about the safe commodities proffered elsewhere.

A Man's A Man, 1962

A Man's A Man was written between 1924 and 1926 and was first produced in 1926, when Brecht was twenty-eight. These dates are important, for they represent Brecht on his way to The Threepenny Opera produced two years later, long before the emergence of his mature work in 1943. To put it another way, A Man's A Man reveals Brecht passing from the bitter anarchy and semi-expressionism of his first two plays to the acrid irony and distorted lyricism of the famous musical work, but still far from the lofty dispassion and semiclassicism of *Galileo* and *Mother Courage.*

Yet all of Brecht—though raw—is present in *A Man's A Man.* That is why Eric Bentley, who translated the play, was right in adapting it in the vein of Brecht's later manner. There are more songs in the present production than Brecht wrote: the others are Bentley's—and are not bad. The satiric captions we read between scenes are also by Bentley and quite Brecht-like. Since Brecht himself was an inveterate adapter who altered his texts from production to production, Bentley in his adaptation is following the master's tradition.

There is in *A Man's A Man* a certain folk naïveté: Brecht always retained a strong peasant strain. The plot of *A Man's A Man* is extravagant—a sort of Teutonic tall tale. This is sharpened by a latter-day savagery in the George Grosz manner. The vocabulary veers toward obscenity as the delivery barely suppresses a jeering anger, a shrill mockery, when it does not mount to a roar of derision. This is the voice of the disillusioned German after the First World War—a voice typical of Left and Right outrage: the personal and social despair of the German people at that time was capable of turning in either direction.

The play is about brainwashing. It is above all antimilitaristic. Brecht broadens its message by toying with time and place. It is set in 1924 but Queen Victoria still reigns. It takes place in India but its pagodas and priests are Chinese. The soldiers are British but their bellow is of Berlin.

Beneath the "propaganda," Brecht is saying something ambivalent. (There is far more ambiguity in Brecht than many who think of him as a Marxist suspect or will allow.) The key sentences in the play are these: first, the lines of the song which go "A man's a man is Mister Bertolt Brecht's contention. However that's something anyone might mention. Mister Brecht appends this item to the bill: You can do with a human being what you will"; second, the line "One man is no man."

This means that such a nice chap, the little (Irish?!) man Galy Gay, the play's central figure, under the pressure of certain circumstances can be turned into a killer. It also means that men are socially conditioned; that they have no permanent or inherent personal characteristics—that the individual alone amounts to very little. This is both an empirically justified and a terribly dangerous doctrine. If it were not for the fact that we recognize Brecht's hatred of war and imperialism, the thesis might be accepted by a Fascist. But though Brecht was ideologically an anti-individualist, he was a very independent (as well as a highly gifted) individual; therefore his work always strikes a note of skepticism and betrays symptoms of inner laceration. One phase of his writing shows him as favoring collectivism on "scientific" grounds, or for the public good; another archly, almost surreptitiously, implies that nothing is certain about man: it is possible for him to remain a man come hell and high water because of an incorruptible and unpredictable essence which makes him a man —not a machine. This is the secret and saving grace of the Brechtian temperament.

No production of *A Man's A Man* that is not German can be wholly adequate. The German audience of 1919 to 1929 created this play nearly as much as its author did. Its humor and bite, its references and its emotional bias, its color, smell and sound are unmistakably of its time and place. Among the actors of its first productions—it was revived several times before 1933—were such players as Peter Lorre and Alexander Granach, men of outstanding talent who were as emblematic of the period as the text itself.

Lacking these elements and the necessary resources for its complete theatrical realization, the production of *A Man's A Man* under John Hancock's direction is nonetheless intelligent and to the point. The use of the masklike makeups is stylistically appropriate, the music by Joseph Raposo, though without the authority of Kurt Weill, Paul Dessau or Hanns Eisler, still retains the depressed sweetness and the nasal "drag" of what has been called the Brechtian minor, strongly reminiscent to a foreign ear of the songs Marlene Dietrich made famous in the days of her debut. The production's scenic scheme also functions.

John Heffernan, who is something of a clown, manages, curiously enough, to be more convincing in the dramatic scenes that describe the anguish of a man torn between the need to preserve his identity and the weight of the forces that compel him to forgo it than he is in the comic scenes, which are, in fact, underwritten. Clifton James, Harvey Solin and Maurice Edwards also meet the production's requirements with professional aptitude.

Though not one of Brecht's wholly successful plays, *A Man's A Man* is immensely superior to our customary stage fare nowadays, so one can confidently recommend it to people interested in the theatre as expression rather than as diversion.

Mother Courage, 1963

Bertolt Brecht's *Mother Courage* is a beautiful play. Written in 1938–39 and first produced in Zurich in 1941, it is one of the peaks of dramatic writing in this century. Its production by the Berliner Ensemble in 1951 under the direction of its author and Erich Engel ranks among the truly great works of theatre art in our time. Done all over the Continent, the play is a modern classic.

I say all this at once because I wish my readers to see the play, despite the severe shortcomings of its production under Jerome Robbins' direction.

I cannot predict what an audience unfamiliar with the play will think of it now, but I hope that the New York production will not be used as evidence that Brecht is the bore which some folk through inverted snobbism (or ignorance) have recently declared him to be, and which he was in certain unfortunate American productions. My guess is that, despite present handicaps, the play still comes through to the audience with some part of its force and grandeur intact.

It requires great artistry for a modern writer to achieve pristine effectiveness and epic scope with apparently primitive means. That is what Brecht has done. There is something almost medieval, peasantlike and penetratingly poignant in the simplicity of *Mother Courage*. Brecht possesses folk canniness and mother wit, a shrewdness of vision based on intimate experience of life's basic realities. He is both skeptical and direct; his language combines the accents and vocabulary of street and stable with the purity and majestic rhythm of Martin Luther's Old Testament German. The play seems massively sculpted in wood.

Mother Courage is not "propaganda"; not an antiwar tract. It is a comic narrative that mounts to tragedy. Its central figure is a woman without a "soul," an earthbound creature astray in the miserable current of history. Virtually illiterate, Mother Courage makes a bare living, supports her three children (each the off-spring of a different father) by supplying odds and ends—brandy and belts, chickens and buttons—to the roving armies (Catholic and Protestant alike) during the Thirty Years' War in the seventeenth century. She has allegiance to no cause but survival and the care of her brood. She is a pack horse and a "profiteer" of war. She has not the dimmest idea of what all the shooting is about. Nor does she ever grow wiser, learn a lesson. But the war deprives her of everything—her goods, her children, her indomitable vitality. The only heroic and enduringly innocent person in the play is Mother Courage's daughter, who is a mute. Brecht's use of her in the play is a masterstroke.

The play opens on a note of gaiety—like the exciting, hopeful, first days of war. Mother Courage's two sturdy sons are pulling the wagon which conveys her wares and in which she and her family live. "Here's Mother Courage and her wagon!" the quartet sings. "Hey, Captain, let them come and buy! Beer by the jug! Wine by the flagon! Let your men drink before they die!" It's a lark! Slowly, very slowly over a period of twelve years, Mother Courage and her children cross Sweden, Poland, Germany. The wagon ages, diminishes and ends as a shadow of itself—still a burden to "Courage," who now all alone keeps dragging it through the wasted towns and war-torn countryside.

Much of the play is funny with harsh humor and wry wisdom. There are no villains, barely any sentiment, little pathos. No one preaches, no slogans are enunciated, and even the interpolated songs, which serve as choral comment, might be taken simply as "entertainment." All is impersonal; yet in the end we are moved and feel close to life.

The original text contains nine songs. I have the impression that several of these have been cut in New York—probably because, if they were retained, the time allowed to sing and play them might exceed twenty-four minutes and the Musicians' Union would list the production as a "musical." According to the regulations, this classification would entail the employment of twenty-four musicians at heavy cost.

My supposition strikes me as typical of the obstacles that stand in the way of a fitting production for such a play as *Mother Courage*. But there are obstacles beyond this perhaps minor one (the words of the songs—superb in the original and still admirable in Eric Bentley's translation—are imperfectly heard as they are delivered in this production.

The Brecht (Berliner) production is so intimately related to the text as to seem identical with it. (That is what I mean when I speak of "theatre art.") The actors, the direction, the sets, the props and the time allowed at the Berliner Ensemble for all these to become part of a unified fabric and meaning are what made *Mother Courage* everything I have declared it to be. Very little of this is possible in our theatre.

Anne Bancroft, who plays Mother Courage, is a charming actress with a heart-warming smile and a generous honesty of spirit. She is too contemporary, too locally urban, too young, too soft to do much more than indicate the part. (She puts on age by an obvious change of wig; the later one being much too white.) Of the land, the soil, the devastation of the world she crosses, there is hardly a trace. Most of the company is in even sorrier plight. Zohra Lampert as the mute daughter is appealing. Barbara Harris as a camp follower is an actress of exceptional gifts. Hers is the best performance, and her last scene as the gilded, disease-ridden whore turned into a puffy "colonel's lady" is, despite a note of burlesque, a treat.

The sets are simplified beyond Brecht, whose visual austerity was so artful that Parisian critics when they saw his production spoke of its several hundred shades of brown. But if Robbins wanted his sets (credited to Ming Cho Lee) bare, why did he have all sorts of journalistic photographs projected against the background to make "editorial" points where none are needed? Indeed, in view of the play's style, they are altogether pointless. A revolving stage is imperative for this play; it evokes the sweep of Mother Courage's endless trek across Europe. Pulling the wagon in circles around a stationary stage, as Anne Bancroft and the others are obliged to do, simply looks silly. The props, themselves works of art and so much part of the play's "feel" in the original production, are now Broadway routine.

The inscriptions introducing the scenes should be shown on a screen if they are to retain their fine gravity; they should not be spoken by actors with little voice or impressiveness of manner.

The idea of having all the members of the company introduce themselves by name (Anne Bancroft, Mike Kellin, Gene Wilder, *et al.*) is a parody of Brecht, whose style, while eschewing the illusionism of the naturalistic, is more *real* as well as more theatrical than most of our so-called realistic productions.

If Robbins wanted to do an original production he should really have been original; otherwise he should have remained as faithful to Brecht as materially possible. In one respect fidelity and duplication proved a mistake: while Paul Dessau's score was ideal for Brecht's words it does not blend happily with Bentley's.

For all that, and though hardly any translation can do Brecht's writing full justice, *Mother Courage* manages to remain impressive.

The Resistible Rise of Arturo Ui, 1963

The incoherence of the American theatre was oddly exemplified by the production of *Arturo Ui*. Brecht's *The Resistible Rise of Arturo Ui*, written in 1941, was never produced or published during the playwright's lifetime. It could not have been produced in Europe during the war, and he probably thought it inappropriate to the immediate postwar period. When the play was finally presented in Berlin it was directed by two of the Berliner Ensemble's younger directors. I was scarcely aware when I saw that production that its language was a parody of passages both from Goethe's *Faust* and from Schlegel's translation of Shakespeare. What was inescapable was the effect: a parable which, though blatant and madly hilarious in spots, was also full of terror, an infernal vision. A group of American and English theatre folk who saw the play with me would not allow the slightest criticism of it. To them, the production was a masterpiece, a perfect wedding of content and form.

In Warsaw, where I again saw the play, the production was even more grim; it retained hardly a trace of farcical caricature. The set appeared constructed of steel, a vise in which all the characters (and the audience) were caught. When at one point I laughed, members of the audience glared at me as if I were a Fascist or a fool. In Paris, too, the play attracted a large popular audience, not as a fun show or as an exercise in style and scenic virtuosity, but as a revelation of something the audience had experienced, something in which it had been and might still be implicated.

Why was the play produced in New York? Because the remarkable English director Tony Richardson convinced the canny producer David Merrick it might be as great a hit here as it had been in Europe—besides being very "artistic"? Because it was high time that Brecht made it on Broadway, and of all his plays this light one on a familiar theme (the rise of Hitlerism) had the most salable elements? Was this, moreover, a chance to show what that excellent actor Christopher Plummer could do with a character part?

I sat in the audience frustrated, exasperated, very nearly prostrated. In many ways Plummer's performance was brilliant. His crippled (Brooklyn-Bronx, Third Avenue) speech was accurate and funny, his voice as moldy as his diction, his body bent as if he had been living most of his life in a dank cellar. He was a wanly pathetic crumb of a man, dismally charming, almost lovable. As an isolated portrayal, the performance could inspire nothing but admiration.

There were clever directorial touches. The sets, though too spacious and placed too far back from the curtain line (so that much of the text, though shouted, was hard to hear), were drawn in cartoon fashion and were not without point. The costumes were grotesque vaudeville; the makeups were masklike, though neither funny nor macabre. The doggerel translation was agile, but failed to convey the mock-heroic associations with classic models which justified Brecht's use of verse.

All this might be applauded by folk in search of something different and "experimental." It certainly was not commonplace Broadway fare. But what exactly was the purport of it all?

Brecht's play continues a line which may be traced back to his early *A Man's A Man* (page 58). That play was a fable of the brain-washing process. "You can do with a man what you will. Take him apart like a car, rebuild him bit by bit. . . ." A mitelike creature is transformed into a killer. In *Arturo Ui* a psychotic creep becomes the scourge of an entire community through the ferocity of his hysteria, the savagery of his henchmen, the depravity or cowardice of its rulers, the fright of its citizens. Ui, a microbe injected into the nonresistant pulp of a debilitated society, spreads disease and disaster. He infects by the intensity of the fever that possesses him. He mesmerizes his fellowmen through the reverberations of his screaming wretchedness in their sick souls. His success makes him seem shrewd and grandiose to the crowd he has stupefied. This happens in a mythical "Chicago" which is a real Germany and, by extension, Europe. Brecht's epilogue sounds the warning, "The womb from which this beastly thing issued is still fecund." That is the meaning of *The Resistible Rise of Arturo Ui* for its audiences abroad.

In New York, the play was intended as entertainment. The production set out to prove that Brecht can be funny, as good a showman as any in our neighborhood. Every one of the production's employees improvised his contribution independently of any objective other than that of putting the show over. Thus, facile local jokes were introduced, as well as snatches of old-style "liberal" propaganda. (A Negro woman hurled obscene imprecations against the evils of our times; there were allusions to the John Birch Society, etc.)

The production made no *statement* because it had no central theme or valid motivation. The "fun" was spoiled because somewhere in the hash there were fragments of Brecht's bitterness. The effect was, therefore, not only confusing but at times embarrassing and painful. For *theatre* to exist there must be something clearly at stake in which the audience, both as protagonist and chorus, can play a role. Our *Arturo Ui* was an exotic circus in which each participant provided a sideshow of his own. It was a display that never became a play.

Albert Camus

Caligula, 1960

ALBERT CAMUS' *Caligula* is replete with atrocities and is a
profoundly moral play. For Camus was above all a moralist. This does not mean that his play is without dramatic power.
But like most parables its interest inheres in its ideological content more than in its surface story. That is one reason why the
play, for all its record of vice and crime, does not deeply shock or
move us. We know that its savagery—though historical—is only
symbolic.

Written in 1938—when Camus was twenty-five—*Caligula* reflects a sensitive man who came of age in an epoch of concentration camps and civic nihilism. More important than this is the
atmosphere of despair at a time when intelligent and educated
people had begun to question all traditional values—when, as I
once heard Camus express it, "music had lost melody, painting
form, poetry rhyme and meter, thought conviction, history sense
and religion God." Nothing seemed left but a bleak emptiness in
which everything is possible because everything is permitted. Expression in this wasteland without limits could become only violent or mad. Fierce and bloody action itself appeared to cause no
human repercussion.

The young men of France felt themselves spent. When war
broke out in 1939 and France collapsed, shaming itself not only
by defeat but by the behavior of so many of its most respected
citizens, there seemed nothing left to do but abandon oneself to
the filthy tide or rebel. Many of those who rebelled (like Camus)
did so not in the name of their country alone nor in the name of
any certified value—for they were skeptical of all explicit values

—but from a sense of the spirit within them, a spirit we might call the remnant of human feeling which miraculously (or mystically) rejects the brutal disorder that nature and society perennially foster.

Caligula attempts through an inverted idealism to attain freedom by imitating the anarchic ferocity of life and destroying all that he and the world had hitherto regarded as sacrosanct or proper. He becomes a logical killer by pursuing the illogic of nature and society—archkillers themselves. The end of such action is a secretly desired suicide; for a man cannot deny life without eliminating his own. One cannot destroy others without creating an aloneness more terrible than death. No individual can sever his connection with his fellows; who says connection inevitably says love—no matter how the word may be distorted.

In reviewing Stuart Gilbert's translation of Camus' plays last year (Justin O'Brien's translation for the stage is much better) I wrote that they were important rather than good. I meant that while Camus' plays—to me *Caligula* is the most interesting—are the emblem of a generation and a clue to much that has been thought, written and painted and has happened not only in France since the war but to some extent almost everywhere in the West, they are not completely realized works. The writing—while distinguished—does not achieve the white heat or specific imagery of poetry, the characters and scenes attain only a general or moralistic definition.

Camus himself seems to have sensed this, for he acknowledged the play's shortcomings and spoke of *Caligula* as an actor's and director's play. To this and to all I have already said I should add that, for all its flaws, I found that the play merited and got my absorbed attention, that it is, in short, a superior piece with trenchant passages throughout. The production—simple to emaciation in 1945 Paris, where it was a tremendous success with Gérard Phillipe—here leans to the spectacular.

I have been told that Camus advised Sidney Lumet, who directed the play, to eschew the obligatory austerity of its original production. Perhaps Camus thought our audiences might find a stark presentation forbidding. But I am not at all sure that there is not some other style for the play which would be neither bare in the manner of an impoverished Paris nor costly in keeping with our prosperity. I am sure that Broadway, with its high prices—

behind and in front of the curtain—does not provide the most favorable conditions for the mounting of such a play.

Sidney Lumet's direction is intelligent, faithful and sometimes ingenious. Yet all the details of the production struck me as being somehow irrelevant. One cannot help being "held" by the lighting, the set, costumes, etc., but I could not really like them, because in some peculiar way they all seemed foreign to the author's idiom. They are too elaborately decorative to suggest classic restraint, too mechanically modern to be inconspicuously beautiful. Kenneth Haigh's Caligula is creditably, even impressively sincere, and accomplished to a degree. It lacks only the astringency of intellectual anguish and tragic dimension. The straightforward intention and diction of Phillip Bourneuf, in the role of a humanist, reach the mind.

Shelagh Delaney

A Taste of Honey, 1960

A *Taste of Honey*, by Shelagh Delaney, the young English-woman who wrote this play at the age of nineteen, is at once an example of the new "lower-class" milieu which has recently become an object of fresh interest on the London stage and an expression of a state of mind now becoming universal among those who share the spirit of our youth. It reflects a world in which everything once regarded as scandalous and abnormal is taken almost casually.

In Miss Delaney's play a somewhat loose lady arrives in a slum district of a Lancashire town with her seventeen-year-old illegitimate daughter. The girl resents her mother and continually insults her; the mother swears back and suggests that she is going to abandon the girl, who behaves as if she would not mind that at all. The girl has an affair with a Negro sailor who never turns up again, becomes pregnant by him and in the absence of her mother (who disappears for a while to marry her lover) is befriended by a homosexual boy whom the girl has met at an art school.

All this is conveyed with humor, tenderness and very little sentimentality. We see that the girl, who declares she hates love, craves it desperately; we realize that the constant wrangling between mother and daughter is a perverse form of attachment and dependence. The relationship between the girl and her homosexual protector is perhaps the nearest these people will ever come to gestures of pure devotion. The author eschews pathos in telling of these events or in presenting her characters. They are the flotsam of modern civilization—we might once have called them "waifs"—but the feeling the play communicates is "Aren't we all?"

The world here is stripped bare of everything but its lonely souls whose impulses are all toward some form of friendly connection that is achieved only in fits and starts. Nothing on the outside seems to help these people; they are all cut off from what might be called society. These human beings are darling insects who lack all hypocrisy and whose direct expression of natural appetites includes spiritual as well as physical traits.

It is an endearing play. The directors—following the original Joan Littlewood production—frame it with jazz music, the nervous melancholy of which flavors the basically naturalistic text. There are other little condiments—like having some of the characters speak to the audience—which somehow "lighten" the atmosphere. This is characteristic of the new trend in contemporary drama (*The Hostage* [page 43], *The Connection*, etc.). The cruelty and terror of the essential matter must not be taken "tragically." Since life has become very nearly meaningless—in terms of the old tenets which nobody seriously believes—let us not be ponderously "square" in presenting it.

Joan Plowright is touching and oddly enchanting as the girl: she is plain, with eyes that fairly pop and gleam with wonder, mischief, curiosity and understanding. Her performance is funny and lovably lyric; it gives the play a little less "weight" than it had in London, where the excellent actress who played the girl was more earthily sensuous and violent. The present directors—Tony Richardson and George Devine—tend to call on the actors to play for laughs, which makes the play seem less original and less innocent than it truly is. For the quality that chiefly marks this shabby folk tale is *innocence*.

Jean Genet

~~~~~~~~~~

The Balcony, 1960

JEAN GENET'S brothel in *The Balcony* is a house of mirrors, a temple of illusion—one might say art itself—where things are truer than life. In this brothel—where there is more obscenity than sex—acts turn in on themselves (as in art) and thus achieve a certain purity. They have no practical consequence. What the brothel does is give men a presentment of their dreams in their essential meaning. The patron who impersonates a bishop realizes and enjoys the cruelty which is at the root of his absolution, the "judge" his kinship with the criminal, the "general" his taste for command.

The ambitious of the world also aspire toward the glorification or perfection of image which is the service the brothel performs. The workers of the world are in revolt. The brothel alone seems protected. The revolution is drowned in blood. When its leader comes to the brothel it is to become the glorified simulacrum of his captors and rulers—and he castrates himself in doing so. The dictator (the chief of police) becomes the new Hero—dominating even legitimate royalty and the lords of religion, justice, war. This Hero—vulgarian without accredited lineage—who has always yearned to become a great figure in the brothel's galaxy—need no longer do the work which has raised him to power. Having established himself and dug the people's faces in the mud with their orgastic consent, he will now rule by his legend alone—the aura of grandeur which the art-institution of the brothel has given him. Some people still remember their moment of revolt, secretly murmuring, "the rebellion was wonderful"—so that despite their defeat they may some day rise again.

Is this confused? Not very. Genet's construction is as nightmarish, perverse and chaotic as the creations of our fantasies, but like them it has its own illuminating vividness, its lurid clarity and a language—as intensely solid as a classic—which gives the play a substance that cuts through the darkness. I suspect that Genet belongs to a category of artists who, while marginal to the mainstream of major work (that which possesses great duration and broad applicability), retain a certain symbolic significance for their time. Such artists act as a ferment, giving rise to what may be described as a salutary disease—through which we recognize what is happening in and troubling the epoch. These artists do not reveal the world as it is or we as we truly are: they isolate and bring into view the symptoms which threaten us. They are portents and protests. Hence their value—for in art everything must be said, everyone must be heard. To feel and understand what is ailing us is more curative than the balm of the bland entertainers or the engaged propagandists.

France has produced more such artists perhaps than any other modern nation. De Sade, Huysmans, Lautréamont, Jarry, Laforgue, Artaud, maybe even Rimbaud, not to mention certain other of our contemporaries in Paris—novelists, playwrights, poets, painters—belong to this special artistic manifestation. America is too young for important artists of this sort to emerge. When they appear here they usually seem imitative or phony—bad boys aping mythical monsters. It is true that we are beginning to be so infected, but the circumstances which make a Genet authentic are still a bit remote. So *The Balcony* is mostly an oddity with us, a sideshow novelty.

If José Quintero's production is far from being an organic embodiment of the play, one must at least credit it with earnestness of effort in a supremely difficult task. Resources beyond the capacity of any American management are required. (I have heard that there have been some excellent productions in Germany.) The present production is distinctly superior to the one I saw in London in 1957. Nancy Marchand here plays with authority and intelligence. Salome Jens is attractive with the ambiguous glow needed for the occasion, and David Hays as designer is appropriately inventive within the limited means available. The cast as a whole plays arduously. But one regrets the opportunity missed to make the production as hauntingly alluring and gravely demoniac as it might be.

The Blacks, 1961

André Gide once said that when you ask a question of a philosopher you end by not understanding the question you asked. And Poe once warned that the truth is often to be found not at the heights we try to reach but in the valley which is clear to our sight.

I was reminded of these two remarks as I overheard or read various comments on Jean Genet's *The Blacks.* There is a tendency to explain so-called *avant-garde* drama (or painting, poetry, etc.) in such terms that it becomes not only unenjoyable but hopelessly unintelligible. Sartre has on several occasions explained Genet so superbly that his exegesis needed more elucidation than Genet's work itself. I have sometimes feared that these virtuoso explications might affect Genet as much as they frequently confuse the reader or spectator.

All this is to say that *The Blacks* (when you see it) is not an obscure play. Do not try to "comprehend" the problem of its method or the conundrum of its metaphor. If you dwell on these you may talk interestingly but you will miss the *play.* It is a strong, hard, scandalous and utterly fascinating masquerade. It is also one of the most original theatre pieces of our day.

Genet calls it a "clown show." It presents what he once described as a "true picture born of a distorted image." The elegant and vicious ritual of *The Blacks* is a work of pure hatred. It is an elaborate *coup de grâce* struck against the white man's distrust, fear and abhorrence of the blacks. It is an ironic howl at and mockery of everything the paleface thinks, says and, in furtive guilt and repressed aversion, fails to say against the dark-skinned peoples. It also unleashes the fury of the blacks themselves against the white ruling minority. The fiercely polished language Genet employs and the splendid colors arrest our attention like the gleam of a beautiful dagger directed at our throats. We stand in horrified hypnosis at the sight of the imminent (and playful) slaughter like the bewildered bull confronted by his magnificent killer.

It is all done with a grin which has little humor, though it will provoke a frightened laugh. This cold, dazzling smile dispels any suspicion that it might contain love or tenderness. As Verlaine wanted to wring the neck of eloquence, so Genet beats down the possible emergence of sentiment. In the decadent mode we might say that *The Blacks* is a perfect crime.

The play is very French. It contains something of the pride of classic seventeenth-century rhetoric with the outrage of the more vehement symbolist poets, in addition to the latter-day jamboree of journalese and topical, editorial allusions. Paradoxically, it communicates neither warmth nor passion—for murder may be haughty. No matter what initial impression we may get of confusion, the pattern of the whole is shapely and formal.

The first half of the performance is more successful than the second; the play seems too long. But perhaps it is a mistake to divide the play by an intermission. Perhaps it should be maddeningly, intolerably protracted, like a refined torture. Then it would not appear to fall off a bit but become clearly what it is: a calculated cruelty.

There may be, as I noted, different interpretations of Genet's plays according to the spectator's tastes and interests. This is particularly true of *The Maids* and *The Balcony*. In its meaning *The Blacks* is simpler than either of these. My own view—and it is a point I should like to emphasize—is that for all the anarchy and personal stress of Genet's dramatic work it is social and "revolutionary." *The Blacks* is not the kind of play of "social significance" that we are accustomed to: it is not melioristic or benign. It is dangerously explosive; and that is one of its virtues.

Most plays dealing with the race "problem" (or prejudice) are pathetic, constructive, patient. Genet, poet and criminal, is a scourge. In the end his destructiveness is salutary, an assassin of hypocrisy, a bomb dropped on mediocrity and complacency. The contemporary French exasperation—the savagery of which we tend to underestimate as we underestimate everything that threatens—is on its moral level a signal to the world for the need of a not-too-long-to-be-delayed self-transformation.

If an extension of the play's content is sought I should say that beyond the limits of its material lies another (perhaps unconscious) intent. The blacks are not simply the Negroes but all the scorned, neglected, oppressed, ridiculed people thrust out by established society. The play may be thought of as a plea and a protest for the outcast—of whom the blacks are the symbol. But it is a plea and a protest of a man who no longer permits himself the luxury of forgiveness.

Admirably translated by Bernard Frechtman, the play is directed with a firm and skillful hand by Gene Frankel. The masks and costumes are in a properly weird style; the whole production shows care and intelligence. It seemed to me at one moment that an element of glamorous mystery was missing, but on further reflection I have come to believe that the almost machinelike precision and clear brightness of the production's atmosphere may possess its own mystery—the modern one in which the strangely contortionate conformations of assembly-line gadgets are placed nakedly on bare planes against neutral horizons, as if everything were in order.

One is not sure that all the actors understand the full meaning of the words they speak, but this may add a certain desirable impersonality in the proceedings. The cast is generally fine. You may pick your own favorites. Mine were Helen Martin for the easy sense she made of her lines, Ethel Ayler for the stunning aristocracy of her beauty, Godfrey Cambridge for his hang-dog characterization, Louis Gossett for the acute venom of his gaze.

Jean Giraudoux

Duel of Angels, 1960

JEAN GIRAUDOUX's *Duel of Angels*, beautifully translated by Christopher Fry, has been given a handsome production under the skillful guidance of the English dancer-choreographer-actor-director Robert Helpmann. Vivien Leigh, looking altogether lovely in superb gowns by Christian Dior, speaks admirably in a voice that is both caressing and provocative; she has probably never acted better. Mary Ure is a bit overbleached for my taste, but she also fills the eye with grace.

The text itself—it is Giraudoux's swan song and was first produced posthumously in Paris—has always struck me as somewhat ambiguous. Therefore, though it is certainly one of the superior offerings of the season, I feel slightly ambivalent about it.

The play is another of Giraudoux's paradoxical variations on a classic theme—in this case the legend of Lucretia—and deals, as does so much of his work, with the subject of purity. What is meant by purity in this instance is sexual purity (in *Ondine* and *The Enchanted* the purity is of another kind). One might say that purity here has its most popular Gallic connotation: conjugal purity and its converse, adultery. At the end of the play, with the suicide of Lucile ("Lucretia"), a procuress says something to the effect that purity cannot live in this world—a conclusion which Giraudoux has dramatized before.

What troubles one is that Lucile is made to seem—apart from her beauty—a thoroughly bigoted figure, certainly not appealing. Paola, who represents the sophisticated rationalization of the worldly Frenchwoman (the play is set in the South of France in the mid-nineteenth century), makes Lucile appear almost ridicu-

77

lous, though at the sight of Lucile's dead body Paola is non-
plussed and admits that Lucile may have been right. We wonder
whether Giraudoux meant us to feel that absolute purity must
seem either absurd or hypocritical to the normal mentality—as
idealism always strikes us in everyday life—because it is so rare
as to be out of place in this world. One is not altogether sure
where Giraudoux stands. Does he wish to infer that purity by its
uniqueness is something of a threat to us and in its own way
wrong, even "bad"?

On further reflection, I hardly think this interpretation, though
admissible, is what Giraudoux intended. And here a subtle point
of theatrical treatment comes into play, one also involving national character. For I am fairly certain that, though the French
are usually considered more tolerant than the English or the
Americans in regard to marital infidelity, the French audience did
not laugh at Lucile as the American, or at any rate the Broadway,
audience does. I believe the Parisians must have taken Lucile at
face value as an inspired person (if only symbolically so) whose
example of sexual high-mindedness was a kind of poetic reproof
of their looseness. One is a sinner only if one believes in sin, and
the most frivolous French audience is sufficiently penetrated by
its cultural-religious tradition to believe in sin. We, on the other
hand, are free without foundation; we are not sure of anything
either in our orthodoxy or in our emancipation. As a result we
laugh at Lucile, whom we take to be a nuisance, and side with
Paola, who is shrewd, perceptive and above all gay and amusing.

In this half-spoken and semirevealed conflict of attitudes, our
audience regards *Duel of Angels* as essentially comic, in which
case it is very nearly an immoral or a misanthropic play. (Incidentally, Lucile's husband is shown to be a conventional prig,
entirely inferior to his wife.) But I suspect that for all the play's
wit and polished detachment, Giraudoux meant it to have a tragic
emphasis: he is *for Lucile*. (The play's original title is *Pour Lu-
crèce*.)

A striking example of the contradiction between the text and
the audience's reaction to it is the last scene, in which the procuress despoils Lucile's corpse of its treasures—the triumph of evil
as it were; clearly not a comic moment. But the first-night audience laughed at it, not only because the curtain speech was read

with an ineffectual lightness, but because the interpretation of the play as a whole had led the audience to believe that this too was to be taken as a keen joke.

What I think happened is this: the play is difficult because the part of Lucile is not written as consummately as that of Paola. (Also the leading lady—Vivien Leigh—plays Paola opposite a much less vivid actress.) Then the interpreters—the director and the others—like their audience are not impressed by Lucile's (and probably Giraudoux's) moral position. Finally, since the play is so elaborate and elegant in language as to need a special style of presentation to make its particular manner conform with our ordinary demands for "realism," a directorial compromise was effected by placing the emphasis on good looks, suave decorum, salon flair, comedic airiness, a balletlike picturesqueness in the manner of Constantin Guys' drawings—and a minimum of feeling. The result is civilized, smart, fashionably glacial and—thinking of Giraudoux—perhaps false.

Rolf Hochhuth

~~~~~~~~~~~~~~~~~~~~~~~~~~~~~~

The Deputy, 1964

THOUGH THERE may be doubts as to the merit of Rolf Hochhuth's *The Deputy* as a play, there can be no question as to the absorbing interest of its material. The blunt fact is that I found myself so intent on the subject that I very nearly ceased to concern myself with the performance as an evening in the theatre.

Before saying anything further about *The Deputy*—which has been produced in Berlin, London, Paris, Vienna, Stockholm, Athens—I should like to comment on the implications of that opening remark.

It is nonsense to maintain that we see and judge plays entirely in the light of their "creative" values. If we have no personal relation to a play's human content we are not likely to understand it at all or care anything about it. Imagine a person incapable of passion at a performance of *Romeo and Juliet* or *Tristan und Isolde*. True, there would still be the language of the one and the music of the other, but even these would lose their affective force for such an auditor. He might well ask, "What's all the excitement about?"

Allardyce Nicoll, the English theatre historian, made a point some years ago at an international drama conference, citing a passage from my book *The Fervent Years* which describes the opening night in 1935 of Odets' *Waiting for Lefty* as follows: "When the audience at the end of the play responded to the militant question from the stage—'Well, what's the answer?'— with a spontaneous roar of 'Strike! Strike!' it was something more than a tribute to the play's effectiveness. . . . Our youth had found

80

its voice. The audience was delirious. It stormed the stage. . . ."
Professor Nicoll held that such a response to a play was a form of
mass hysteria and thus not a proper attitude for a theatre audience. It lacked the necessary objectivity for artistic appreciation.

Perhaps so. We always hope for and seek perfect unity between form and content in a work of art, but I suspect that
complete "Apollonian" detachment from the sources of an artist's
inspiration—the living matter which generates his work—is even
more foreign to relevant judgment in the arts than is complete
identification with those sources. I very much doubt that the
Athenians who attended the plays of Aeschylus, Sophocles,
Euripides and Aristophanes viewed them with the contemplative
calm presumed by doctors of aesthetics to be the correct frame of
mind for cultivated enjoyment. All of which makes me sympathize with the critic who, when asked about his favorable review
of Dore Schary's *Sunrise at Campobello*, "You really liked the
play?" answered, "I liked Roosevelt."

An evaluation of *The Deputy* at this moment is difficult, to
begin with, because while it was written as a Schiller-like epic
drama—the published text would take more than six hours to
perform—each of its versions has had a different translator and
has been staged and cut by a different director. Even more taxing
to strict criticism, an ambiguity in the dramatist's motivation has
led to a confusion in the audiences' reception of the play everywhere.

Apparently Hochhuth set out to write a dramatic "poem" on the
existentialist question "Why should a young Jesuit priest, martyr-
ing himself on behalf of the Jewish victims of Nazi savagery,
cling to his belief in God when all the evidence of his actual
experience contradicts any rational justification for such faith?"
But this theme was lost sight of in the development of the work
because the author was carried away by the more burning question of why the Christian world—embodied in its most organized
Church—failed to protest the blackest crime in history: the sys-
tematic slaughter of six million Jews between 1941 and 1944. The
outraged moralist and historian in the author superceded the religious artist.

The climactic scene of the play becomes, therefore, the one in
which Pope Pius XII (Pacelli) refuses to denounce the Nazi ac-

tion against the Jews or to abrogate the Concordat between Hitler and the Church. It makes the play appear to be primarily an attack on the Pontiff and, by extension, on the Catholic hierarchy.

This is a distortion of the play's significance and value. It should not be construed as anti-Catholic. Even the Pope's role in the dramatic context should not be considered central. The play's real protagonist is Father Fontana, whose tragic outcry and assumption of Jewish martyrdom lie at the heart of Hochhuth's message. What the play tells us is that we all share in the guilt of those years, for none of us acted with sufficient vigor, none of us protested bitterly, clamorously, specifically enough. The governments of Britain and France, to go no further, are as open to the play's accusation on this score as was the Church's chief deputy.

If the audience misses this point, its failure is largely due to a weakness in Hochhuth's dramatic thinking, his inability to bring the play's larger issue and the detail of its scenes into focus. Father Fontana is less vividly and convincingly drawn than are his more compliant fellow clerics. Yet, despite these grave defects of dramatic statement, it would be false to deny the play's hold on our attention or its power to stir.

Herman Shumlin's production is unfortunately not nearly as gripping as it should be. It lacks impetus and bite. Jeremy Brett is a good choice for the role of Fontana, though his part seems underwritten in this version. But most of the cast on the second night, except for Fred Stewart as an unctuous cardinal, struck me as insecure, either from insufficient rehearsal or lack of aptitude.

Emlyn Williams, on the other hand, possesses all the skill and authority needed to play the Pope, but his (or the director's) choice of interpretation was misguided. It damages the play to make the character soft or to suggest, even in the slightest degree, a suave insincerity. The part is not written that way. From a political standpoint, the Pope's arguments are "sensible" enough. His behavior toward the Italian Jews was irreproachable and his general attitude in the circumstances was less reprehensible than, let us say, that of Chamberlain in respect to the situation in 1938. The part could and should be read with dignified strength, masterly self-possession and with the firm conviction that the Pope is "right."

Eugene Ionesco

The Bald Soprano and Jack, 1958

EUGENE IONESCO's one-act plays *The Bald Soprano* and *Jack* interested and entertained me. The question raised by most people who have seen Ionesco's plays here, in London and in Paris is, "Are they a manifestation of a significant new dramatic personality or mere French flummery?"

The first thing that strikes me about Ionesco's work is its theatricality. What Ionesco does is to take ideas which are now in the air—some people would say à la mode—and make arrestingly vivid stage images of them. The effect in general is usually macabre and witty while the writing is both sprightly and sharp with overtones of pathos.

Overlong, *The Bald Soprano* illustrates the featureless inanity of lower middle-class domestic relations: the lack of connection between man and wife, among neighbors and between individuals and their ordinary environment. Men and women today, Ionesco implies, hardly recognize each other, especially if they have lived together a long time: their homes are blank spots in space and all live in mechanical response to one another and to the world. The fashionable word for this state of being is "alienation."

Kafka gave this mood its classically contemporary expression. The surrealists have added something to Ionesco's palette and the perennial Parisian flair for spicy nonsense (nonsense may have meaning) has added to the recipe.

Jack is a fiercer, rather than funnier, variation on the basic theme. It is also more ambiguous, for Ionesco will not be pinned down so that anything altogether precise may be deciphered in his plays. There is a constantly waggish elusiveness to avoid any completely rational or logical connotation. This adds an element of mystery (or mystification) to the picture.

Jack might be called The Family Nags the Son Into Marriage. After the discontented and uncommunicative boy has been bullied into seeing his prospective bride—child of a rich bourgeois household—and he begins to speak with her, she overcomes his reluctance or fear by a wild outburst of erotic wooing to which he finally succumbs. At the end we see him prostrate under the solemnly ritualistic gaze of both families. Has sexual contact with his bride killed him or has he just passed out with passion? The answer is perhaps more pertinent to a psychiatric investigator than to an audience.

All this is very colorfully communicated—the family in this instance are circus folk—with fundamental (artistic) clarity. My saying this may strike the reader as a pose. *Godot* clear? *Endgame* clear? And now this Ionesco clear? Attentive spectators will find these plays understandable—particularly those I am now reviewing—if they do not seek to grasp every word in a literal or information-bearing sense. What must be followed is what the eyes take in (for example, the weird clock in *The Bald Soprano*) and the *line of action* in each scene. The form of the plays rather than the details of each speech carries most of the message. The speech is understandable too, but in a suggestive or "symbolic" rather than a strict sense. The whole is related to meaning as we know it in contemporary painting and in modern verse. What is mainly to be noted in such a play as *Jack*, for example, is that traditional scenes from bourgeois drama with almost conventional action (the mother entreats, the sister reasons, the father moralizes, the boy protests, the would-be in-laws storm, the boy begins to yield, the bride cajoles, love scenes ensue, etc.) are transformed into grotesqueries by the author's thematic intention and poetically stylized dialogue.

It may be difficult to determine at present whether Ionesco's plays will eventually seem more clever than truly felt. His view of life is certainly not mine. But every phase of feeling, every aspect of truth—no matter how strange—ought to find articulation in the theatre. Ionesco utters his truth in specific stage terms which are startling and often brilliant. What he has to say, moreover, is justified by the routine of our daily living. The lack of spiritual content in our civilization has been the major outcry of European drama since Ibsen. Ionesco has carried this idea to the climactic point of savage caricature.

Rhinoceros, 1961

Rhinoceros is Eugene Ionesco's "popular" play, or, as he himself has said, the play he wrote *pour le public*. It has been a success in Paris, in Germany, in London (in good measure due to Laurence Olivier's participation), and now it has been cordially received by a press which was generally indifferent to Ionesco's shorter works.

The play's career makes a lively bit of theatre history. In Paris an American writer of *avant-garde* tendencies assured me that *Rhinoceros* was perhaps the only one of Ionesco's plays which was totally without interest for him, while at the same time an English critic affirmed that it was the first Ionesco play which was not rubbish. Nigel Dennis, English novelist, playwright and critic, complained that the play was too explicit and thus lacked the imaginative piquancy of Ionesco's *The Chairs;* Kenneth Tynan, in London, where most reviewers favored the play rather than the production (directed by Orson Welles), declared that the production was good but the play bad—but I rather suspect that Tynan's seeming prejudice is dictated by his admiration for Brecht, whom Ionesco scorns. Sartre—another author about whom Ionesco is icy—deems *Rhinoceros* to be a play for the complacent, because it does not really make clear why a man should not become a "rhinoceros"!

With such a background of controversy—and having myself seen the London production—I approach the statement of my present reaction with particular care and caution. There is no use in a critic's pretending that he is never influenced. He would be less than human—therefore a poor critic—if this were so.

I advise my readers to see the play. It requires no courage—at this point—to say that it is the most interesting play of the season. (Of course, like all comparative superlatives the remark is somewhat empty: it has been a dismal season and *Rhinoceros* cannot properly be linked with *A Taste of Honey* or even *The Hostage*.) What may certainly be affirmed is that *Rhinoceros* is entertaining and, whatever one's estimate of its underlying spirit, significant. This is sufficient today to make it important.

The play was originally a short story; it is overlong as a three-act play. Its apparent point is made at least three-quarters of an hour before its final curtain. I speak of an "apparent" point because there is something more in the play's message than is contained in the symbol of men who turn into rhinoceroses—the comedy and terror of conformism. For the play, despite the central figure's ultimate defiance of bestiality, is essentially anarchistic, bitter, very nearly hopeless.

The rational mind and logic are absurd, Ionesco tells us; they have little relation to the truth (which is the chaos) of life. Intellectuals are fools. Most organized radicals are not only clowns but robots—ready under pressure to swing from extreme Left to extreme Right. The conventional middle-class gentleman is a moron; the smooth little subaltern of the business community is a fraud; favored hirelings of the *status quo* are grotesque; the sweet young thing whom we regard as the sweetheart of the world is spineless. Ultimately, they all turn into monsters of blind energy, cruel forces of destruction.

A little man—confused, uncertain, without direction except for some nameless grace of disposition—will resist, though he too is probably doomed. (He acknowledges that the person who wishes to remain an individual always ends badly.) Destined to defeat or not, he does resist—all by himself—which may be described as a *pathetic* absurdity. In almost all the other Ionesco plays the counterpart of Berrenger (the helpless "hero" of *Rhinoceros*) is always done in by the Monster—the mysterious Evil which dominates all. In this sense *Rhinoceros* may be said to mark an "advance" for Ionesco, a stirring of conscience against complete despair, an anguished sign of protest against surrender.

Philosophically this is an unsound, as well as an unsatisfactory, position. Humanly, it is quite understandable: many people the world over feel as Berrenger does, both lonely and afraid of others. Historically, it is typical of the state of mind of a large part of the French intelligentsia today. At worst, its attitude is preferable to the nonawareness and spiritual inanition of, let us say, the ordinary American playgoer. Ionesco's merit as an artist is that he finds theatrically telling means to reflect this contemporary fright. His plays are brilliant statements for the stage; his, therefore, is an authentic and original theatre talent.

Ionesco has said that his work has been stimulated by Kafka and the Marx brothers: it expresses apprehension through gags. In Joseph Anthony's direction of *Rhinoceros* (more engaging than that of the London production) only the gags are effective. The first act (the most successful of the three) is generally hilarious—though there is a faint touch of college theatricals throughout. The latter impression is due to the fact that we get very little sense of how the fun and games relate to the central theme, which is not at all funny.

The slightly Disney style at the beginning is not only childlike but rather childish and when protracted makes us surmise that we are witnesses to a one-joke affair. But this is not really the case. From the outset the play's final act and particularly its crucial last speech, which approaches the tragic, should have been kept in view. What is required by the material is not so much "Kafka *and* the Marx brothers" as Kafka *within* the Marx brothers. The present production has no true style because each of its elements apes whatever farcical trick or serious sentiment seems to be indicated moment by moment, and does not convey a sense that all of the play's aspects interpenetrate to form a single Idea with an indivisible meaning. Thus, the last scene of the play descends to the level of a rather flat realism.

Still the "show" makes for a good evening with, as they say, loads of laughs. Complimentary remarks might be made about everyone—Eli Wallach for his bewildered sweetness, Morris Carnovsky for his expertness at rendering innocent idiocy, Anne Jackson for her cuteness, etc.; but the outstanding performance is that of Zero Mostel, whose penchant for Rabelaisian antics of inexhaustible comic verve and inventiveness makes the conversion of his bonehead bourgeois into a roaring pachyderm seem masterfully easy, despite the perspiration. My only reservation on this performance is that the final emergence of the character as a rhinoceros should be indicated by a horn thrust through the bathroom door rather than by the actor's own Gargantuan baby face.

Ann Jellicoe

ᗰᗰᗰᗰᗰᗰᗰᗰᗰ

The Knack, 1964

THE AUTHOR of *The Knack,* Ann Jellicoe, now thirty-six, wrote the play about three years ago. It is a ripple in that "new wave" of English writing which has enlivened the London stage since 1956. To say the least, it is fun.

I identify it in this unassuming fashion because, as with many plays of its kind, there is a temptation to treat it as esoteric. It might be preferable, to begin with, to view *The Knack* strictly as entertainment—as one might judge an extended but on the whole well-sustained revue sketch.

The subject is sex: the sex of the British "bohemian" middle class. Sex, unrelated to love or passion, has lately become an obsession with the English. I do not mean that there is "more" of it now than at any other time, but that a fascination with the discussion of sex even more insistent than indulgence in it has become ever more prevalent since the war. There is little that is morbid in this, little that is even sensuous; it is for the most part facetious. It is a symptom of a social transformation, a breakaway from rather than a breakdown of old class restrictions and phobias.

There are three young men in *The Knack.* One appears "neutral," either because he has arisen above sex or is incapable of rising to it; he is characterized by a certain asperity of intelligence. Another is eager for the experience of sex but utterly inept at it through timidity. The third has become expert in its pursuit through a basic lack of feeling. With him it is a kind of professional interest to pass the time in a world in which nothing more substantial exists. The locale of the play is a bare room being haphazardly painted, though it looks as though no one has the slightest intention of ever furnishing it. Into this vacuum comes a seventeen-year-old girl, fresh and fat from the provinces. She fears and craves the advances of practically any (or all) three fellows. She is ignorant, dense and utterly natural, both predictable and unpredictable: in a word, altogether *ready* for the seduction which she will call rape. There are several determined assaults on her virtue, followed by retreats, thwarted skirmishes, renewed forays and finally no consummated action.

The play is what the French might call a clown show; it never states a case. It is "crazy"; yet its characters' eccentricity—for example, when three of them enact the playing of a piano on a bedspring—is not so remote from the actual behavior of young folk today who will beguile themselves in some such way to fill the emptiness of the hours.

The talk is both terse and loose, epigrammatic and repetitive, extravagant and dry, pointed and inane. We laugh and at the same time ask ourselves, "Where are we?" We are here and now, very much in the midst of today's bewilderment (especially in certain English circles): sportive, "civilized," spiritually null and void. There is a faint odor of homosexuality on the premises.

The play has something of Harold Pinter's weird bleakness, together with the variety-hall travesty of London's "Crazy Gang." It hovers about the Theatre of the Absurd but never really enters.

Finally, it is a clever stage piece. It lives on action—sound, speech and movement—all of it zany yet never less than lucid. One need not concern oneself with how "good" the play is nor how seriously one has to take it. As spoof or symbol it has unmistakable merits.

The production is brilliantly directed by Mike Nichols and the cast is excellent. Brian Bedford in the tart humor of his indifference, Roddy Maude-Roxby in his numbskull naïveté, George Segal in a studied and somehow stupid sexual aggressiveness are all first rate. But Alexandra Berlin in her maddening innocence, as deceptive as guile, is perhaps the best. By total involvement in, and seemingly unconscious abandon to, the lunacy of the commonplace, Miss Berlin achieves the wholeness of a true creation.

LeRoi Jones

～～～～～～～

Dutchman, 1964

D UTCHMAN indicates the emergence of an outstanding dramatist—LeRoi Jones.

His is a turbulent talent. While turbulence is not always a sign of power or of valuable meaning, I have a hunch that LeRoi Jones' fire will burn ever higher and clearer if our theatre can furnish an adequate vessel to harbor his flame. We need it.

He is very angry. Anger alone may merely make a loud noise, confuse, sputter and die. For anger to burn to useful effect, it must be guided by an idea. With the "angry young men" of England one was not always certain of the source of dissatisfaction nor of its goal. With LeRoi Jones it is easy to say that the plight of the Negro ignited the initial rage—justification enough —and that the rage will not be appeased until there is no more black and white, no more color except as differences in hue and accent are part of the world's splendid spectacle. But there is more to his ferocity than a protest against the horrors of racism.

Dutchman, the first of Jones' plays to reach the professional stage, is a stylized account of a subway episode. A white girl picks up a young Negro who at first is rather embarrassed and later piqued by her advances. There is a perversity in her approach which finally provokes him to a hymn of hate. With lyrical obscenity he declares that murder is in his and every Negro's heart and were it to reach the point of action there would be less "singin' of the blues," less of that delightful folk music and hot jazz which beguile the white man's fancy, more calm in the Negro soul. Meanwhile, it is the black man who is murdered.

What we must not overlook in seeing the play is that, while this

90

explosion of fury is its rhetorical and emotional climax, the crux of its significance resides in the depiction of the white girl, whose relevance to the play's situation does not lie in her whiteness but in her representative value as a token of our civilization. She is our neurosis—not a neurosis in regard to the Negro, but the absolute neurosis of American society.

She is "hip": she has heard about everything, understands and feels nothing. She twitches, jangles, jitters with a thin but inexhaustible energy, propelled by the vibrations from millions of ads, television quiz programs, newspaper columns, intellectual jargon culled from countless digests, panel discussions, illustrated summaries, smatterings of gossip on every conceivable subject (respectable and illicit), epithets, wisecracks, formulas, slogans, cynicisms, cures and solutions. She is the most "informed" person in the world and the most ignorant. (The information feeds the ignorance.) She is the bubbling, boiling garbage cauldron newly produced by our progress. She is a calculating machine gone berserk; she is the real killer. What she destroys is not men of a certain race but mankind. She is the compendium in little of the universal mess.

If *Dutchman* has a fault, it is its completeness. Its ending is somewhat too pat, too pointed in its symbolism. If one has caught the drift of the play's meaning before its final moment, the ending is supererogatory; if one has failed to do so, it is probably useless.

Dutchman is very well played by Jennifer West and Robert Hooks.

The Toilet and The Slave, 1965

LeRoi Jones' two "new" plays—*The Toilet* and *The Slave*—were written before *Dutchman* (page 90). They are not as successful artistically as the later work. In the hardware blonde of *Dutchman*, Jones conceived a concise and piercing dramatic image for the killer our society generates through its metallic emptiness.

Still, the new plays stunned and shook me. After an initial

discomfiture, I ceased to examine them as "dramatic fare" and began to think of them as symptoms. By this I mean that I cannot dissociate them from the hoodlum world we now inhabit. *Dutchman* was an angry play; *The Toilet* and *The Slave* are rabid. They are full of the rage which *precedes* anger, for anger has a definite form and a clear objective; rage only smolders and explodes.

Frustration breeds rage. It is caused by the contradiction, confusion and suppression of strong feeling. It therefore expresses itself in semiarticulate speech and violent action. Hoodlums are creatures consumed by the fires and fumes of frustration.

The language of the new Jones plays (particularly the first) is entirely naturalistic. Adolescents in our big city ghettos speak exactly as do the characters in *The Toilet*. Nor is the choice of the play's locale, a toilet in a boys' high school, gratuitous. The fight —very nearly a general massacre not without its "geniality"— would take place there. Still, it is part of the poet's inspiration— and Jones *is* a poet—to make the words used and the setting chosen emblems of the inchoate savagery which possesses him, his characters and, to a degree unsuspected by most of us, our civilization as a whole.

After searing our sensibilities with indiscriminate brutality, *The Toilet* gets to its point. In an oblique way the play is a study in hypocrisy. The two youths who beat each other nearly to death are secretly and shamefacedly in love with each other. That the love is between black and white as well as being homosexual is undoubtedly significant, but far less significant than that we are made to realize that its frustration must result in the most shameful and horrifying cruelty. What is wrong with the play, what delays our realizing its meaning till long after it is over, is that the reasons—aside from the obvious ones—for the suppression of love are not sufficiently suggested. We are given only the harsh anecdote and the dreadful environment.

Frustration again is the root sentiment in *The Slave*. The central figures are a Negro poet turned race terrorist and his former idol, a white college professor. In this play, expression is more literate because what is said concerns the futility of the white man's liberalism and the hysteria its failure causes in the souls of those who suffer most through that failure. But the situation and the atmosphere are so insanely extravagant that these issues do not emerge as ideas at all. (Perhaps they are not meant to.) What is actually communicated is the sense that our incapacity to make true contact with one another must head our world to a hopeless, shapeless shambles—destruction and annihilation without a "lesson." Glimmering through the play's hectic verbiage and opaque argument, glimpses appear of the mangled love the Negro harbors for his divorced white wife (a love heated by lust, which is an attribute of its frustration) and his distorted and poisoned veneration for the white professor who educated him and finally robbed him of his wife.

I do not "admire" these plays or call them "good." But despite their malformation and immaturity I believe them important. They are to be heeded. They say "Beware!"

About Leo Garen's direction, Larry Rivers' sets, the acting of Al Freeman, Jr., one can only note that they are part of an evening we shall not soon forget.

Robert Lowell

~~~~~~~~~~~~~~~~~~~~~~~

The Old Glory, 1964

ACCORDING TO the playbill, "The American Place Theatre exists to foster good writing for the theatre. It hopes to accomplish this by providing a place, a staff and a broad program of practical work to American writers of stature: our poets, novelists and philosophers who wish to use the dramatic form, and to serious playwrights."

I heartily approve of this purpose because I always wish to encourage every effort to break the bonds of Broadway. (I am also in favor of increasing production on Broadway by making its organization less burdensome—probably an even more difficult task.) I dispel from my mind the fact that very few modern poets, novelists and philosophers writing in English have written viable plays. Playwrights have often proved themselves poets; poets, novelists and philosophers rarely become effective playwrights. Still, I am convinced that it is highly desirable that writers not primarily identified with the theatre be pressed into service so that they may help freshen the field. One further thing should be said in this connection: just as Mallarmé warned Degas that poems were not made with "ideas" but with words, so drama is not made with ideas or words but through the development of human action given life within certain specific technical limits.

The American Place Theatre has begun its official existence well by offering the work of Robert Lowell. One listens with respect and, in regard to language at least, with pleasure, to every word this poet sets down. Lowell's *The Old Glory* is a triptych of three one-act plays related to American history from 1630 to 1800. There is throughout a thread of feeling and thought characteristic of the author's spirit.

94

Since the presentation of the three plays was found to be too
long for comfort, the first of the series, "Endicott and the Red
Cross," has been dropped. That is a pity because, while it does
not have the "kick" of the last and longest piece, "Benito Cereno"
(from a story by Herman Melville), "Endicott and the Red
Cross," as a clue to Lowell's statement, is perhaps the most telling
of the three plays.

I cannot say much about "My Kinsman, Major Molineux," the
second section of *The Old Glory*, because, while its form and
import are evident in the production, only one or two of the
actors who play it are wholly intelligible. I could make out no
more than half of the spoken text.

When the performance of "My Kinsman, Major Molineux" was
over, I murmured to a friend who sat in front of me, "This is a
subversive play; I'm going to report it to the authorities!" I suspect that my feeble quip represented a certain intuition. There
is a subtle and gnawing skepticism in Lowell's soul—and all
skepticism is subversive!

After a somewhat extended prelude of talk—*good* talk, though
the suspense it is meant to engender verges on the self-defeating
because we are not made sufficiently aware of what portends—
"Benito Cereno" ends with the slaughter of Negroes on a Spanish
slave ship. The Negroes had mutinied against their captors,
killed the shipowner and taken over the rule of the vessel. They
plan to force the captain of an American merchant ship to sail
them back to Africa. When the massacre (at the hands of the
American captain's sailors) is over, the leader of the Negro
mutiny defiantly proclaims, "The future is black." Delano, the
American captain, replies, "This is your future," and empties all
six barrels of his pistol into the Negro's body.

An exciting conclusion. But what is "the future" Lowell suggests? That murderous suppression of Negroes will continue for
160 years and more? History has corroborated this. And it goes
without saying that Lowell is a man of goodwill who abhors
violence. Yet the play is ambiguous. It is ironic and disturbed. It
is not tragic as much as pained and bewildered. It leaves us
shocked and strangely dissatisfied. Lowell, it would appear, is no
kin to the American captain; nor, though he understands him, is
he really sympathetic to the Negro rebel. Lowell is more like the
overpowered Spanish grandee, Benito Cereno, sensitive, lofty,
impotent.

"My Kinsman, Major Molineux" (in which only Thomas J. Stubblefield is wholly distinct of speech) is called a "political cartoon." A cartoon is a simplification or an exaggeration of a supposed verity. In this short piece (it takes place on the eve of the Boston Tea Party) the activists on both sides, those opposed to the king as well as those loyal to him, are shown to be pimps, prostitutes, fairies, hypocrites, turncoats—all more or less covered with slime or gore, sometimes both. Are we to understand that, like all revolutions, ours came about through such agencies? Perhaps so. Certainly we are not made to believe that Lowell "regrets" the upheaval which made us independent. What then? The question hangs in the air. Lowell is not telling: he smiles and is troubled.

The piece omitted in the production of *The Old Glory* is, I repeat, the most significant and the most admirably written. It, too, represents the conflict in early colonial times between the Puritans, who will forge the new world unfettered by England, and the more cultivated Anglicans, who are to be driven from power. Endicott, the Puritan leader, plagued with doubt, speaks such pithy lines as "I now understand statescraft: a statesman can either work with merciless efficiency and leave a desert, or he can work in a hit-and-miss fashion and leave a cesspool." Endicott, in whose every utterance we detect an element of indecision, finally takes a stand against the English because they would impose a royal governor. He exercises the necessary severities on the milder and more compliant colonists. Before doing so, he promises to make a speech denouncing the Stuarts and the Pope, with additional talk about liberty of worship and the like.

When he is assured that these points will make a noble speech, he says, "No, it turns my stomach/It will be a hollow, dishonest speech, half truth, half bombast . . . but my speech will be practical." When he has concluded the speech and is complimented on it by a fanatic community Elder who declares that it is "the finest speech I've ever heard outside the pulpit," Endicott says, "I don't suppose so, I wasn't really listening." He had not spoken from conviction but from a need to prevent his own breakdown. He anticipates the much more pragmatic American captain of "Benito Cereno," who admits, "Nothing relaxes order more than misery. They [the slaves] need severe superior officers."

Liberal, Lowell is an aristocrat to his very marrow. He is incapable of, as well as horrified by, the "merciless efficiency" needed for strong rule, and he is disquieted by the "cesspool" which results from leniency. Dismayed by the equally appalling courses of action, Lowell as a poet turns inward and reveals the terms of his distress obliquely.

Such men cannot govern. A hesitancy in decision and discipline makes them similarly ill at ease when they try to exercise the definition and command of the stage. Still, one hopes that Lowell will be impelled to continue his theatre writing, for his is an authentic voice. I should be glad to have him attempt to dramatize his disquiet more amply. He is not alone in his searing and sacred dilemma.

It would be wrong to say that Jonathan Miller has directed the two plays with "merciless efficiency"; but it is nonetheless true that his meticulous direction, though it lends his production a very polished, even handsome, surface (no point is slighted, no intention is permitted to escape our notice), tends to sacrifice certain values. The sharp stylization of the "political cartoon" appears to obstruct the actors' diction. More practiced actors compose the cast of "Benito Cereno"—everyone speaks well—but the stringency of direction tends to rob the actors of a certain "humanity," thus reducing the possibility of a warmth which might add a larger dimension to the play. Nevertheless, Miller has managed to catch some of the hard, dry, tight cleanness of Lowell's writing. The over-all mechanics of staging (including the treatment of sets, makeup and costumes) are thoroughly skilled.

Roscoe Lee Browne, Lester Rawlins and Frank Langella make us look and listen. They are faithful to their masters, Lowell and Miller.

Eugene O'Neill

~~~~~~~~~~~~~~~~

The Great God Brown, 1959

PRAISE THE Phoenix Theatre for producing Eugene O' Neill's *The Great God Brown* anew. George Jean Nathan thought it O'Neill's best play, an opinion I do not share, but one step toward the making of a true theatre in our country is the production of old plays of merit.

It is not sufficient, though, that such plays be seen merely as new "shows"; they should be comprehended as part of a development in their author's work and as part of our own history. It is no longer of first importance that O'Neill used masks in this play, a device considered highly "experimental" in 1926, when the play was originally presented. What is important is the play's theme and the anguish O'Neill imbued it with. The theme is the practical man's envy of the artist and the artist's jealousy of the dominant practical man—a peculiarly American theme in the period of the play's conception.

O'Neill probed further than this bald statement might suggest. He saw the American businessman—for that is what Brown represents, though O'Neill made him an architect—becoming infected with the artist's yearnings and unable finally to realize himself either as one thing or another. Brown suffers some of the inner dissatisfactions which plague and impel the artist without possessing the artist's sensibility or skill. More strikingly, O'Neill portrays his artist, Dion Anthony, as a trammeled human being, really a half-artist with a gnawing sense of inadequacy in his philosophy, his personality and his adjustment to life. That is a crucial American tragedy: the incompleteness of American civilization as it focuses in the individual.

This sounds old-fashioned. Today, only a brief "moment" since the dilemma appeared poignant in the growing American consciousness, terms and circumstances have altered their outer form. The businessman of today is emotionally more complacent: if he appreciates the artist's function, collects paintings, attends concerts and reads certain books or book reviews, he expresses his disquiet otherwise than O'Neill's Brown. Similarly, the artist today seems to have taken his "proper" place in our society, so that with a little maneuvering, rationalization, psychoanalysis and publicity he can feel pretty much in the same boat as the Browns. The result is that they are both prepared to moan in monotonous chorus about taxes and the threat of atomic extinction.

The core of the matter, however, is not changed as much as we pretend; if we believe otherwise, that is chiefly because we rarely think of any "core" at all, except to indulge ourselves in a specious vocabulary of high-brow platitudes. O'Neill was no intellectual; if his play suffers in form and thought as well as in clarity, its impulse and source are nevertheless real and deep.

In O'Neill's work as a whole the theme of *The Great God Brown* recurs again and again in the most diverse guises; and if we refer even cursorily to O'Neill's life we become aware that the conflicts which made the theme urgent were rooted in his relationship to his father, his mother, his brother. A blood tie binds *Beyond the Horizon, Desire Under the Elms, Marco Millions, Long Day's Journey Into Night, A Touch of the Poet* into a single underlying meaning: the individual American has not reached fulfillment; he is not full grown; neither as a doer nor as a feeling person has he yet made peace with himself or with the world, and all the blather about the "American way of life" will not heal the sore.

Note too that O'Neill's artist, for all his mockery of Brown, is not presented as a "genius." It is always clear that O'Neill never thought of himself as a master in any way. He identified himself with derelicts and failures. He has no heroes; all his central figures yammer and yearn, curse and are as much lost as Yank the laborer in *The Hairy Ape*. Immature on the level of ultimate power, O'Neill is the dramatic poet of our own immaturity—which in his work is not merely an artistic or an intellectual flaw, but a lacerating wound.

You may be embarrassed by some of the awkwardness and

feeble verbiage of *The Great God Brown,* particularly in the last act; and you can, if you wish, disparage O'Neill, in academic loftiness, by comparing his plays with the best work of the European playwrights of the past forty years. The fact remains that he is not only our most important dramatist, but one whose total product is, even in some of its faults, more truly relevant to the American people—whose "story" after all concerns the whole of modern society—than any other dramatist of this period anywhere. .

The Phoenix Theatre production under Stuart Vaughan's direction is much more obviously stylized than the original production directed by Robert Edmond Jones. The new production is perhaps more lucid than the early one, or let us say less "mystic." It is intelligently executed throughout. I also believe it likely that the comparatively young actors in the present production—Fritz Weaver, Robert Lansing and the others—"understand" the play and their parts better than did those of the original cast. Yet I cannot suppress the feeling that the emotional resources of our present generation of actors are not as rich as those of former years. The distinction is not one of talent: it has much to do with the times. Today we are perhaps more troubled and possess less actual experience. Our lesions nowadays seem to be chronic and, so to speak, automatic, whereas the older acters were more truly engaged in the world and in the living theatre. They had *earned* their neuroses.

John Osborne

〰〰〰〰〰〰〰〰〰

Inadmissible Evidence, 1965

SEVERAL ENGLISH critics whom I respect were less than luke-warm about Albee's *Who's Afraid of Virginia Woolf?* but were rapturous about John Osborne's *Inadmissible Evidence.* I point this out not as a comment on the plays or on the critics, but to emphasize that art and literature are not inevitably international in value. Critics are parts of communities, each with its own particular history and need. *Inadmissible Evidence* was a great popular as well as critical success in London; it has not been well received here and is probably destined to a brief run.

There is still a "dream" in *Virginia Woolf,* as well as a jocu-larity, which helps keep the play's sting from being poisonous. Though *Inadmissible Evidence* begins with and occasionally reverts to stream-of-consciousness monologue, it contains no "dream"; though it crackles with sharp phrases which startle us to a guffaw, it is not at all humorous. It is a display of English nausea.

The absence of a dream is its underlying theme. Where in our lives is there anything to rouse us to significant action, to some sort of substantial idealism, to a belief or a cause which might lead us to a struggle worth the candle? In fact, says Maitland, the man who submits evidence against himself, "I've never dis-covered what is [worth the candle]." Everything has gone stale, flat, acidulous.

The English see in Maitland a "hero" of their day, the present archetype of the educated middle-class Britisher. He works hard without a sense of purpose. He has little except a routine relationship to his job. He has only a nagging affection for his wife, a nervous yearning for his mistress, a spastic impulse toward every pretty girl he encounters and with whom he copulates in a fog of befuddlement. His children are slightly repellent strangers. One of the most eloquent, indeed brilliantly written, speeches in the play is Maitland's denunciation of the "cool" generation, addressed to his daughter, about whose age he is in some doubt. He is addicted to pills. A solicitor, he is losing his professional grip. He sees all his clients as one dismal, distracted creature no better off than himself. "I, myself, am more packed with spite and twitching with revenge than anyone I know of. I actually often, frequently, daily want to see people die for their errors. I wish to kill them myself, to throw the switch with my own fist." The man spews spleen.

Jimmy Porter in *Look Back in Anger* was bitter about England after the war. It had lost its ancient stature. Now, says Maitland, "I'm not the one on any side. I don't have any idea of where I am." Even more to the point he exclaims, "Britain's position in the world. Screw that. What about my position!" Because there has been this apparent change from a degree of social consciousness in Jimmy Porter to Maitland's despair about himself, it has been said by a number of English critics and at least one American critic that *Inadmissible Evidence* is the profounder, the more universal play—a modern tragedy.

No doubt many Englishmen see themselves in Maitland. They honor Osborne for articulating their inner distress. (Outwardly —and this is one of Osborne's beefs—they are much too patient.) He exposes their concealed wounds, their soul-sickness. His play is a document: it *does* reveal their weariness, their atony, above all their desire to sneer at themselves. In this, together with an extraordinary faculty for derision in passages of coruscating rhetoric, lies the strength of Osborne's play.

Still, it is a social symptom. It is not true that Maitland embodies the condition of man. At the most, he is an Englishman, and only of one sort. To be sure, he has his counterparts in other countries—but with distinct differences. Even the morally debilitated American has more youthful zest and thus a semblance of hope, of going somewhere, getting some place. There are large areas of the world in which the Maitlands hardly exist at all. They are the product of political stagnation brought on not by fear or an intellectual incapacity to change but by a society divided within itself: one part clinging to a traditional past which has become a fading memory, the other unsettled because it does not know what the future will look like. Maitland is an image of a festering England.

I say "image" because Maitland is not a *man* at all. He exists as an idea, not as a person. He is a composite of observations, reflections, confessional epigrams. He is the spirit that denies itself. The man who supposes himself a Maitland deceives himself. Maitland is a collage of traits and effects adding up to a gigantic grimace. He is truth only as a caricature is truth. The material of *Inadmissible Evidence* might prove far more cogent as a series of sketches, pathetic-comic.

There is talent in the enterprise, but not for tragedy or great drama. Apart from the unmistakable literary flair, it is a talent for catching the mood of a period, a sense of what is in the air, the gift of the adman of genius. This is coupled by what is deepest in Osborne: an outraged disaffection, a self-loathing projected as a contempt for society. None of this is irreconcilable with an irrepressible ambition.

I admire the phenomenon; I have a sneaking sympathy with it, and for all the above reasons (not excepting my own admiration) I find it hateful. It is antibiologic. Men have a life wish far more potent than any death wish. It is the life wish which must be perceived and made sensible to us in every work of art no matter how "black." It is the quickening spark which creates whatever is real and meaningful to us in the world—including expressions of anguish. Ultimately no true work of art can be a depressant. The "downbeat" is only an outcry, sometimes a howl of affirmation.

There is too little of this in *Inadmissible Evidence*. There is barely a trace of compassion (or passion of any kind) in the play. Everything hangs fire. Actually there is no situation, only a state of mind. Therefore nothing can move or be moving. Maitland's clients are not convinced of their case; they are undecided as to whether or not they demand judgment. Maitland's last words as he remains alone in his office are, "I think I'll just stay here. Good-bye." He does not want to become other than he is. His psychologic posture is to sit contemplating a supposedly injured thumb, murmuring, "A little tumor. On the end

of another." For the English audience *Inadmissible Evidence*
became a formidably impressive piece of publicity, reading: Sign
of the Times. In this it succeeds too well.

Anthony Page's direction is excellent; the cast on the whole
is very good. This is especially so, among the lesser parts, of Ted
van Griethuysen as a "symbolic" homosexual—latent in almost
every aspect of thought, work, play or misdeed.

Nicol Williamson's performance as Maitland is a technical
triumph. The part is exhausting because *Inadmissible Evidence*
is virtually an overextended one-man show. What is especially
remarkable about Williamson's performance is that he forces one
to listen to and to hear every phrase of the two- and three-page
speeches. Not a line or a nuance is scotched or dropped. Still,
from this appearance alone, one is unable to assess Williamson's
full measure as an actor. At times he is as intolerable as the
character he portrays—nasal in speech with a ringing, uninflected
voice except to the extent to which he is able to make such an
utterance as "How are you?" an oily snarl of disgust. There is
in the performance a kind of unvarying proficiency of delivery
which may be required by the assignment or intended to maintain the style of heartlessness which is perhaps desired by
author and director. Feeling seems largely absent, or perhaps it
has been avoided as evidence of sloppy sentimentality.

Harold Pinter

The Caretaker, 1961

IN ITS OWN WAY Harold Pinter's *The Caretaker* is a perfect little play. Like the work of Samuel Beckett, it is a terrifying comedy. I mention Beckett, not only because Pinter has acknowledged his indebtedness to the Parisianized Irishman, but because *The Caretaker* is a variation on the Theme that has begun to haunt the stage since the younger men of the theatre began waiting for Godot. This does not mean that Pinter is not an original talent: the specific English accent of his play lends it its own stamp.

I am sure Pinter detests the reading of symbols into *The Caretaker*. It is written with so much raciness, so definite a tang of British weather that one barely notices the degree of the play's abstractness. Its three characters are named Mick, Aston and Davies; the house in West London where the action takes place reeks of the wetness, the slovenliness, the mold and decrepitude of many buildings in that neighborhood. And while the play is streaked with humor, it might appear almost meaningless were it not for the ideological patterns it suggests.

The details are graphic and striking enough to be memorably self-sufficient (which is always true in a work of art). Yet they call for interpretation, even if the author were to protest that a particular interpretation, or any interpretation, belied his purpose.

Aston, a strange young man who dwells in a run-down flat in a battered and leaky house, brings home an old derelict named Davies, whom he has saved from a beating in a pub where the old man was presumed to be doing some menial job. The old wretch (ever since the war he has been going under an assumed name: Jenkins) is a malodorous grotesque—craven, boastful, aggressive. He hates foreigners (especially blacks) and is lazy and mendacious. Yet he is pitiful in his stupid pride. Aston sees through the sham and invites him to share the disheveled quarters.

Davies shows little gratitude. He begs for new shoes but is not satisfied with any of those offered. He grumbles over the placement of the bed in which he has been put up. He groans and makes ugly sounds in his sleep—keeping his host awake at night. When he learns that his benefactor was once subjected to shock treatment (Aston was committed to a mental hospital because he was a "dreamer"), Davies abuses him for not treating him as well as he should. Davies also turns for help to Aston's brother, Mick, who actually owns the house which he has bought to keep his brother in safety. Mick hardly ever speaks to his brother, though he seems semibenevolently to watch over him. Unaccountably, Mick toys with and torments old Davies and threatens him when Davies refers to Aston as a "nut." Ultimately, Aston orders the old man to get out; his complaints, his ungratefulness, his dirtiness are insufferable. Then the old beggar cries out: "What am I going to do? Where am I going to go?"

Each of the three characters seems to dwell in a world apart from the others—and from everything else. They repeat themselves endlessly but never make themselves understood. Each on his own is cruel to the others.

Who are these people? What do they signify? One is not supposed to be entirely sure. But is not Mick, the laconic prankster with his deliberate double-talk and barbed mystifications, a kind of godhead—angel and devil in one? May not Aston, crucified for his idealistic dreaminess, be a sort of Christ figure? And could not the curmudgeon Jenkins-Davies, in search of the papers which will identify him and prove who he "really" is, stand for mankind itself? He is asked to be a caretaker, but he has neither aptitude nor appetite for the job. No one knows what his "game" is; the final verdict passed on him in the play is that he must be gotten rid of because he makes "too much noise." The house which he is asked to guard is so run down it is hardly worth the trouble of anyone's care. Aston, who had hoped to make something of it, who had tried, at any rate, to protect the poor, harmless creature whom he had invited to share his digs, now dreams only of building a new shelter of fresh, clean wood—a healthy place somewhere in the nearby premises.

Pinter's refusal to make the play as neatly (or platitudinously) intelligible as this is probably justified. Plays like *The Caretaker* owe some of their fascination to ambiguity. But this ambiguity covers what is inherently a simple—perhaps too simple—design. Hence they disturb without actually moving us. The artistic plan is narrower than it pretends to be; the ambiguity is an unconscious spiritual device whereby the author, uncommitted in his soul in relation to the bewilderment and anguish life causes him, remains congealed in his quandary—a situation which may after all be easier to bear than an outright decision as to how to resolve or change it.

It is a tribute to the talent and value of *The Caretaker*—one of the most representative plays in the contemporary English-language theatre—that it can provoke such thoughts, conjectures and perhaps controversies.

Almost as remarkable as the play itself is its production under the direction of Donald McWhinnie. He has achieved that rare thing in the theatre: a true marriage of text and performance. Donald Pleasence as Davies is funny, obnoxious, astonishing, mysterious. His manner ranges from the fiercely vulgar to the apocalyptic. (How his voice echoes when he utters his last cry of abandonment!) His flailing gestures, frightening and incoherent, seem to beat the air with nameless yet vehement queries and protestations. The emotional result is awesome rather than tragic or even pathetic—in which respect it partakes of the quality of the play itself. This is true too of Robert Shaw as the play's impotent "redeemer," caught in the vise of a pity that fails to console. There is a coldness in Alan Bates' consummate portrayal of the inexplicably good-bad "landlord"—utterly real in its English impassivity, a kind of muted familiarity which in its unyielding objectivity is as fatal as a god's final judgment. Play and production wound and adhere to one's spirit like the impress of a tattoo.

The Dumbwaiter and *The Collection*, 1962

Without being on the creative level of *The Caretaker* (page 105) or his first play, *The Birthday Party*, Harold Pinter's *The Dumbwaiter* and *The Collection* extend our understanding of this interesting dramatist.

There is a paradox in the combination of these two one-acters. The more effective and the better played is *The Collection*, but I was more fascinated by the not-so-efficient *Dumbwaiter*. Though shorter than its companion piece (and earlier in composition than either *The Caretaker* or *The Collection*), *The Dumbwaiter* aims higher and its method is subtler. It is written as a comedy sketch, but is nevertheless wholly symbolic. Yet there are no "mists," none of the deeply intoned incantations, commonly associated with symbolism.

Two cockneys, speaking the monotonous, barren language of the uneducated and unimaginative, are discovered to be hired gunmen who kill without malice or personal motive apart from their "profession." (The failure to use an authentic London dialect in the production is unfortunate; it deprives the piece of needed color.) The gunmen's victims are not only persons unknown to them but "objects" whose identity is hardly distinguishable by them. We see the gunmen in a dismal basement, lying on two miserable cots and waiting for orders to proceed to their murderous destination. They wait—and here there is an echo of the "waiting" in Beckett's plays—when strange things begin to occur. A packet of matches is suddenly slipped under the door. They do not understand the source or meaning of this "gift," but they decide to use it so they can boil water for the indispensable tea. But the gas range does not work. "Why did he send us matches," one of them asks, "if he knows there was no gas?" And we begin to perceive the play's drift.

Then, just as surprisingly, the dumbwaiter bangs down with a series of orders for all sorts of fancy foods. The place they are in, they surmise, must once have been a restaurant. Though it is now gutted of all provisions, they respond to the peremptoriness of the demand by sending up silly substitutes for the ordered dishes.

The orders now come down faster and ever more furiously. They are in despair as they respond with hysterical impetus. They cry out to explain their inability to supply the orders and to find out who exactly is issuing them: "What's the idea! What's he playing games for?" There is no reply. It may be possible that the final order is for one of the men to kill the other; the impulse and tempo of obedience make it not at all improbable that this order too may be carried out.

The intention is clear. (Why does such a simple plot structure baffle so many in the audience—particularly those practiced playgoers who are expected to understand it?) Man immured in penury, discomfort and airless constriction, is bound to carry out the commands of a master whom he does not see, know or fathom—commands he obeys in mechanical haste as if he were gripped by a tic. And if this is not true of man in general, it might be inferred (for Pinter will not say) that it is certainly true of man today; and the play, if one wishes to ascribe to it something less than a metaphysical interpretation, might be set down as a protest, albeit a hopeless one, against the pressure of our industrial civilization.

This, however, sounds more pretentious than is Pinter's spare treatment. His play is a swift image halfway between humor and horror. But its production is imprecise and undistinguished.

The direction by Alan Schneider and the acting—particularly by James Ray and Henderson Forsythe—in *The Collection* are much more pointed and therefore, as I have indicated, make for a better "show." It is unnecessary to summarize the plot of *The Collection*. It too has its ambiguities—does not answer all our questions—but it plays on the themes of jealousy, adultery and the nightmare ambivalence of disturbed marital (or merely sex) relationships, not excluding the homosexual, and is sufficiently clear to almost everyone.

What is astute in Pinter's handling of his subject is that nearly all the impulses involved are only partially expressed and thus emerge only as possibilities. There can be no Othello or Iago in such a situation because modern man (and woman) disapprove of jealousy and the acts of violence arising from it. They therefore attempt to repress them, so that finally they (and we) begin to doubt the reality of their feelings. Am I really "fit to be tied" because my wife has been unfaithful? Can my contact with that man be really considered "an affair," or did I just toy with the idea of such a contact? If I were certain that he or she has had an affair would I divorce, maim or murder, or would I go on living with my mate in tortured or "sophisticated" indecision, the possible infidelity forgotten or forgiven because I am unsure whether I also "transgressed"?

The Collection reveals another curious aspect of Pinter's technique. His plays work because they are constructed as *melodrama*. They possess a taut, suspenseful quality that serves to give intensity to the suggested emotions. These are rarely probed because, for emotion to be full-bodied and secure, clear values must exist, and Pinter's theatre implies either that we have none or that those we have are peculiarly vague. The shadow of the suggested emotions keeps us theatrically excited even before we realize—and even if we do not realize—their specific substance. This technique is so marked in *The Collection* that we are led to suspect it of a certain slickness. The trick may conceivably end by deceiving its author. *The Caretaker*, for all its effort to suppress it, has feeling; *The Collection*, almost none. As a substitute, it employs tension.

The Room and *A Slight Ache*, 1964

The Room and *A Slight Ache*, advertised as the *New Pinter Plays*, are not new at all. The first—Pinter's earliest piece—was written in 1957; the second was originally televised by BBC in 1959. They make a very interesting evening. In fact, I rate *A Slight Ache* as highly as anything Pinter has given us. It is a little masterpiece.

Both plays are "mysteries." Like most of Pinter's work they are sustained by suspense. Technically, they are melodramas, which is an excellent, indeed a classic, formula for playmaking, but I call them "mysteries" because there is something religiously ineffable about them. They speak a strange tongue but the effect is that of saying things so fundamental that reducing them to concrete explanation is somehow to deform their relevance.

The Room is the more obscure of the two plays. It is not made to be "understood." It is intended as something to feel. It is all fun, folly and fright. The fun results from the language used by the drab folk huddling in a miserable room in an anonymous lodging house in a nondescript London neighborhood. This room, which should inspire claustrophobia (and pneumonia), is a kind of dank hiding place from the horror of the streets. Pinter is a past master at recording the inanity which marks the small talk of the English poor. Its repetitious monotony and ineptitude make us laugh to begin with and end by making us shiver. This speech is not merely characteristic of a locale or a class; it evokes a moral landscape.

In this landscape monsters appear: some eventually prove themselves harmless; in others the grotesque becomes murderous. They are emblems of the world's stupidity, unhappiness or insane violence. I will not disclose what happens in *The Room*, but if I were pressed I would say that the Room happens!

A Slight Ache is much more intelligible. But though it can be recounted as a story, odd but lucid, it is almost as mysterious as the first play. Edward, a middle-class husband, and his wife, Flora, notice an old Matchseller who has chosen to post himself outside their house on a quiet country lane, close to a monastery where hardly anyone passes. No one ever buys the old man's matches or gives him alms, yet rain or shine he stands in the same place without a word or a gesture. Edward, suffering from a slight ache in his eyes, is perturbed by the Matchseller's peculiar presence and insists on calling him into the house for questioning. The man enters, never utters a sound, barely moves except to sit down when he is asked to. This failure to respond to courtesy or to quizzing drives Edward into a frenzy, to breakdown, finally to a confession of abject impotence in everything. Flora receives the Matchseller in more kindly fashion, even feels toward him as a mother, and possibly as a mate. He is dirty, his smell is repellent, but he needs only a good wash and scrub (which she undertakes to give him), after which she will fondly keep him in the house.

Let us say that the Matchseller represents existence itself. It is ugly, it is uncommunicative, it is without clear meaning or specific identity—except that it is there. Edward contemplates it, finds it unsightly, tries to shut it from his mind, becomes fascinated by it, and finally succumbs in helpless awe before it. The actual confrontation with it makes a gibbering idiot of him. The woman, Flora, responds to it with an instinctive embrace: she accommodates herself to it and domesticates it with tenderness.

That is how I saw the play. You may see it quite differently and so may I on another occasion. Pinter may have had other ideas in mind. It does not matter. The play entertains, holds and moves us. Its vocabulary.has moved upward in the class scale. Edward and Flora are literate folk but what they say is just as conventional and obtuse as the cockney talk in *The Room*. In Pinter, speech is always used as if it were an obstruction to human contact. But the play achieves a sort of poetry, the tension of a slight ache which adumbrates tragedy.

The performances are well directed by Word Baker—particularly in the better of the two plays. The set, too, in this play has been craftily designed by Ed Wittstein—excellent use being made of slight means and limited space. Frances Sternhagen is admirable in both plays, though certainly more authentic in the second. She is one of the many unheralded actresses of quality in which our theatre abounds but rarely employs to their (or our) advantage. Henderson Forsythe as Edward also serves with conviction and address.

The Lover and Beckett's *Play*, 1964

Words have become so debased or featureless in theatre discussion that when a critic calls a play "interesting," one assumes that he must have been bored by it. I must therefore assert that when I say I found the double bill of one-act plays by Harold Pinter and Samuel Beckett interesting, I want my readers to understand that I mean that these plays merit their attentive consideration.

The Pinter play, *The Lover*, a reformed television script, is the more amusing; the Beckett piece, called *Play*, the more striking. *The Lover* lasts about fifty minutes, *Play* only about fifteen minutes.

There is a certain slickness or "commercial" dispatch about *The Lover*, but it is not, in the author's mind at least, unserious. It is necessary to say this at the outset because some aspects of the play are almost as banal as a revue blackout.

A middle-class Englishman, Richard, married to a young woman, Sarah, lives a double life with her. In the morning and in the evening they are a tidy, traditionally correct, placid couple. On odd afternoons, Richard returns to the house as a tough, disreputable, somewhat depraved character—Sarah's "lover." Sarah, in turn, greets her "lover" as a wanton whose technique of enticement must have been picked up from a textbook issued by a low-grade movie magazine.

In the evening, when a sedate Richard returns, he frequently asks about Sarah's lover; at the same time he confesses his own affair with a dissolute woman who is little more to him than an erotic convenience. This routine continues for some time, until one day Richard announces that Sarah's liaison is insufferable and that he no longer will tolerate her afternoon escapades. Richard's jealous tantrum frightens her until she realizes that to appease him she must enact the trollop with him, the gentlemanly Richard!

The conduct of the play's action, which combines a touch of Strindberg with a larger dose of burlesque, is insidiously clever and passably unwholesome. What intrigued me more than the play's game is the degree to which audiences, particularly in England, take the play as something more than entertainment. Is it received as a metaphor for a psychological truth (we want our wives to be our whores), or as the symbol of a wish, or simply as a "teaser"? Pinter's ambiguity in this respect is cunning. Is the play the reflection of a peculiarly English mental and moral disarray, to be studied by sociologists and psychoanalysts, or just a joke? Pinter's attitude is noncommittal. He retires from the scene like the Cheshire cat—without the smile. Perhaps he, himself, is puzzled. We laugh a bit and remain ever so slightly disturbed.

Beckett's *Play* is less "fun," but is a further instance of his genius. I cannot say that I "like" it; it is the kind of work which exists in such a way that the question of my, or your, liking it becomes irrelevant. It is a thing in itself.

The stage directions as Beckett himself set them down furnish a clue to his style:

> *Extreme front, touching one another, three large white urns, one yard high, from which three heads protrude through holes*

*close fitting to their necks. . . . [They] face undeviatingly front
throughout act. Age: indifferent. Appearance: indifferent. . . .
Faces impassive throughout. Voices toneless except where expression indicated.*

Whom do these "heads" speaking from their (funerary?) urns
belong to? W. 1, W. 2, M. (Woman one, Woman two, Man.) The
play is the essentialized comic-tragedy (or "metadrama") of
adultery: the eternal triangle. The dialogue is uninflected by any
readily defined emotion or climax. At times each of the figures
speaks some incomplete phrase typical of his or her thought.
Often they speak simultaneously—not always intelligibly—and in
a semimurmur affecting us like the rustling of leaves or the
whisperings of the dead.

The triangular situation begins hilariously as a vulgar commonplace. Slowly a sense of boredom, then of guilt, then of regret, then of hopeless indifference and finally of utter forgetfulness steals over the three livid figures immersed in their urns as if
in a gray sod, nearly mute and altogether meaningless. It is almost too awful to be sad; too disheartening to be tragic.

You have heard of the Constitution being written on a postage
stamp or of the Lord's Prayer being engraved on a pin. Beckett's
Play is like a statement of the polygamous sex-agony inscribed in
sure shorthand strokes.

This leaves me dissatisfied, dumbfounded. But who says
Beckett hoped to satisfy me? There is acute pathos here, but so
compressed that one is not permitted a sigh or the shedding of a
tear.

Scientists have said that there will come a time when a small
pill will replace a full meal. The pill takes less time to consume
and will furnish us with all the needed vitamins. Perhaps so. It
will indicate progress and certainly be "modern." Unregenerate
hedonist that I am, I shall always prefer a banquet even though it
may make me sick.

Still, Beckett is a master. As director, Alan Schneider is his
obedient servant.

Murray Schisgal

Luv, 1964

A STRIKING OBJECT lesson in the making of a play might be given if it were possible to see the London production of Murray Schisgal's *Luv* followed immediately by the one now on view here.

It happens that I was asked two years ago to review the play in London for *The Observer*. It struck me then as an amusing spoof with some arid moments when the play dwelt overlong on its parody. In New York, where it is perfectly cast with Eli Wallach, Anne Jackson and Alan Arkin, brilliantly directed by Mike Nichols in a set crisply styled for attractive fun by Oliver Smith, and suavely lit by Jean Rosenthal so that a night scene manages to look both atmospheric and cheerful, the play is a clean hit, a continuously engaging event.

It is not simply a matter of its having been "improved"; without noticeable addition to the text, it is almost a new play. It kids the stereotypes of our everyday talk, the self-pity in which so many of us indulge, propped by the dumb jargon of analysts, permissive pedants, the theorists of our aches and pains whose diagnoses so often sound like commercial blather on behalf of TV nostrums. The properties of love-love-love as a cure for every discomfort from chilblains and heartburn to metaphysical anguish are thoroughly travestied. Lampooned even more is our mania for temperature-taking to measure the degree, duration and dimension of our "loves."

The peculiarly American style employed is related to clowning in the manner of a sophisticated Sid Caesar. The comment is neither deep nor cutting, but it *is* hilarious. The objects of ridicule are neither confronted nor transcended; they are negated by a hop, skip and jump of irreverent tomfoolery.

Something more should be said about Mike Nichols' inventive fancy, as well as about the finish with which each bit of action is accomplished. The gags become cunning notes of imaginative statement, comparable to a fine flourish of ballet movement. Examples of this are present at the curtain of both acts. Eli Wallach's ecstatic leap onto the lamppost when freed of his wife; Alan Arkin's climb up the same lamppost to get away from his symbolic nemesis—a dog threatening to use the man's leg as a place of convenience.

Wallach is all sweet exuberance or lovably idiotic despair; Anne Jackson is all foolish earnestness and silly severity; Arkin's voice, unresonant with a doggedly nasal vehemence, adds to an immense self-absorption that results in portraiture as classically indelible as the work of a master caricaturist.

Peter Weiss

Marat/Sade, 1966

EVERYONE SHOULD be grateful to the Royal Shakespeare Company of London for bringing to New York its production under Peter Brook's direction of Peter Weiss' *The Persecution and Assassination of Marat as Performed by the Inmates of the Asylum of Charenton under the Direction of the Marquis de Sade*. Whether or not you are going to like it, you ought to see it. For when all is said and done—and much is done and said through the hubbub of the performance—the production is a fascinating entertainment. For scrupulous care in makeup, for subtlety in costuming, for ingenuity in dealing with movement, for the feeling of novelty throughout, New York has not seen the like in a long time. We witness here what a well-organized repertory theatre of talented players and leaders can accomplish.

Much of the talk during the intermission of *Marat/Sade* centered on Peter Brook's "use of space." It is indeed brilliant. So is Richard Peaslee's incidental music. Even more persuasively theatrical are the sound effects—for example, the employment of the wooden platforms as "drums" to be struck by whatever objects are available to the actors. Brueghel, Bosch, Goya have provided models for the visual aspect of various figures. There is a memorable grouping in which the actors' faces alone are seen, their bodies being submerged beneath the stage floor. The impression is that of a heap of severed heads tossed helter-skelter on the ground. There is witty business to match the playfulness of the text, such as the pouring of red paint from a pail to indicate the shedding of the people's blood, changed to blue when the aristocrats' blood is spilled, and then to milky white when Marat finally succumbs to Corday's murderous knife.

More impressive perhaps than all this is the actors' zeal, their unrelenting concentration and byplay so that nothing on the stage is allowed to become static or to fall out of line. Even the musicians in the side boxes participate in pantomime. Voices are resonant, diction is admirable, though I could not always make out the words of the ensemble singing.

The kind of acting demanded, though physically strenuous, is of the simplest sort, requiring attitudes and postures rather than intimate emotional transfiguration. The well-managed trick for most of the cast is to show that the "actors" of the play they are presenting at Charenton are syphilitics, spastics, catatonics, schizophrenics, paranoiacs, manic depressives or otherwise debilitated persons, none of them consistently able to remember the script's lines or to keep within the confines of the author's (de Sade's) scenic scheme. The team work is exemplary.

Of the individuals in the excellent company, Ian Richardson as Marat, Patrick Magee as de Sade, Robert Lloyd as the fanatic Jacques Roux, John Steiner as an aristocrat afflicted with satyriasis, Susan Williamson as Marat's ever faithful mistress, Simonne Evrard, Michael Williams as the Herald (master of ceremonies) deserve special mention, though my particular favorite, an actress of insidious attractiveness, is Glenda Jackson as Charlotte Corday.

Apart from noting "the use of space," the professionally oriented playgoer may speak of Brecht and "alienation" or of Artaud's "theatre of cruelty." The production is punctuated by frenzied paroxysms, as the text is replete with images of extreme violence. There is also—and this is not as noticeable in an English translation as it would be in the original German—a good deal of expressionist hysteria (abhorred by Brecht), a kind of roaring and macabre lyricism.

It should be noted in regard to influences, which though they have a certain interest do not affect the heart of the matter, that while many of Brecht's devices are employed—the most salient being the use of remote historical material to make topical points —certain elements in the production, almost baroque in their profusion and nerve-racking in their intended impact, are antithetical to Brecht. It should also be said of a production in which the staging very nearly swallows the script that Weiss' text might be produced with less emphasis on the hectic and

bizarre and that the insanity of the characters need not have
been rendered with as much graphic distortion as Brook has
employed. In that case, although the results would not be quite
so showy, we might more readily discern what Weiss had in
mind.

What is certainly untrue, as some have intimated, is that there
is no *play*, no meaning or message in Weiss' writing. Here we
come to the question of the evening's real worth, of which discussion limited to its stage excitement is actually an evasion. (Do
you go to the theatre to enjoy "the use of space"?) In Germany,
where it was first produced, *Marat/Sade* was preeminently a
political play. (To be sure, it also reveals Weiss as a master of
the theatrical medium, quite apart from Brook's contribution.)
It is a particularly German political play though its author lives
in Sweden and stresses his internationalism. There is a reference
to the "Final Solution" (the Nazi extermination of the Jews), but
the issues raised extend beyond such history. Even allusions to
"wars whose weapons rapidly developed by servile scientists
will become more and more deadly until they can with a flick
of a finger tear a million of you to pieces" are not of the utmost
moment here.

Marat/Sade is a debate within its author's spirit. The political
issue which gave rise to it is the division of Germany (and the
rest of Europe) into capitalist and Socialist camps. In this play
Weiss stands between the two camps. He sees fascism beaten
and capitalism still oppressively hypocritical. He sees an apparently victorious socialism lead to a crippling conformity.
His skepticism turns to bitterness, anxiety to despair. Man is a
destructive beast, as Weiss' de Sade (who arrives at his sadism
through masochism) says; the people still demand a revolution
which will realize the everlasting dream of peace, plenty, freedom of conscience and expression.

Again and again, as the songs in *Marat/Sade* voicing this
dream are turned into satires, Weiss mocks the idea that any
political action can end oppression. He seems to be saying that
all determined struggle in this direction, the promises of all
social, cultural and religious institutions, end in betrayal. Remember that all the central characters in the play—including the
most articulate, the ultra-radical Marat and the mortified de Sade
—are demented, their world a madhouse.

Weiss does not make the Marat/Sade duel a one-sided affair. He tosses and turns in indecision. The final lines of the play are Roux's outcry "When will you learn to see, when will you learn to take sides?"—an outcry stifled by the people's trancelike march and shouts. Yes, one must take sides, but isn't there something futile, Weiss infers, in it all? To which, Weiss or Brook has appended an ironically facetious speech telling us that we can compose our own moral, draw our own conclusions, from the proceedings.

That I am not wholly mistaken in my interpretation I call Weiss himself (apart from his text) in evidence. He has recently announced that since the writing of *Marat/Sade* he has changed his attitude, he has decided to take sides: he has become a Socialist. But for the playgoer or the critic it is perhaps not initially imperative to declare oneself on the validity of Weiss' position in this play but simply to recognize that the play aims to illustrate the anguish of decision, the gravity of the human problem involved: that social change always entails the possibility of sanguinary upheaval—a price too terrible to pay in view of man's disposition to turn the most high-minded enterprises to mediocrity and, in the end, to perpetuate injustice.

Yet I left the theatre unmoved, almost indifferent. (I was reminded of Tolstoy's quip about Andreyev: "He wants to frighten me, but I'm not scared.") I am moved by the "coolness" of the Berliner Ensemble in Brecht's *Mother Courage*. In like manner, I am truly concerned about Galileo's dilemma in the same author's account of it. With *Marat/Sade* I am left only with a sense of an adult entertainment—surely a precious boon these days—rather than stirred by any vitalizing thought or feeling about the play's subject matter, ostensibly of crucial importance.

It is true that when Coulmier, the asylum's supervisor, jumps up to intervene—after Roux has shouted, "Once and for all the idea of glorious victories won by the glorious army must be wiped out. Neither side is glorious"—with the admonition "This is outright pacifism. At this very moment our soldiers are laying down their lives for the freedom of the world and of our world," the audience applauds (and how delighted many of us are that it does) in recognition of the attack upon a contemporary parallel. Still, I venture to say that it is not really engaged in the play's theme, never truly disturbed by the cardinal question raised, or stimulated to search itself for an answer. LeRoi Jones' savagery (another sort of "theatre of cruelty") appalls us. *Marat/Sade* converts all our political and intellectual concern into display, an artful fun house, a magnificent toy. It is distinguished decoration, first-class theatrical "salesmanship."

Whether or not this is due in part to the sort of brilliant direction Brook has given the play, the fact remains that most of the text, though cleverly or cutely phrased in deliberate doggerel or near verse, is trite. There are long passages popularizing primary existentialist pronouncements as understood in cafés and often reduced, despite Germanic vehemence, to a facile pessimism very comforting at bottom to the presumably despised bourgeoisie.

Since *Marat/Sade* is a dramatization of political inconclusiveness or nihilism, a position which many smart folk nowadays equate with true wisdom, I shall set down my own sentiments in regard to the misgivings which the play enunciates.

Yes: the French Revolution was followed by Napoleon's autocracy, the hopes of the early Russian revolutionaries were mangled into Stalinism, the war against Hitler has brought Germany, France and Italy to various degrees of stultifying complacency. History offers no guarantees. If pressed hard enough, men will assert their livingness to the point of bloodshed to achieve what they deem to be a better life. Man moves and sometimes fights because he *is* man and wants to make a world according to his material and spiritual needs. This is an impulse, if you will, a fact of nature, to which I say "yea"—no matter how often history appears to negate man's efforts. One does not even have to believe in Progress to assent to and justify the never-ending struggle. As long as there are creatures on earth more sentient than computers, men will, because they must, make choices, and they will not be deterred by what wiseacres in the future may decide as to the sagacity of these choices. When asked, "Is life worth living?" Samuel Butler answered, "That is a question for a foetus not for a man." To despair because man's extreme efforts to modify conditions of social injury or physical misery frequently result in new humiliations is to be either an intellectual sissy or a moral coward.

The best compliment I can tender *Marat/Sade* is that it has provoked me to this declaration. And if anyone argues that in approaching the play in this manner I have exceeded the bounds of the "trade," that is, gone beyond the theatre, I must once again affirm that unless theatre and theatre criticism do this they both become paltry and inconsequential. "He knows no drama who only drama knows."

Tennessee Williams

~~~~~~~~~~~~~~

Sweet Bird of Youth, 1959

TENNESSEE WILLIAMS' *Sweet Bird of Youth* interested me
more as a phenomenon than as a play. Its place in the author's development and its fascination for the audience strike me
as more significant than its value as drama.

Williams is a romantic; one of the characteristics of the romantic is a pressing need to reveal himself. Though the play's
narrative is realistic, the characters are frequently called upon to
address the audience directly. Both in its content and its form one
senses the author's urgent impulse to say everything he feels right
out. Here I am, he seems to be telling us, naked and unabashed,
and I am going to speak my piece. At the end of the play the
central character turns to us and says, "I do not ask for your pity
or even your understanding. I ask you only to recognize me in
yourselves."

What is it we are asked to recognize in ourselves? That we
are corrupted by our appetite for the flash and clamor of success,
that we are driven to live debased existences by the constrictions
and brutality which surround us, that the sound instincts of our
youth are thus frustrated and turned to gall, and that we have an
inordinate fear of age, for the passing of time makes us old before
we mature.

There may be truth in this. More important is the manner in
which this truth is conveyed. Chance Wayne is an average small-
town boy born and reared somewhere on the Gulf Coast. At the
age of seventeen he has an idyllic affair with a girl of fifteen. But
because he is poor, the girl's father—political boss of the town—
calls an abrupt halt to the romance. The boy goes to New York in

123

the hope of becoming enough of a big shot as an actor to impress the folks back home. Because he has good looks but very little training, he gets nothing but jobs in the chorus of musicals. He also gives unbounded satisfaction to numerous women.

He is drafted for the Korean War and he suffers the awful fear that his splendid youth will be cut off by mutilation and his ambition thwarted by death. After his release from the Navy one of his jobs is that of masseur at a Florida beach resort. He earns money on the side as a gigolo. One of the women he encounters is a fading movie star in flight from impending failure. Her terror makes her take refuge in drugs and promiscuity. Chance Wayne brings her back to his home town. He clings to this woman—whose whore he becomes—because he plans to make her the key to a Hollywood career for himself. To make sure that she will live up to her end of the agreement, he uses a dictaphone to blackmail her—she has confessed to having smuggled the hashish they both smoke. In the meantime, he uses her Cadillac and takes her money to spend conspicuously so that his former girl, her father and the boyhood friends will be awed by his "position."

At some point before these latter events, Chance had resumed his affair with the girl who is his true love. Sometime during his career as a gigolo he had contracted a venereal disease and had unknowingly infected his beloved. Her father has her undergo an operation which renders her sterile. The girl bids the boy—still ignorant of what has happened—to leave town for good lest her father have him killed.

There are many more details portraying the girl's despair, the vile hypocrisy of her father, the maniacal vindictiveness of her brother, the savagery of the town's political gang. In the end the movie star, who for a moment had shown signs of compassion for the boy, abandons him because she has made a Hollywood comeback and can think of nobody but herself. By remaining in town after he has been repeatedly warned to get out, the boy virtually invites the castration with which he has been threatened.

I have no categorical objection to this heap of horrors. I can believe that they occur in life, indeed that they have occurred. But the telling of this story is very close to lurid melodrama. What saves it from being just that is the fluently euphonious idiom and vivid grace of Williams' writing. Even more telling is Williams' ache and what might be called his ideology.

Is there any virtue at all in Chance Wayne? Williams names it. Chance has given *great pleasure*. He is consummately male, a wonderful lover. When he hears that a Negro in his town has been castrated for assaulting a white woman, Chance cries out, "I know what that is: it's sex envy"—which is surely the author's comment rather than the character speaking. Sex potency is held forth as a special order of merit bestowing amnesty for every misdeed.

Williams does not ask us to admire the boy, but the whole play suggests that he is sufficiently typical to induce us to share some kinship with him. A nonentity can be made central to a modern tragedy as is Clyde Griffith in Dreiser's book, but the novelist did this by weaving a web of environmental circumstance so complete in each detail that we are objectively convinced. Taken literally, Chance Wayne is an atrocity. He is not a real person but a figment of Williams' commanding sentiment.

The simplification and distortion which mark the portrait of Chance are evident in the play's other characters as well—schematic types whose bareness is covered only by Williams' colorful verbiage. The movie actress is the best of them, for there is a grotesque humor about her—a kind of wry pity not far removed from contempt. The most crudely drawn figure is that of Boss Finley, a caricature of a Dixiecrat, a dirty dog beyond compare, more bogey than man. Indeed, there is something about all the people in the play which seems calculated to scare us to death.

Much of what Williams has attempted to say here has been implied in some of his earlier plays, but they had more texture in characterization and reality. What we suspect in *Sweet Bird of Youth* is that Williams has become immobilized in his ideology; that it has not been refreshed either by any new experience or by mature thought. He has only become much bolder. The result is that we feel in this play an inverted sentimentality and a willful stress which produce more ugliness than lyricism or credence.

We know that a great part of what Williams feels about American life is valid; many novels and sociological studies in the past thirty-five years or more have helped us recognize its validity. So it is perhaps useful for Williams to alarm theatre audiences still largely protected from the rumor of the real world. Scandal on Broadway may be beneficent. But I observe that the audience at *Sweet Bird* is entertained rather than stirred, piqued rather than sobered. It does not truly believe what it sees; it is simply enjoying a show with a kick in it. And this lack of shock may be attributed to something specious in the stage proceedings.

The production, directed by Elia Kazan, is admirably cast throughout: Paul Newman, Sidney Blackmer, Diana Hyland—all are good. Geraldine Page as the movie star creates an especially striking image—more on the comedy character side than on the pathetic. A sure and sharp showmanship is always manifest. The sets, though bare, are prettified by Jo Mielziner's sumptuous lighting.

The Night of the Iguana, 1962

Some years ago, defending a novel by a famous writer which had been thoroughly roasted in all the reviews, Tennessee Williams said that he liked the book because the novelist had succeeded in thoroughly exposing his inner being. That is a romantic view of the function of art, but since all works of art do in fact reveal the men who made them—though I doubt that it is their main purpose or value—I am not prepared to contest Williams' defense.

While Tennessee Williams' latest play, *The Night of the Iguana*, is certainly not strict autobiography, it does give us an idea of how Williams sees and judges himself. At the moment, this seems to me the most rewarding aspect of the play, though not the only one. Indeed, it is easy to assert that it is the best American play of the season—since there is nothing else to stand beside it.

There is sentimentality in all of Williams' work, but in *The Night of the Iguana* he is not trying to show himself in a favorable light. The reverse may be closer to the truth. If there is pardon in the play, it results from confession and self-castigation —which is one of the forms a puritanic romanticism takes.

The central character is the still young Lawrence Shannon, an Episcopal minister who has shocked his congregation by denouncing its God and substituted for Him a pantheistic deity, or to put it more plainly, a god as amoral as the forces of nature themselves. Shannon's church is closed to him and he has become a tourist guide in Mexico. He takes pleasure in showing his (American) clients the shady or seamy side of the places they visit, not only because that is what attracts him but also because it fascinates them. He is given to promiscuous fornication—usually with young persons, even minors.

The personal association is clear, is it not? A man of religious disposition desires to spread the Word, but the old God of vengeance is too narrow and shallow for him. Since he cannot renounce instructing and preaching, he must bring to everyone's attention the secret and foul byways of man's experience. Unless these are disclosed life cannot be wholly known or accepted. (This too is what *audiences* hunger to have displayed in a repressed and morally worried community such as ours.) To dedicate oneself to such instruction may have its reprehensible side, but there is a grave mission in it as well.

There is very little indulgence in the portrait of Reverend Shannon. He meets a beautiful and very spiritual New England spinster who travels about with her grandfather, once a well-known minor poet. To support themselves in their extensive peregrinations she paints watercolors and he recites his verse in hostelries, restaurants, holiday resorts. The girl is chaste without strain, pure without vanity. She understands all, forgives all. She is the image of what the outcast preacher considers almost sacred. He knows he cannot corrupt, break or defile her. She has her own strength. Nor can he ever measure up to what she embodies. So he reconciles himself to becoming the companion in waywardness of the lewd and gusty lady whose hotel is the scene of the play. Smiling ruefully, Williams must be content (like his poet) to set himself down as "frightened me."

If one does not perceive the drift of *Iguana* in its relation to its author's legend, the play may seem meaningless, shapeless, a little unreal. Every character is more conceptual than specifically true. (I must allow, but find it especially difficult to believe, that Shannon was ever an ordained minister.) Yet such is Williams' talent that the play breathes with its own artistic life.

The writing, to begin with, is lambent, fluid, malleable and colloquially melodious. It bathes everything in glamour. Colored lights seem to illuminate all the play's people, lending them an odd dimension. I do not care for the hinted psychoanalytic explanation given of Shannon's behavior, but one cannot resist Williams' intuitive invention. For example, cavorting through the seedy Mexican hotel is a chorus of comic maenads in the shape of German (Nazi) tourists—so many fat grubs infesting the place with a sick-making health.

These and the terrifyingly funny secondary characters—the hysterical girl Shannon has seduced (it is interesting to note that he maintains the girls have seduced him), the righteously indignant American schoolteacher infuriated by Shannon—all form part of a picture that not only lends the play credibility but an extraordinary vividness.

A born dramatist, Williams writes wonderful acting parts. The cast has been admirably chosen. Margaret Leighton glows with a subtle flame which conveys a sense of mystery, pity and awe—almost pictorial. Bette Davis, in perhaps the most soundly written part, is ablaze as the sullied bacchante who owns the hotel in which she and the apostate will continue to sin. Patrick O'Neal has the right mask for Shannon—wracked with fever, guilt and a depraved saintliness which somehow resembles asceticism. O'Neal's is a real characterization, though in avoiding gush he appears a little dry, perhaps depriving the personage of lyricism. (It may be a fine point of interpretation whether this is desirable or not.) Patricia Roe and Lane Bradbury are highly effective in smaller parts; Alan Webb, who plays the nonagenarian poet, is, as always, a complete craftsman. Oliver Smith's set—the seedy hotel rank with undergrowth of strange flora and fauna—is one of his best. The company plays well together, to the credit of the director, Frank Corsaro.

Theatre Across America

Crisis on Broadway

1961

THE ONLY CONCLUSION I can come to on reading the six reports which appeared in *The New York Times* on the Broadway crisis is: "No foundation all the way down the line." This applies not to the *Times'* journalistic efforts but to the thinking about the theatre—in the theatre—which the articles reflect.

To begin with, there is scarcely any agreement as to the facts. What are some of the matters which one might suppose to be beyond dispute? Attendance in the Broadway theatre has fallen from 12,300,000 in 1930–31 to 8,100,000 last season. The theatre's physical plant has diminished from sixty-six houses in 1931 to the present thirty-three. Forty-six new shows were produced last season, a record low, as compared to the more than two hundred produced in 1926–27. Hardly any of the better productions of nonmusical plays were of American origin. Is there a crisis? One of the reporters summed up the reaction of the theatre people he questioned as "absolutely yes—definitely no."

One producer is quoted as having said, "I think Broadway is entering a renaissance. We are on the verge of a boom." (This producer has had an exceptionally profitable year: three musical hits and an English "prestige" play.) Another producer who has lost his backers considerable sums of money in the past but who made some last season with a two-person revue goes so far as to say that "the financial plight of the theatre is exaggerated."

The crisis—acknowledged by the majority—was brought to public attention not because so few plays were produced last season but because so much money was lost. Hardly any nonmusical play, except for *Mary! Mary!*, showed a real profit or even paid all its costs. It is now feared that the conduct of the "legitimate" theatre will soon become a wholly quixotic enterprise and ultimately altogether unfeasible.

The suggested remedies are, first, the elimination of federal and city entertainment taxes; second, adjustments by dramatists, stars, directors, scene designers on royalties, and, third, the abrogation of certain onerous rulings by the stagehand and musician unions. So far only the Dramatists' Guild has agreed to any concession in the matter of royalty payments—*provided* stars, directors and others follow suit.

The federal and city taxes have not yet been reduced. On the other hand, it is expected that tax privileges on expense accounts for entertainment will soon be rescinded—a severe blow to the sale of orchestra seats bought by so many businessmen whose theatregoing seems dependent on their expense accounts. What is also noteworthy is that the tax on theatre tickets is part of the *entertainment* tax, which places nightclubs on a par with the theatre.

This points to the core of the trouble. Though Senator Javits, in an honorable attempt to aid the theatre through legislation, speaks of it as "a cultural expression," almost everyone else discusses it primarily as a business. For example, one of the arguments advanced in behalf of the community's taking an interest in the theatre's prosperity is that if the theatre were to disappear, other commerce—restaurants, parking lots, garages, taxis, ticket brokers—would also suffer!

There is no question that business organization must play a vital role in the conduct of all theatrical enterprise. But if the theatre is a business chiefly aimed at a profit, then it follows that if a profit is not forthcoming it must and should disappear—unless, like the railroads, its continued life is held to be a matter of public interest and need.

Even the Broadway aphorism tells us that "show business is no business." One of the reasons for the thoroughgoing confusion and muddleheadedness of our theatre world is that willy-nilly the theatre is not *essentially* a business. Even the most hardened or money-minded showman has something of the gambler (that is to say, the artist) in him. We in America have forgotten this or were rarely obliged to remember it—as long as business in the theatre could go on as usual.

The theatre as a private enterprise has existed for at least three hundred years. But almost every country in Europe has recognized that the theatre is part of a nation's patrimony and must therefore be subject to some sort of public control through government (royal, princely, civic or national) agency. Thus in France, Germany, the Scandinavian countries, and now even in England (not to mention most of the Iron Curtain countries even before they were converted to that metal) not only are partial government subsidies provided but regulations as to the number and use of playhouses have been set down. (Napoleon took time on his Russian expedition to rule that the Comédie Française must always keep low-priced—5 franc—seats available for the poorer public.) Some part of the country's theatre establishment —and very often the best—was protected so that it might serve its true function as an expression of the nation's spirit, its emblem. The theatre is one of the means by which a society realizes itself.

In America, for historical reasons, the theatre has never been seriously viewed as being integral with the respectability of our social life. It has been assimilated with our business community, in which success (or profit) becomes the symbolic as well as the effective goal. In a normal economic situation this does not necessarily exert disastrous influence. But when the economic balance in the community is upset, our theatre—now ideologically as well as practically dependent on the profit or pure business motive— must be stricken with paralysis and threatened with extinction.

Talent for the theatre and an appetite for it are still abundant. And theatre folk being what they are, germinal artists, the theatre goes on in our country in a schizophrenic state—half crazy from every point of view and less than half as proficient or useful as it might be.

Let us consider one minor point among the various statements in the *Times* reports by producers on matters of settings and stagehands. Some say that settings should be simplified—to reduce costs, and perhaps also because simplified sets are more "artistic." Others, on the contrary, are entirely satisfied with huge expenditures for "scenery"—when the productions they have spent the money on *prove profitable*. The question of artistic fitness in each instance is gauged by the measure of box-office success rather than by the style of scenic investiture demanded by the text. Certain plays which demand large-scale production—many sets and numerous actors—must virtually be ruled out as prohibitively costly, no matter what their intrinsic merit.

When profit becomes the chief criterion or proof of excellence, understanding of the theatre must become distorted. Business standards replace all others. The preferred actor is the one who will sell the most tickets—if nowhere else, at theatre parties. The most important director is the one who has had the most recent hits. The best scene designers are the ones whose work has graced the greatest number of smashes. This way of thinking makes sane judgment impossible, even *in matters of business.*

No wonder then that the dramatists, presumably the pivot of the theatre organism, are among the most frightened of all show folk. To write a flop is not only an economic blow; it is moral disgrace, a loss of status. Is it possible to write in such an atmosphere? Ah, but the "real" writer will never cease writing. Of course not; the question is what will he write?

Present circumstances—inevitable from the false premises on which the theatre has been obliged to operate—poison the whole theatre: the audience, the critics, the very air of the playhouses. The trauma thus created has made the past fifteen years the age of the middleman, or agent. They are the "victors," the lawgivers. There are now agents for everyone, including the audience. This is the end result of our "realism," "practicality" and nonartiness.

Certainly I favor the reduction of taxes on the theatre. (I also favor special tax benefits, such as obtain in France, for accredited theatre folk and artists in general.) Whatever immediately practicable remedies to small specific ills can be achieved must win our unqualified endorsement. But I suspect that very little will get done through ordinary Broadway channels. The provision made by the Dramatists' Guild in regard to the curtailment of royalty payments will not be acceptable to most stars, and certainly not to their agents. The same holds true for most of the others—directors and scene designers—and with a certain justification.

One agent very sensibly says, "I am willing to gamble, but it should be a concentrated effort by everyone. Are the theatre owners ready to make concessions? The unions? The producers? Is the producer willing to let the other people participate proportionately for gambling with him?" The theatre is a collective (or corporate) art. It must be managed that way. It is perhaps the model type of organization for the industrial as differentiated from the craft union. But at present the theatre is being run as a business in which every man looks out for himself as good old-fashioned business dictates. That is why we are at the point of collapse.

Yet in collapse may lie our only hope. Health may be restored through breakdown, as to a degree it was during the thirties. The theatre may have to be beaten into sanity. Reason (or art) may return to the theatre when "business" has done almost everything possible to kill it.

Already there are signs of this even in the very chaos which *The New York Times* series exposes. Our audiences—as developments off-Broadway to some extent indicate—are becoming ever-more aware of values different from those which obtain on Broadway. Community theatres are growing on a more extensive scale than before. Such projects as the civic theatre in Minneapolis and the Lincoln Center in New York may be auguries of a salutary change.

Not everyone inside or outside the theatre today deems it peculiar to think or speak of the theatre in the terms I have so often employed in these pages. My "pessimism" is intended as a creative implement. Before the theatre changes there must be some "new" thinking. We will not go far, even "business-wise," if we confine ourselves to so-called practical assumptions that are incompatible with the nature of the material at hand. We must be persistent and dogged. Relief will not come overnight. In the meantime we must do the best we can. The first step may be to sharpen our theatrical *intelligence*.

Minneapolis

~~~~~~~~~~

The Minnesota Theatre Company, 1963

MINNESOTA should be a proud state, as Minneapolis is a lucky city. They have taken a step which marks a signal date in American cultural history: they have opened the Tyrone Guthrie Theatre, the most ambitious civic theatre project in this country outside of New York.

This fact alone seems to me to outweigh all other considerations in regard to the first three productions. (The fourth production, *Death of a Salesman*, opened in mid-July.) To argue whether or not the presentation of *Hamlet* in modern trappings is justified strikes me at this juncture as essentially irrelevant. What is significant in the Minnesota venture is the attempt to create a repertory theatre on a high professional level away from the shambles of New York's entertainment market.

What we need in this country is not so much more and better "shows," but the image and fact of a Theatre. Thus far we have none of any conspicuous stature. The more fuss and excitement there is over this or that sensational hit show (even when it is a truly good one), the farther we remove ourselves from the very concept of a Theatre. For a Theatre is not the business of putting on a series of brilliant "attractions," but a unified effort to create an artistic identity which bespeaks the life of both the company and some important segment of the community.

The Minnesota Theatre Company is not yet, and for some time cannot be, such a unit. Its importance is that its organizers, Oliver Rea and Peter Zeisler, with the support of public-spirited sponsors in Minneapolis and a gratifyingly large number of citizens in the area, plan to make this dream come true.

136

The circumstance of Tyrone Guthrie's stewardship as Artistic Director for at least three six-month seasons is both fortunate and dangerous. Guthrie is one of the world's most gifted stage directors. He is a person of large human scope and a craftsman with talents which approach genius. He is an immediate and invaluable asset in the formation of a company on a level of unquestionable theatrical competence. But unless he serves to lead the company to an independent and permanent career, unless he makes everyone responsible for the company's future realize that it must stay and grow after his tenure expires, his individual "stardom" may prove as detrimental to the venture as it is now vivifying. In the making of a true Theatre the director's (or leader's) function is not only to present notable productions, but to educate both audience and artists in the nature and meaning of the institution as an abiding expression of their lives.

The acting company is not and should not now expect to be a "great" company. It is an honorably able one. Its first three productions afford aspects of genuine satisfaction.

I find myself rather impatient with the debate as to whether modern dress and "props" (bowler hat, trench coat, tennis rackets, electric flashlights, etc.) are appropriate to the production of Shakespeare's plays. Offhand I would say that modern clothes in these plays are more emphatically *costumes,* more blatantly eye-catching, even more "stagy," than any sort of traditional dress. But I am unwilling to take a categorical stand. On the whole, the costuming of Guthrie's *Hamlet* is attractive and in some cases witty.

Hamlet is a play of which I am able to follow the plot but have never been able to fathom the meaning. The number of explanations I have read or heard have served to intensify my confusion. I have yet to see a production which had its own unmistakable thought. But perhaps it is in its very mystery or complexity that some of the play's extraordinary fascination lies. I am certain only of one thing: that it is not about a man too thoughtful to take action. If anything, Hamlet is too active.

I have never seen a "definitive" Hamlet (what would that be?), nor has the play in production ever shaken or thrilled me to my depths, as many lesser plays have. The best Hamlets I have seen have impressed me only in bits.

Guthrie's *Hamlet* is a production in which the actors—some of

them do very well in serving his view of scenes and characters—
are employed to fulfill a design rather than to embody their own
(or whatever may be taken to be Shakespeare's) substance. This
is not a *Hamlet* without a Hamlet (George Grizzard, who is an
excellent actor, does certain scenes and speeches eminently well);
this is a *Hamlet* performed by a company loyally subservient to
the director's intentions. Thus we see in Lee Richardson's Claudius a king who is disturbed, dishonest and yet an ordinary
respectable and sensual stuffed-shirt politician—which may represent Guthrie's comment on most men of state.

I followed this four-hour (uncut) version of the play with almost unremitting attention, for Guthrie never does anything that
is altogether without originality. Never before, for instance, have
I seen the opening of the "Get thee to a nunnery" sequence
played as an impassioned love scene turning to fury and frustration when Hamlet realizes he is being spied upon. There are
several such episodes which, in addition to their exciting choreography or staging (the "Play" at the court), make this production a
far more stimulating event than most of the more critically applauded presentations of *Hamlet* seen in New York since John
Barrymore's day.

What American actors everywhere need for their personal
equipment more than anything else at present is further and more
exacting speech and vocal training. What the Minnesota management must unfailingly provide next season is more rehearsal
time. Four weeks of rehearsal for such plays as those in the
present repertory are an absurdity.

Molière's *The Miser* is a challenge. It is a slight and comparatively short farce, and as a French play (avarice may be universal, but French avarice is proverbial) it still retains a certain bite
in the sprightly or dancelike dialogue, a great part of which in the
original constitutes *morceaux d'anthologie*—passages for perennial quotation. Such plays are difficult to translate theatrically on
our stages. Douglas Campbell has done this by weaving the simple pattern of the play into an elaborate fabric of crazy-quilt
humor within a huge framework of stage business.

The plan succeeds with the Minneapolis audience, which is
convulsed by Hume Cronyn's fantastically energetic clowning
and is delighted by the pretty costumes and the director's inventions. But they all came to be too much for me: the scheme was

too evident and elaborate, everything was stretched to a scale that ultimately defeated (my) laughter. A fear of Molière's foreign idiom and modest proportions (within the large theatre and its extensive open stage) seems to have impelled the director to make us forget that there ever was a play there to begin with. The result struck me as a very clever improvisation around a vacuum.

Of the three plays, the one I found most affecting (this I believe to be the general impression) was *The Three Sisters*. Guthrie's production is intelligently aware of the text. Though I found only one performance more memorable than the rest—that of Claude Woolman as Tusenbach—and I am not at all certain that the arena stage is helpful to Chekhov, the play once again wove its soul-stirring spell as few plays of modern times are able to do.

The Three Sisters is a work as pertinent to Minneapolis in 1963 as it must have been to Moscow in 1901, a poem of our age-old yearning for a full life.

This delicious comedy which makes us weep should be made a permanent item in the personal repertory of every civilized citizen everywhere. What does it matter whether Guthrie's is as good a production as we can imagine or might find elsewhere; has Minneapolis ever seen the like and do we ever see such a play anywhere more than once in a blue moon?

Let Minneapolis applaud and persevere, and let the rest of the country emulate and improve on this Midwestern example.

The Tyrone Guthrie Theatre, 1964

The Tyrone Guthrie is a laugh theatre. Though certainly versatile, Guthrie's directorial forte is comedy—swinging, vaulting, saltatory. It can be lusty though asexual. It is understanding but not "psychological." It is intelligent rather than profound. It has a healthy, open-air quality. It is fearless because it is without malice.

In the present season's program something of this rubs off on productions which are not directed by Guthrie himself. This may be due not simply to the infectiousness of Guthrie's influence but to the general youthfulness of the company, which is eager, earnest, unaffected, capable and emotionally callow.

Another element which contributes to the lightheartedness and light-headedness of this theatre's tone is its audience. It is receptive, full of goodwill, unspoiled, theatrically unsophisticated. It seeks entertainment and is ready to be impressed by culture. Finding culture in the theatre's plays it is gratified, but one feels that above all it supposes that its theatre's mission, through its leading director, is to make it laugh. There is nothing particularly wrong in this, but I wonder whether in the end the audience may not come to the conclusion that, since serious drama is neither forbidding nor heavy, it is synonymous with just plain fun—a bright kid's view of art.

There is a festival air about the Tyrone Guthrie Theatre which may ultimately serve to give it a resort atmosphere. What is missing is the feeling that the theatre may also be a place of challenge, of virile engagement in matters which concern us most directly.

Ben Jonson's *Volpone* is the best of the four productions. This savage comedy is a masterpiece of robustious writing; if it did not possess so great an intellectual scope, if it were not so full-blooded and biting, it would be gross. It is a veritable onslaught of vehement action, torrential verbiage and truculent laughter. Jonson's target is not merely avarice or the pursuit of gain but man's inability to resist their effects. "All the wise world is little else in nature, but parasites or sub-parasites." No wonder Joan Littlewood has called *Volpone* the greatest dramatic indictment of capitalism.

Guthrie's playfulness makes Jonson appear more good-natured than he is, but I yielded completely to the sweep of the director's pace and comic inventiveness. In its own special terms, Guthrie's production is a brilliant translation of the text into stage business. He is at the top of his form, incessant in physical riot and rip-roaring tricks of sight and sound. Guthrie will sacrifice verbal intelligibility to the essential scenic meaning of each episode, and it is surprising that we understand so much of the language. Indeed, it must be said that speed, along with laughs, is another fetish of the Guthrie Theatre. In this production the company has made a considerable advance in its capacity to combine rapidity of movement with clarity of speech.

On leaving *Volpone,* I was chiefly aware of Guthrie's triumph. Actors are his tools. Still, actors may learn as much from him in dash and courage as they may possibly suffer in some other respects. Guthrie usually neglects or disregards those elements of acting which do not relate to colorfulness, theatrical zest and virtuosity. That is why his productions tend, for all their graphic muscularity and fleet power, to strike us sometimes as humanly meager.

Besides the direction in *Volpone,* one remembers with satisfaction Tanya Moiseiwitch's artful arrangements of the stage and splendid costumes, as well as the arresting makeups she has designed for the well-played characters of Voltore, Corbaccio, Corvino (Ken Ruta, Robert Pastene, Claude Woolman). Douglas Campbell as Volpone is wholly the director's willing and affable instrument; George Grizzard brings to Mosca his gift for honeyed mockery. In Guthrie's treatment both are less vividly sinister than they might be.

Henry V loses much in not having a heroically inspiring king and, though Guthrie has staged the battle scene ("Once more unto the breach. . . .") with exciting naïveté, the production seems diffuse. (The diction, inferior to that in the Jonson play, may have deteriorated because of the strain of two performances of *Volpone* on the previous day.) The Fluellen of Ed Flanders is excellent. Characteristic of Guthrie's amusing, but occasionally distracting, detail is the opening scene, in which the Archbishop, magnificently robed, scratches his backside while speaking of state matters. The audience smiles, but does not listen to what is being said.

Inattention may not matter much in this instance, for *Henry V* is part jingo pageant and part salty skepticism about the cause and nature of war—a mixture difficult to unify into a coherent statement. Shakespeare, who saw many sides to every question, sometimes strikes one as being both timeserver and heretic. *Henry V* is less adept at this game than some of the other Shakespearean "histories"—perhaps because the characters of Bardolph, Nym and Pistol are not as pointedly funny as they should be, nor as well integrated into the play.

Shaw's *Saint Joan* is the Minneapolis box-office smash. It is probably much less familiar to audiences in the Midwest than it is to us. Besides, is it not the story of a little girl—a sort of girl scout!—who made good? There is something disarmingly candid in Shaw—a trait often overlooked in discussions of his work—and the production, directed by Douglas Campbell, highlights the play's fairy-tale aspect. The audience responds wonderfully. How it laughs in contentment when Joan, the brave little yokel, worsts all the famous fatheads and frauds around her. I enjoyed the audience's delight at the play more than I did the interpretation on the stage.

Joan is an innocent (Ellen Geer, who has a winning American wholesomeness and pluck, inescapably conveys that quality), but she is also a *saint*, that is, a power. More than that, she is over-powering. She has to be stopped, done away with, because like all fanatically persistent moralists, she is a pest, a threat, unbearable to the ordinary. Joan fulfills her function: her driving will sweeps away the resistance of the staid, she pierces the dead-weight of cautious common sense like a steel arrow. Hence, though she wins in history, she must lose in her person. She herself recognizes this, but cannot and does not wish to curb her force and fail her fate. Though Shaw is unable to achieve trag-edy, his play has a tragic dimension.

There is hardly anything of this in the Minneapolis production; we get only smiles, benevolence and sentiment. The company, the direction, the audience make this inevitable.

But how did Alan Schneider, who directed *The Glass Menag-erie*, succumb to the spell of the Guthrie Theatre? The play, a delicate fragment, a sensitive rumination, has taken on a brash note of guying comedy in which a meddling mother crushes her daughter while her son finds relief in movies and outbursts of contempt. "Momism" must be something more than an American myth, because the audience seems to echo the filial defiance hap-pily. Once again it has a grand time—laughing.

Perhaps Schneider felt obliged to do something new with Ten-nessee Williams' script. Laurette Taylor made Amanda a poig-nantly pathetic figure in which our laughter had no trace of scorn, only compassion. But it was more than Taylor herself which endowed the original production with glamour. The setting, the music, the sound of the several voices, the woundedness of Anthony Ross' Gentleman Caller, all contributed to the play's lyricism, a lyricism which mitigated and ennobled the writer's bitter recollection of his youth. The decision, if it was a decision, to make the play more forthright and funnier was a grievously mistaken one. If the choice of interpretation was guided by a fear that the open stage and the largish theatre might dissipate the efficacy of a "twilight" treatment of the play, it shows a lack of confidence either in the play or in the company.

Whatever the cause, *The Glass Menagerie* has become a comedy of small-town family bickering rather than an elegy of reconciliation with a painful past. In such a case one must absolve the actors of all blame. But to speak of "blame" may be inappropriate because here, too, the audience seemed wholly satisfied.

Despite my disapproval of the handling of the play, I was glad to see it because it offered me an opportunity to cast a retrospective glance at Williams' career. It has become a widespread critical habit to express regret that Williams abandoned the gentle key of this play for the harshness of most of his later writing. Seeing *The Glass Menagerie* again, I became more than ever convinced that *A Streetcar Named Desire, The Night of the Iguana* and several other of Williams' plays possess greater dramatic impact and weight than does *The Glass Menagerie,* which, for all its melancholy charm, is a slight work to which the finest American actress of our time lent unforgettable fragrance and glow.

It takes time to develop an important theatre. The Tyrone Guthrie Theatre has already rendered its community a signal service. My strictures, more rigorous this year than last, are a recognition of the importance of the venture.

San Francisco

The Actor's Workshop, 1963

WHILE THE NEW Minneapolis theatre looms, The Actor's Workshop of San Francisco has been building from the ground up. For eleven years now the small band of fanatics led by two determined and knowledgeable college instructors—Jules Irving and Herbert Blau—have been struggling to create a Theatre in this city gaily indifferent to the art. I have the impression that they have succeeded.

The statement is tentative because I have seen too little of the Workshop's program to pronounce a firm judgment. But observing the company at rehearsals of Genet's *The Balcony* and seeing its production of Brecht's *Galileo*, I am impressed by the freedom, intelligence, ability and security of the company as a whole. These people know what they want; their commitment is not transient. They are here to stay.*

The Workshop operates two theatres. One is a 660-seat house on the second floor of the Marines' Memorial Club (actually a hotel); the other, seating about 140, is a former nightclub below street level. The larger theatre is occasionally rented out for meetings and entertainments of various sorts, and the Workshop staff is frequently obliged to remove its scenery and props to make way for these occasions.

The two theatres, small though they are, are more than the company began with. The early days were given over to little essays in a tiny studio which Irving and Blau rented to conduct

---

* Blau and Irving are now the artistic directors of the Repertory Theater of Lincoln Center.

their first experiments. The possession (on a rental basis) of the present quarters is the "monumental" sign of the company's increasing growth and prosperity. For only in the past two seasons have the company's efforts been rewarded by the Ford Foundation's attention and funds.

The first sum of money was granted the Workshop with the stipulation that professional actors be brought in from New York. Last year the Workshop was permitted to use the Foundation funds as the theatre's directors saw fit—that is, to develop and retain their own resident company. Now the organization is sufficiently established and solvent (on an extremely modest basis) to contemplate the purchase of a house of its own. A theatre—at present devoted to burlesque—has been chosen and a cash offer made.

The history of The Actor's Workshop has been written by Herbert Blau (*The Impossible Theater:* Macmillan). It is the story of idealistic ambition, strain, discouragement, renewal and quixotic persistence. Serious theatre work in our country can be achieved only at the cost of personal hardship and dogged effort. Stamina resembling folly is indispensable. It may also be fun for the proud, the disoriented, the single-minded and the strong. In such enterprises the normally easy-going and practically well-adjusted are most often the "rats" who abandon ship.

At present The Actor's Workshop commands a permanent company of about thirty-five (besides part-time adherents), a company that is resolved to remain permanent. The main body of actors do not take their participation in the Workshop program as a "showcase" for Hollywood or Broadway. (When will New Yorkers and others realize that New York is a province?) A number of the actors—very few of them native to San Francisco—have been at the Workshop for more than five years. Will the Tyrone Guthrie Theatre (page 136) be able to develop such a company? Not, I venture to say, for some time. And without the formation of its own *esprit de corps*—faith, technique and style— the creation of a theatre is barely possible. The Actor's Workshop is at the moment almost the only American organization that has embraced its community and settled down to its own work as an independent artistic unit.*

* Most of the San Francisco company is now engaged at the Repertory Theater of Lincoln Center.

The Workshop's greatest successes in the past have been *The Birthday Party* (Pinter), *The Balcony, Waiting for Godot, The Crucible* (Miller). The plays being prepared for next season are Pinter's *The Caretaker*, Williams' *The Night of the Iguana*, Webster's *The White Devil*, Aristophanes' *The Birds, The Taming of the Shrew* and a new American play. Seven new productions are presented each season, formerly in repertory arrangement, now for a run of about five weeks. The aim has been to keep the theatre active most of the year.

The Workshop's public and actors have become so used and partisan to plays of the aesthetic "Left" (Genet, Pinter, Beckett, *et al.*) that when plays like Shaw's *Major Barbara* or Anouilh's *Becket* are done, worry is expressed that the organization may be going "square"!

The directors are talented. Besides the two leaders, new directors are being developed (one of them is an actor in the company). There are also guest directors: Alan Schneider staged a new American play some time ago, and next season Carl Weber of the Berliner Ensemble will put on Brecht's *The Caucasian Chalk Circle*.

The rehearsals I saw of *The Balcony* (now being "revived" under Blau's direction) reveal an individual and imaginative approach to the play. Blau is an intellectual, which in no way prevents his having lively production ideas. What I particularly liked about the scenes I saw rehearsed was the assured treatment of the specifically erotic aspects of the play, which in most productions I am familiar with were veiled as much as possible so that the audience might not suspect Genet of being merely "sensational"—hence no artist!

The *Galileo*—also directed by Blau—is one of the few successful "unBrechtian" productions of that master's plays. Blau's production has a kind of vigor—perhaps I should say "punch"—which does not belie the play's intention or fail to preserve its innate hauteur. For what so many directors of Brecht's plays overlook is the elegance, the aristocracy, of his manner. There is an elevation and grandeur in most of the later Brecht plays that is closer to the classic tradition than to the contemporary. He is never dry or pedestrian; his work for all its down-to-earth "factualism" has breeding and grandeur. The Moscow *Threepenny Opera*, for instance, has a Russian gusto and warmth but lacks something of the subtle refinement which dwells within that work's raffishness.

The Workshop's *Galileo* is designed with distinction in a style influenced by the most modern schools of art. Various San Francisco sculptors and painters were invited to contribute individual costumes and props, most of which add sharp notes of interest to the production. The company's acting has a certain unschooled roughness without awkwardness or self-consciousness. It is intelligent acting, full-bodied, confident and forthright.

At a first quick glance at the company I am reminded of Blake's aphorism "If the fool would persist in his folly he would become wise."

Challenge of the New Theatres

1964

THE "BREAKDOWN" of Broadway, the consequent propaganda for the theatre's decentralization, the aid of the foundations, the spread of university and community stages, the "cultural explosion" have all led to the establishment of a number of new repertory or semirepertory theatres—with more or less permanent staffs—from New York to California, in the South and the Southwest. We have reason to be pleased, but it is too soon to celebrate. As Van Wyck Brooks many years ago said (in effect): America is the land of promising first acts.

An American characteristic which may frustrate our hope in the new theatres is impatience. We must not expect miracles overnight. Time is required to mature all concerned: the directorate of the various theatres, their personnel, their audiences. We have no settled tradition to proceed from. We must learn.

The first step is to define aims. The repertory system by itself is a measure of convenience; it can prove a drawback. A permanent company should be a great asset; it may turn into a deadweight. A subscription audience is extremely useful; it has occasionally acted as a block.

It is not enough to say that the goal of the new enterprises should be to offer "good theatre." As Stanislavsky told Norris Houghton, no one has ever deliberately tried to found a bad theatre. Nor can each of the new companies strive for exactly the same ends. Much depends on where each theatre is situated and the conditions under which it is obliged to operate, the audience it hopes to attract, the very structure of the building it must occupy.

The Repertory Theater of Lincoln Center will serve New York. It cannot do everything for New York which New York needs, nor can it do everything at once. (It promises a studio auditorium for special productions when its permanent quarters have been built.) New York should have several similar theatres, as London at present has three, Paris four, Moscow many. It is a sign of sanity that the organizers of the Repertory Theater of Lincoln Center recognize that even if they play at capacity for fifty-two weeks every season they cannot look forward to a profit! The theatre is not a merchandising business any more than is a library, a museum or a symphony orchestra.

Countries which have long theatrical histories may maintain theatres especially designed to preserve those traditions. That is the chief purpose of the Comédie Française, and to some extent this was and is the purpose of the Old Vic and of the Shakespeare Theatre at Stratford-on-Avon. It is largely true of the various state or municipal theatres in Germany. Most European countries have produced dramatic literatures rich enough to sustain such theatres over the years.

America has not (though there are more American plays worth revival than we suppose). Certain choices are open to the founders of the new theatres. A choice which is really no choice at all is to announce that one is going to present a series of good plays. The question to be asked is: good for what, good for whom?

A company of actors unprepared—that is, not specifically trained—to do Elizabethan, Restoration or Classic Greek plays deceives itself and its audience when it undertakes to stage them. I could list a whole shelf of masterpieces—by Strindberg, Kleist, Racine, Calderon and others—which would doom any company offering them in the wrong place at the wrong time. Their *audiences* are not prepared! Remember that Beckett's *Waiting for Godot,* eagerly received and thoroughly appreciated in scores of university theatres throughout the country, flopped on Broadway despite an expert cast. The same is true of so relatively forthright a play as Sartre's *No Exit.* The circumstances—costs of production, price of seats, the whole atmosphere and mental disposition

—on Broadway are inimical to the proper reception of such plays. The audience is a theatre's leading actor!

The Tyrone Guthrie Theatre in Minneapolis (page 136) made a wise choice of plays for its first season. *Hamlet*, Molière's *The Miser*, Chekhov's *The Three Sisters* and Arthur Miller's *Death of a Salesman* are suitable to any American city of like size. But note in passing that *The Miser*, performed in a sort of enlarged "revue" style, and *Three Sisters* were more popular than *Hamlet*, done by actors not wholly up to the demands of that formidable play. It is a moot point whether it is better to do a great play with mediocre means than to do a lesser but still worthy play more congruously.

It might be desirable to institute a theatre entirely devoted to "difficult" or *avant-garde* plays (a) if the director, actors and others are equipped to do them well, (b) if there is a sufficient number of people in the community who wish to see such plays, and (c) if the financial support at the theatre's command can be counted on for respectable productions of these plays. One must remember always that we are speaking not of the desultory production of separate plays but of a continuous program of production.

To present plays by Ghelderode, Beckett, Ionesco, Genet or even more recent examples of "adventurous" drama, in addition perhaps to plays like Büchner's *Wozzeck* and Strindberg's *Dream Play* or his *Ghost Sonata*, without reference to all the above considerations would be as much an artistic misdemeanor as a sign of organizational ineptitude. There is little point in speaking of the theatre as a social art and ignoring in practice the actual society in which the theatre finds itself. ·

Most of the new theatres—particularly those in cities unused to a steady regime of substantial fare—will, to begin with, have to be eclectic in the manner of the Tyrone Guthrie Theatre of Minneapolis. If a university is able to finance a professional company on any long-term basis—as has occurred to some extent at the University of Michigan—the theatre may take greater risks. No theatre may look forward to a secure future where it is expected to prove a "smash" with its initial productions.

Beyond the practical considerations of the problem there lies the root question of what constitutes a true theatre. The answer once given by the great Russian director Vachtangov was couched in the special jargon of his time and place (Moscow,

1919), but it is nonetheless exact: "A theatre is an ideologically cemented collective."

This bespeaks not what we call a "policy" but a fundamental Idea. This Idea—religious, social, aesthetic, political or only "technical"—must inform the entire theatrical community from dramatist to minor player and apprentice craftsman. Such a theatre is not intended as the stage equivalent of a library (offering the Hundred Best Books) or a museum for the display of masterpieces. A true theatre creates from its Idea; it educates its members in the Idea and generates production methods from it. The Idea is born of an impulse in the society in which the theatre's artists live and is directed toward that society. Dramatists and interpreters are interrelated as kinsmen in a common movement immanent in the social unit of which they are at once the projection and the instrument. Thus the career of such a theatre will take on the kind of character and meaning we find in the work of an individual artist.

Such unity was more or less spontaneously achieved in the Classic Greek, the Elizabethan and the seventeenth-century French theatres by virtue of the homogeneity of their respective cultures. Unity of this kind is extremely difficult to arrive at in our day—especially in America. Still, something of this aesthetic-social concord has been attained.

Besides its purely professional reforms, the Moscow Art Theatre in 1898 declared its purpose to be the creation of serious art for the People. By the "People" the leaders of that famous institution chiefly meant the middle-class intelligentsia and the educated working class. The result was a theatre which explored many avenues of theatrical expression, though its signal contribution was consummated in the production of plays by Chekhov and Gorky. With further development along these lines the studios of the Moscow Art Theatre (virtually new theatres) veered at first toward a sort of Tolstoian mysticism and then proceeded to radical departures from realism, as well as to more pronouncedly social objectives.

By 1935, the Russian theatre had branched out into extremely diverse aesthetic manifestations. Its progress was then impeded by a politically oriented campaign against "formalism," when a very restrictive interpretation of "Socialist realism" was imposed by main force.

Though the Theatre Guild between 1919 and 1929 was hardly

a theatre in the sense I have indicated, it did make a valuable contribution in organizing audiences through subscription and in maintaining a fairly consistent program of the kind of contemporary European play which had up to that time been considered caviar to the general. The Theatre Guild represented the new cosmopolitanism of New York's middle class shortly after the First World War. In 1928, the Theatre Guild adopted Eugene O'Neill, scion of another body, the Provincetown Players.

The Group Theatre (1931–41) was the first, and so far the last, conscious effort in America to create a theatre exemplifying both an aesthetic and a "philosophic" attitude. Its first emphasis was on a unity of technique—particularly in regard to acting; its second was the enunciation of what it held to be the temper of American life of the time. The combination resulted in the emergence of a playwright from its permanent acting company: Clifford Odets. He was in effect not only the Group Theatre's typical figure but that of the decade.

What Idea will motivate each of our new theatres? That is for each of them to decide for itself, depending on the composition of the companies. Without some coherent Idea to impel it, an Idea which each group must learn to formulate for itself and exemplify in its action, none will survive beyond the flush of its first flight.

It is my personal conviction that every true theatre must sooner or later produce its own native playwrights. (The Group Theatre presented plays by Paul Green, John Howard Lawson, Dawn Powell, Maxwell Anderson, Sidney Kingsley, before it reached Odets' *Waiting for Lefty* and *Awake and Sing*.) This does not mean that all other dramatists are to be considered "alien"; it means that somehow all the plays produced by a true theatre must more or less serve as "original" expressions of the group (directors, actors and others) who compose its membership.

Such a theatre does not follow fashion, however attractive, up to date, "advanced"; it bodies forth its own spirit. It should be conceived, not as an interpretive vehicle, but as a creative organism. It may find material in old plays of any period from any land, but in this kind of theatre such plays become its own plays, a facet of its own "message." This implies no distortion of revered texts in the manner of certain early Soviet productions. (Though I confess a preference for Meyerhold's staging of Gogol's *Inspector General* or the Jewish Chamber Theatre's

mounting of *King Lear* in Moscow in 1935 to most of the "faithful" or faceless Shakespeare productions in America and England.) Classics are produced in my "ideal" theatre, not solely
on account of their literary stature but for their relevance to its
audience. The outstanding example of this sort of theatre for the
past decade or more has been the Berliner Ensemble, whose guiding spirit was Brecht but whose productions have not been confined to his plays. A large community may have several such
theatres with differing Ideas. If they are truly theatres each will
create its own identity.

For these theatres to exist and flourish, more than a collection
of expert professionals is required. The theatre as it develops
must *school* itself for the tasks it envisions. We have as yet no
single body of theatre craftsmen capable of coping with the
wide range of styles which the perspective of our dramatic heritage offers. We must be modest even as we are ambitious. The
theatre must not regard itself simply as an arena for the exhibi-
tion of a prize "product," but as the ground for the cultivation on
the broadest possible basis—technical and spiritual—of the artists
and world view it hopes to have emerge.

There are enormous resources of talent in our country, but little
coordinating discipline or formative enterprise. That is why the
theatre has become a hand-to-mouth business instead of what it
was destined to be: a vital expression of adult concern. We are
too concentrated on sensations, names, electrifying phenomena,
bewitching personalities, and not enough on organic growth. We
are eager for the fruit; we do not care about the tree.

With the establishment of the new theatres we have our best
chance for a transformation. But we shall miss our opportunity if
we think of the new theatres in the light of the old. These new
theatres must not be as good or better than Broadway but altogether different. They must forge new paths for actors, dramatists, directors, audiences and the monied patrons. This cannot be
done in a hurry. One, two, or even three seasons will not be
enough.

A Brief History

One Hundred Years in the American Theatre, 1965

WRITING IN 1869, Walt Whitman in his *Democratic Vistas* complains, "Of what is called drama, or dramatic presentation in the United States, as now put forth at the theatres, I should say it deserves to be treated with the same gravity and on a par with the questions of ornamental confectionary and public dinners, or the arrangements of curtains and hangings in a ballroom—no more no less."

Seven months after the assassination of Lincoln in April, 1865, the "hit shows" were *Rip Van Winkle*, with the delightful actor Joseph Jefferson, and *The Black Crook*, the first of our big musicals in which "one hundred beautiful girls in short diaphanous skirts and flesh-colored tights" provided an unprecedented sensation.

This came at a time when our literature had already bequeathed to us *Moby Dick, The Scarlet Letter, Leaves of Grass*, not to speak of Emerson and Thoreau. We can sympathize with Whitman's reaction. But we are less astonished. The theatre is almost always a laggard art.

A single reader may be said to constitute an "audience" for a poem or a novel, one viewer may be sufficient to encourage the solitary artist who shows his painting. Theatre requires a larger number of people to convene at the same set time. The theatre is both a public and a composite art, *social* in the nature of its creation as well as in the circumstances of its manifestation. A history of the theatre must comprise not only a study of dramatic texts but an examination of acting, the mechanics and economics of production and, inseparable from all these, the audiences to whom the art is addressed and from whom it derives.

After they had passed through the primitive state of tribal rites the great theatres of the western world emerged as forms of civic and religious celebrations. State and church—in effect the entire community—supported them. Later, when the theatre was no longer an organic part of governing bodies, when indeed it was frowned upon and its suppression was urged by those who held it to be immoral, the theatre still managed to survive through various devices of aristocratic or royal protection. Despite all the vicissitudes of its history, the theatre was recognized as a social benefit meriting special privilege. In a word, a *tradition* developed in Europe which bestowed care for the theatre.

This tradition was lost in the settlement of America. The Puritans thought the theatre sinful. With a civilization to be built there was no time for such frivolity. By the time the educated minority was able to provide for them, a few playhouses were put up in the main cities of the eastern seaboard. Plays and actors were usually foreign. The best fare consisted of mutilated Shakespeare. There was practically no native drama and hardly any native actors.

When preoccupations beyond those of material needs could be entertained, schools and universities were established, important writers and a few signs of original theatrical creation appeared. One of these was Anna Cora Mowatt's *Fashion* (1845), a satire on the American parvenu, which in our present estimation is hardly more than a chromo. Yet Edgar Allan Poe found it praiseworthy.

That Poe should have welcomed so slight a piece, though he probably would not have deigned to notice its literary equivalent, may appear paradoxical. But this paradox repeats itself constantly. (William Dean Howells in 1891 referred to James Hearne's *Margaret Fleming*, a crude and creaky bit of claptrap, as "epoch-making" because it was the first of our realistic plays.) We may discover a clue in this to the peculiarity of our theatre's progress.

"Hardly anybody listens in the theatre," the Irish dramatist Denis Johnston has said, "to anything he doesn't know already." For a play to prosper it must unite its audience—which to begin

156 THE NAKED IMAGE

with must be homogeneous. A minority attitude, a heterodox premise are divisive, and the theatre's life depends on popularly recognizable interpretations of a common experience. The cultivated handful who were able to appreciate the Brahmins of our literature could not have filled the tiniest theatres of their times.

It has been said—and it is perhaps true—that the liveliest and most representative "theatre" of the period immediately following the Civil War was to be found in the riverboats, in the saloons, in the minstrel shows on the Mississippi and westward. These frolics possessed the rough vigor of their audiences, the hardy folk who were opening the country.

The situation in the East, as we have seen, was that which made Whitman exclaim, "Do you call that perpetual, pistareen, paste pot work . . . American drama?" Still clinging to his faith in the American dream he was dismayed by a society ever more dominated by money values. Capitalism was set on its roaring course of empire building. Fortunes were being made by and for a most fortunate people. It was the Gilded Age. Theatres attracted folk eager to ease themselves with entertainment inducing the minimum of mental strain. The really poor never went to ordinary playhouses and thus poverty was never made the subject of any but the cheapest tearjerkers. A large part of the audience was beginning to free itself from some of its Puritan inhibitions, though the "upper crust" in press and pulpit hypocritically persisted in upholding the Puritan code. Only the smiling aspects of American life or titillating melodrama were suitable material for such audiences. So rage as intellectuals might, the theatre between 1865 and 1890 was, in its own distorted way, a mirror of the times.

Even the intelligentsia does not go to the theatre for literature alone. Native acting during this period improved steadily. If America did not see any good plays (Shakespeare, remember, was bowdlerized), it had the opportunity of catching glimpses of such luminaries as Edmund Kean and Rachel, and later Salvini and Duse. Edwin Booth refined the red-necked robustiousness of Edwin Forrest, America's first tragedian (1806–1872).

The actor-manager Lester Wallack, who beginning in 1861 ran a stock company for twenty years, was patronized by New York's gentry. His theatre was something like a London theatre in Manhattan. He never produced an American play because he found none that was good enough. After Wallack the big "name" producer from 1879 to 1899 was Augustin Daly, who had a sound sense of integral play production. Though he produced Shakespeare with excellent actors, the fare at his theatre was more frequently trash. Daly's "discovery," Bronson Howard, the first writer for our stage to become rich from his work, was the author of *Shenandoah* (1889), a Civil War saga which one cannot read today without indulgent laughter.

The theatre prospered, but because of the advent of realism the playhouses were built smaller. Playgoing became respectable; the social elite or "carriage trade" made it customary. Shows toured the hinterland. The theatre became industrialized. Henry James, writing in 1885, found that "scenery and decoration have been brought to the highest perfection while elocution and acting, the interpretation of meanings, the representation of human feelings have not long been the subjects of serious study."

To appreciate the frame of mind of theatrical leaders at this time one may cite the fact that in 1893 the dignified manager Daniel Frohman rejected Pinero's *The Second Mrs. Tanqueray* (about a woman who had been kept by four men before marriage) because it was "too frank." When it was produced, the reviewer of the New York *Herald* spoke of the play as being "for audacity surely without parallel in dramatic literature." Even as late as 1905, when Shaw's *Mrs. Warren's Profession* was produced (and suppressed), it was said by the New York *Sun* "to glorify debauchery."

Clyde Fitch, the most highly regarded dramatist between 1889 and 1909, was entirely sincere when he wrote, "I feel myself strongly the particular value of reflecting absolutely and truthfully the life and environment about us." He had the impulse to confess himself as much as to reveal the environment, but his play *The Truth* (1906), about a compulsive liar, and *The City* (1909), about the corrupting effects of the Big Town, are rather rickety contraptions. After all, plays, like most of the novels of the day, had to please the Ladies or they would incur the censure of the Gentlemen.

While Edward Sheldon may be credited with bringing social themes to the stage—the destitute in *Salvation Nell* (1908), the "race problem" in *The Nigger* (1909) and politics in *The Boss*

(1911)—the plays themselves are sophomorically inept and timid. (Stephen Crane, Frank Norris, Theodore Dreiser had already written most of their stories and novels.) Sheldon's true vein was that of *Romance* (1913), about the love of an Episcopalian minister for an Italian opera star. A play which harks back to New York in its Age of Innocence, it is chiefly memorable as a vehicle for the glamorous Doris Keane, rapturously admired by Stark Young. There *was* artistic substance in the American theatre of the day—not in the plays but in the players. Otis Skinner, Laurette Taylor, Maude Adams, the Barrymores, and later Pauline Lord, Alfred Lunt and numerous others brought life to the boards.

One notes other progressive signs. The actor Arnold Daly champions Shaw, the intrepid actress Mrs. Fisk and the exotic Alla Nazimova do much to convince the retarded, including the shocked William Winter, the New York *Tribune's* drama critic from 1865 to 1909, of Ibsen's worth.

Most indicative of the community's steadily growing sophistication is the effort sponsored in 1909 by J. P. Morgan, John Jacob Astor, the Vanderbilts, Thomas Paine Whitney and Otto Kahn to establish a "permanent national art theatre." A sumptuous house was built on Central Park West between 62nd and 63rd Streets, at this time an exclusive residential section for the well-to-do, and a remote suburb to citizens of more modest means.

Chosen to direct the ambitious New Theatre was the Harvard-educated Bostonian Winthrop Ames, a man of ability and taste. He enlisted an admirable company and produced Galsworthy's *Strife* (capital and labor), several plays by Maeterlinck (among them *The Blue Bird*) and Shakespeare. It was difficult to find American plays of corresponding calibre (only three, including Sheldon's *The Nigger*, were offered) because few American plays, with only such possible exceptions as Langdon Mitchell's brightly written comedy *The New York Idea* about divorce among the rich (1906) and Percy MacKaye's imaginative *The Scarecrow* (1910), were anything better than hack work.

The New Theatre collapsed after two seasons. Apart from the auditorium's unsuitability for the presentation of modern drama, its poor acoustics, its high prices and its inconvenient location, the reason for the New Theatre's failure was the absence of an audience great enough to sustain a serious repertory theatre.

Yet forces were at work to bring about a distinct change. Contact with Europe began to exercise a marked influence. The culturally alert became acquainted with stimulating and still unfamiliar dramatists (Tolstoy, Hauptmann, Gorky, Andreyev) on New York's Lower East Side—in both Yiddish and German. Little theatres were spreading all over the country so that by 1915 there were nineteen hundred. In 1916 the attractive comedian John Barrymore proved himself an actor of immense emotional power in Galsworthy's *Justice*. New manager-directors like Arthur Hopkins, inspired by overseas example, ventured into new fields which yielded fresh ideas, unusual plays employing the talent of that fine artist Robert Edmond Jones. A number of discriminating critics—their columns full of intriguing foreign references—began to clamor for a theatre in touch with art, literature and life. Chief among them was George Jean Nathan.

Most important, though little noticed at first, were the activities centered in the vicinity of Greenwich Village. The year 1915 witnessed the formation of the Neighborhood Playhouse on Grand Street, The Washington Square Players (transformed into The Theatre Guild in 1919), the Provincetown Players, who were to reappear in the early twenties as a triumvirate of the critic Macgowan, the designer-director Jones and the dramatist O'Neill. These new groups planted seeds from which a proud harvest was soon reaped.

In 1920 we became conscious of the flowering with the production—cautiously introduced at special matinees—of O'Neill's first full-length play, *Beyond the Horizon*. That event marks the *birth* of American theatre as a conscious art intended to contribute to our inner life what we expect of the best literature.

This "birth" in the theatre corresponded to a rebirth in American letters generally. For while the years between 1835 and 1850 gave evidence of our native genius in poem, essay, short story and novel, the fortune-hunting years between 1865 and 1913 had very nearly destroyed vital literary expression. During this interval Dreiser, on the one hand, and Henry James, on the other, dwelled in limbo. This is also true of Whitman, Melville and Thoreau, whose work was known to a rare few only. They came into their own just before and immediately after the First World War.

What made the twenties a feverish and wonderful time was our coming of age in prosperity, in power, in self-confidence, as well as in self-consciousness. This made it possible for us to recognize our character and to acknowledge our shortcomings. Our desire to learn and accomplish things as a great nation lent a tremendous impetus to all endeavors. We became cocky and at the same time self-critical. We were prepared to look at ourselves with unrelenting realism. We were rediscovering ourselves as Americans.

Many thought us fooled by the holiday of our success. Others declared our iconoclasm adolescent. The superficial traits of our Puritanism were raucously shed. Freud began to be read by the literati. We rejoiced in our afflatus and jeered at our rejoicing. Some said that America had become a jungle of competition; others read that Western Civilization was doomed. But whether the diagnoses and prognoses were rosy or black, everything took on a jubilant air.

New York playhouses doubled in number. One hundred ninety-six productions opened in 1920–21; two hundred seventy in 1927–28. The Theatre Guild assembled a loyal body of subscribers which assured its productions a minimum run of five to six weeks. The Guild did many unusual and stimulating plays by foreign authors, as well as by some Americans. After a while it clasped O'Neill to its bosom. Eva Le Gallienne at the Civic Repertory Theatre produced Ibsen, Chekhov and other "standard" European dramatists at popular prices.

Musical comedy, the one theatrical form in which we undoubtedly excel, with truly gifted tunes by Kern, Porter, Gershwin, Rodgers and others, sweetened the surrounding clamor. The Ziegfeld Follies, glorifying the American girl in gorgeous dress and suave undress, served as emblems of our high spirits. Among the lovely faces and the lush furnishings a parade of comedians close to genius cavorted.

The shadowy side of the picture was painted by the uncouth master figure of Eugene O'Neill himself. Apart from his concern with the complexities of personal psychology, O'Neill brooded on the drama of man's soul in America. Something had gone astray. The poet who yearns to explore realms beyond the narrow confines of his job fails to follow his bent and as a result wastes his being. The simple laborer proud of the strength which turns the wheels of our magnificent civilization finds himself scorned and adrift in a mechanism in which he is merely a cog. The artist wishes to attain the effectiveness of the man of affairs; the businessman envies the artist's imagination. Both suffer a sense of incompleteness. The would-be aristocrat from the Old World with his dream of grandeur is rendered absurd in the factory of a materialistic democracy. But without that strain of grandeur the dignity of a true manhood is somehow damaged. The son has little of his pioneering father's grit; the father in his struggle to master the soil of his farm (America?) impairs his capacity to love.

O'Neill dramatizes himself and us as people cut off from but still seeking some principle of coherence. For want of it everyone feels isolated and frustrated. O'Neill's strength lies in the persistence of his quest for a wholeness which has been shattered in the New World. We sicken in detachment from some age-old secret of sanctity. O'Neill is committed to its recovery. He told friends that his never-completed cycle of nine plays would be an epic of America's failure to realize its promise.

The depression of the thirties exposed the moral as well as the social lesion in the national body. Having been wounded where we believed ourselves invulnerable, we began questioning ourselves in new ways. The plays of the depression were not depressed. (Depressed plays appeared in the fifties in a time of prosperity.) The depression was a time of hope. Youth would not accept defeat, would not take "no" for an answer. It condemned the illusions of the previous decade, which had exulted in the fun principle. The thirties sought and found a solution to our dilemma in collective action for social betterment.

The theatre was struck a bitter, though not fatal, blow. The number of productions shrank; playhouses were sold for use as grind-movie emporia and for burlesque shows. Actors left for Hollywood, which prospered because the disconsolate wished to flee the gloom of impoverished homes and streets. The disease wrought its own healing. As Roosevelt aroused the country with his New Deal, so Groups, Collectives, Unions of the theatre were formed. What characterized most of them was the attempt to present plays confronting the times: the condition of the unemployed, the dispossessed, the unprotected worker, the dispirited middle class, the desperate farmer, the threat of fascism. All this was to be done in a new fashion: through organizations which would commit themselves on a *permanent collective basis* to a disciplined practice of theatrical craft.

The theatre of the thirties was thought to be political—a mis-

taken opinion. Its impulse was moral—even moralistic. That is
the essence of Odets' work. He was the era's representative playwright just as The Group Theatre, of which Odets had been an
actor-member, was the representative theatrical organization.
That is why after The Group Theatre's dissolution in 1941, it still
remained an influence in the ensuing years through its former
actors, directors, designers, teachers.

One particular contribution to theatre technique made by The
Group was a way of work which was the heritage of the Moscow
Art Theatre's New York visit in 1923. This was the Stanislavsky
System, which in time—through the Actor's Studio founded in the
forties—came to be known as the Method. While the Method is
presumed to have narrowed the scope of American acting, though
this is not at all its aim or necessary effect, it added a certain
vibrancy and density of feeling to our actors' endowments.

With the scattering of forces during the Second World War
and its immediate aftermath, in which not only The Group Theatre but the inestimably valuable Federal Theatre Project (the
Government's first entrance into the domain of the arts) disap-
peared, a subtle change took place. As business as usual resumed,
there followed a cooling of social fervor which soon turned into a
freeze.

This was hardly noticed at first since Arthur Miller's early plays
and even those of Tennessee Williams sounded a more subdued
and introverted variation on the mode of the thirties.

Social reform had failed to "save" us. Many suggested panaceas
had proved delusive (or so it was thought) and some were considered positively treasonable. The source of our ailments, it
would appear, lay in our unsatisfactory relations with parents,
wives, children. Our traumas—our traumas were to blame!
Though Tennessee Williams' work always had discernible social
connotations, what public and press chiefly responded to was its
private and especially sexual aspects.

The age of conformity and of McCarthy terror drove men of
sensibility into themselves. Young folk exiled themselves in the
ghetto of their egos. The faceless world, all perpetual motion
without any core of meaning, was to be shut out. "Contact," as
someone has said about the new dancing, "went out in the fifties."

Connection with the outside world, now threatened with annihilation, became attenuated. Some solace (or drug) which

might alleviate the pain of aloneness or sink us more deeply into forgetfulness was craved. To be "beat" became an ideal by default. This laid the groundwork for the dramaturgy of the maimed.

The plays of Beckett, Genet, Ionesco, Pinter—usually presented at some distance from the theatre's supermarket—which were expressions of not altogether similar but of equally disabling stresses, became models for American writers. Edward Albee's "permanent vagrant" disturbing the complacent gent on the park bench is a youth who prefers contact through his own violent death at the hand of his neighbor to total neglect. At this moment Albee seems as representative of the early sixties as William Saroyan and Thornton Wilder were, in embodying the spirit of benevolent reconciliation (or "national unity"), in the early forties. Albee testifies to the agony of a society no longer real in which we try to live on debris of exploded faiths, a state which renders us savage.

Though, retrospectively, we may realize that since O'Neill our theatre has turned in earnest to the contemplation of our existence in a manner unthinkable a hundred or even sixty years ago, we remain dissatisfied. Broadway, as the hub of theatrical activity, has become an electrified desert. We still go there though its game is crooked because it is the only game in town! Seventy-five productions a season constitute the norm. At the moment of this writing only musicals and skimpy comedies are produced with much chance of public support.

Movies and television are not the cause of the downfall. It is show business itself which is destroying the theatre. Its arrangements are anarchic; the costs of production are too high, the price of tickets prohibitive. The greedy exactions of the stagehands' unions are not the sole cause for this. They do what all the others do: treat the theatre as a business, which means every craft for itself, every man for himself. This inevitably becomes destructive to an art, the very nature of which depends on the planned and enthusiastic integration of its entire personnel. We have lost the tradition—indeed have never established one—of the theatre as a service, a social need. When business ceases to be profitable it has lost its reason for existence. There is "no foundation all the way down the line," in Saroyan's words, and it will take more than the Foundations to supply one.

Are we to end with a whimper? On the contrary, we may yet see a new beginning. Observation during my travels convinces me that the country is full of talent and appetite for theatre. Young folk are trying to rediscover a true theatre tradition.

The decentralization of the theatre is not the result of any special "idealism" but the response to a need for using all our unused gifts. In San Francisco, in Seattle, in Minneapolis, in Houston, in Washington, in Philadelphia and elsewhere new professional theatres have been, or are about to be, established. This trend is bound to grow.

These theatres aspire to be more than show shops. We are becoming aware that there are other "classics" beside Shakespeare. Many world-famous plays—ancient and modern, in foreign tongues and in our own—are still unknown to our stages because they do not sit well in the maw of commerce. One hears of productions in university and community theatres, as well as in cafés, of plays so "advanced" and "experimental" that even off-Broadway (now being assimilated into the stream of running rats) dares not undertake them. We are also beginning to get free theatre in the parks and on the very streets of certain cities—both in the South and in the North.

New York itself is now endowed with ambitious new theatre organizations. A heavy load of disdain has been hurled at the first two seasons of the Repertory Theater of Lincoln Center—some of it merited but most of it misguided. To found a theatre is not the same as setting up a series of productions. A considerable time of preparation and at least three years of performance are required as a preliminary test. The demand that these new organizations immediately satisfy our hunger for genuine innovation and artistic achievement is a way of applying the old hit-and-flop criteria of Broadway to enterprises with very different objectives and entirely different problems. The sheer fact of the Repertory Theater of Lincoln Center's having come into existence is a step forward. We must hope that the prolongation of its life, no matter under what auspices, will fulfill its serious artistic function.

If it is correct to speak of our theatre as having been "born" only forty-five years ago, we must agree that compared to the long years which went into the making of the Elizabethan, the French neo-classic stages, the recently founded British National Theatre, our theatre is in its infancy. It is part of our immaturity

to expect immediate consummation. The misfortune of our theatre history—due to the absence of a tradition—is its fragmenta-
tion. We always seem to be starting from scratch. But perhaps
this after all is not the case; there may be a continuity which we
do not readily perceive because in our juvenile impatience we are
forever grumbling, "Yes, but what have you done for me recently?"

Theatre Abroad

London

The Proletarianization of the
English Stage, 1961

E VER SINCE 1956, there has been an increasing proletarianization of the English theatre. Like most generalizations,
this one is subject to qualification, but many of the English
people I have spoken to confirm my impression—in pride or pain.
The ordinary English play not so long ago was a drawing-room
comedy; today, the place of action is likely to be closer to the
kitchen. Most English plays of the past were centered in London,
where people spoke smart and light; now the plays are situated in
Manchester, Nottingham, Liverpool, where the talk is fast and
loose, and to many foreigners—and some Londoners—almost
unintelligible.

Of course, the majority of plays in London (as in Paris) are the
conventional stuff one has seen these many years in the commercial theatres of most Western metropolises. The plays we single
out in literary journals usually typify the significant· expression of
the day (insofar as such expression can make its way onto the
stage), but they are not the really popular plays. *Look Back in
Anger* and *The Lady's Not for Burning* were hailed in the press,
but *The Mousetrap* runs on forever.

England is still a class society. But there is a new stress and
strain in the relationship of classes; the contradictions—both
comic and grave—are being more sharply articulated and universally acknowledged.

When I speak of proletarianization of the theatre, I refer not
only to the "new" environments which are being depicted, but to

169

a fresh point of view. The show I most enjoyed is a topical revue, *Beyond the Fringe*. It is a revue in the sense that *The Premise* is one, though the latter is better-natured and less specifically committed to subversion.

The four young men who compose the cast of *Beyond the Fringe* are unmistakably intellectual. One, I am informed, teaches history at a university, another is a practicing physician, still another an accomplished musician. In New York all four would undoubtedly strike our audiences as distinctly high-brow and upper-class. The audiences that are flocking to the show here strike one as being as educated as the players. The most surprising thing about these graduate collegians, apart from the shrewd nastiness of their comment, is their expertness. They clown brilliantly and they convey every nuance of English speech from the adenoidal distinction of Macmillan to the pinched and impassive querulousness of the lowliest worker from one of England's "black towns."

What makes these young men relevant to our theme is that they are iconoclasts. Not only is the Prime Minister quite literally given the raspberry, but in a skit called "Aftermyth of the War," the fond embellishments of war-year memories are fiendishly mocked. The funniest bit of the evening is a Shakespeare parody —text as well as acting are ridiculed—but the most significant moments are those which display a coolly bitter attitude toward the expected extinction of the human race, the refined mumbo-jumbo of the clergy, the still tenacious social prejudices.

Another form of the tendency to proletarianization may be detected in the production of *Romeo and Juliet* at the Old Vic, directed by the young Italian Franco Zeffirelli, whose career hitherto had been chiefly devoted to opera. His *Romeo and Juliet* might be described as an adaptation of *West Side Story*. The junior Capulets and Montagues are Renaissance roughs, well-born Teddy Boys carrying on gang warfare on the streets of Verona between studies and bedroom bouts. Some of the English I met thought the production represented the Method!

I am exaggerating, of course. On the whole, I was favorably impressed by the production: it had character. The intent of Zeffirelli's *Romeo* is to make the play familiar in terms of a certain contemporary naturalism. Romeo and his pals (Mercutio, *et al.*) are obstreperous neighborhood youngsters whose parents have money. This interpretation pleases the younger generation of playgoers here more than anything else at the Old Vic or at Stratford.

There is a certain simple-minded, even an artistic, crudity in this—understandable in view of the stuffiness of so much "traditional" Shakespeare. Perhaps I might not say this if I had not seen a production of *Romeo and Juliet* in Moscow in 1935 which was realistic and grandiose, robust and elegant, virile and profound, popular and magnificent, modern and Shakespearean. But that production had been prepared over a period of nine months.

Though the Zeffirelli *Romeo* is skillfully and interestingly done, the direction has not wholly assimilated its acting. The actors were being *used* to make good points. Romeo and Juliet are alternately made to break down in endless adolescent weeping, the fun among Romeo's buddies is like campus kidding. In genuinely good acting, "points" are absorbed in the behavior of living people so that there seem to be no "points" at all—only human action. Judi Dench, the Juliet of the occasion, is particularly good, but for the most part the actors appear to be dragged along by the direction—to the detriment of both.

The new generation of theatregoers and their critical representatives prefer the raw to the smooth, the stink of the streets to the mustiness of salons. So even a tawdry and untalented "musical" like *Fings Ain't Wot They Used T'Be* (directed three years ago by Joan Littlewood and still running) is admired because it brings Soho garbage and the barely intelligible idiom of ponces and prostitutes onto the stage. It is as far as one can get from Milne and Barrie.

In 1914, the London audience was shocked into its wits by Eliza Doolittle's use of the expletive "bloody." In *Billy Liar*, a family comedy of lower-middle-class life in one of the northerly provinces, the oath is used every two minutes to the audience's undisguised satisfaction. In this play about a youth whose incessant "fantasies" (lies) are supposed to express his desire for a headlong escape from the drab humdrum of his background, the vocabulary hardly extends far beyond the hilarious cuss word, and the action never develops. But the audience is delighted by the picture of what for the theatre had hitherto been an unlikely environment and by an excellent cast. The new London theatre "find," Albert Finney, keeps the show moving. He is an actor of splendid promise; if he hams a bit in *Billy Liar*, it is what the play requires and deserves.

Progress in the Park, by Allen Owun, is a subtler piece of writing. Like *Billy Liar* more novelistic than dramatic in form, it focuses on Liverpool, a city riven by Catholic-Protestant antagonisms. Again there are racy performances, some tangy dialogue, an authenticity of atmosphere and an advocacy of social progressiveness along general "humanitarian" lines.

On the more polished level, *The Devils*, by John Whiting, from a novel by Aldous Huxley (*The Devils of Loudun*), proved a disappointment. There are several fluently written passages, but for the rest this seventeenth-century tale about a priest who excited the libido of nuns in a provincial French convent (and committed adultery with more than one lady of the local gentry) reminded me of certain burlesque aspects of both *The Crucible* and *The Tenth Man*. The total effect of this play is that of a cheap anticlericalism and of a muddy and banal mysticism. The production was poorly directed, badly acted, and ingeniously, impressively and improperly designed.

The designer of *The Devils* is Sean Kenny, whose sets for *Oliver!* (the great musical hit) were last season's sensation. He is unquestionably very gifted. (There is a bullish "run" on his services here now, as there always is in New York for every director or designer who has just scored a smash.) But one fears that all of Kenny's sets may come to look alike and be overexpressive of one special aspect of a play—not always the right one. Kenny's artistic "signature" threatens to deteriorate into formula.

Sartre's *Altona* (originally the *Prisoners of Altona*) was sufficiently absorbing in subject matter to make me "overlook" its production. I do not mean this as disparagement. It is just that I concentrated so hard on the play's dense dialogue that, though I was troubled by the setting (again the "extraordinary" work of Sean Kenny), little else—apart from the dialogue—seemed to concern me. One is absorbed by this play which—against a German background—is about the social guilt of our times.

Sartre engages us here in an intellectual, moral and social combat so strenuous that it takes on emotional dimensions. One is not altogether convinced at the end that the struggle was as vital as it appeared to be, but the fact that one consented to engage in it and felt almost no temptation to withdraw from it—even in moments of near boredom or exasperation—is a sign of a certain mastery.

Altona strikes one as somehow more German than French. In any case, I feel certain that it must be more convincingly produced in Germany (or Sweden) than in France, though it is reported that Serge Raggiani was thrilling in the central role of the original Paris production. The London production (directed by an American, John Berry) shows a devotion to the dramatist's cause which commands respect.

The slickest "performance" to be seen in London at this moment—I refer to the text as much as to the production—is Anouilh's *The Rehearsal,* in a first-class translation by Pamela Hansford-Johnson and Kitty Black. This play about the corruption of the French aristocracy and its dirty drive toward the debasement of innocence is extremely deft, theatrically superb, cleverly up to date and, at bottom, as old-fashioned as Dumas *fils* and rather empty.

It is very well acted, though Alan Badel as the wicked count bent on seduction and destruction struck me as soft rather than savage, and Maggie Smith seemed more like a bluntly sensible cockney girl than a humble example of feminine French sensibility. Still, these two are among the best of the younger London actors.

The Rehearsal is a perfect show for the theatregoer of "middling sensuality." In the more ambitious category, London eagerly awaits John Osborne's next play, *Luther,* with Albert Finney (after its world première at the Théâtre des Nations in Paris), and John Gielgud in Zeffirelli's production of *Othello* at Stratford-on-Avon.

A London Season, 1962

The Broadway theatre season wilts in mid-April; the London season appears to flower in May. Examined separately, the blossoms of the London bouquet are not unfailingly charming; still one is no doubt pleased with the impression of fresh color here.

It is perhaps paradoxical to think of Arnold Wesker's latest play, *Chips With Everything*, at the Royal Court Theatre (the recognized center of England's new drama), in terms of color. It deals with the peacetime training of raw R.A.F. recruits. Yet such is the verve of the production and the vigorous fluency of the writing that one is inclined to overlook the fact that the play is something of a documentary and as such is not quite as memorable as one had at first supposed.

There are very good things in it—apart from the admirable direction by John Dexter and the fine functional settings. A vivid characterization is that of Corporal Hill, who promises his boys a bloody tough eight weeks of drill under his charge. On duty, Hill is savagely sadistic; in the "privacy" of the barracks room where he shares the recruits' "accommodation" he is no worse, and in some respects more considerate, than the others. There are several other sharp thumbnail portraits.

The nub of the play is class conflict in the peculiarly British sense. The educated and well born are one class—more aloof and it would seem impregnable than what wealth makes of an American industrialist or his son. The working class is treated as—and to a large extent feels itself—a race apart; not so much inferior as isolated from the esteem and moral privilege of the upper class. This separation, which one had supposed altered since the war, is still sufficiently marked to provoke anger and scorn among a whole new group of British dramatists, novelists, journalists.

Wesker's play attempts to be "objective" about the situation, but its effect is at once melodramatic, defeatist and, in its psychology, unconvincing. One guileless working-class recruit is broken by brutality; the upper-class rebel among the trainees is insidiously demoralized and brought to heel by having the purity of his motives questioned—a plot turn which is barely credible.

Wesker is a determined Socialist, so one seeks the play's point —improperly perhaps—in that knowledge. One surmises that Wesker is trying to say that the only hope for change is through the resolute struggle of the working class alone; that no solution is to be expected from upper-class idealists.

The cast in *Chips With Everything* testifies to the development in Britain of a group of young players capable of acting realistic plays with disciplined power. The feeling that the evening as a whole inspires is one of devotion, which needs only to be informed by positive aims and by substantial ideas to achieve stature.

Another very important stronghold of the advancing British theatre is the Royal Shakespeare Company, whose director, Peter Hall (now joined by Peter Brook and Michel Saint-Denis), operates not only the theatre at Stratford-on-Avon, but the Aldwych and the tiny Arts Theatre Club in London as well. This organization, built around a core of distinguished actors on long-term contracts, offers a continuous repertory of new and classical plays.

The latest of this company's productions is Brecht's *The Caucasian Chalk Circle*. It has its merits, but my enjoyment was impaired by knowledge of the original German text (Brecht falls flat in any but the most brilliant of translations) and by my familiarity with the work of the Berliner Ensemble, whose long-thought-out and severely meticulous preparation through months of rehearsal cannot possibly be reproduced in the comparatively short time that even so ambitious an acting group as that of the Royal Shakespeare Company is permitted.

I found greater pleasure in John Gielgud's "traditional" revival of Sheridan's *The School for Scandal*, played by one of those expensive, virtually all-star casts, which the London theatre—particularly the H. M. Tennent management—can afford.

I had not seen Sheridan's play (written, in case you've forgotten, in 1777 when its author was twenty-six) for a good many years. It is a delightful piece kept sparklingly alive by the tart prickle of its prose and its gracious humanity. The performance at the charming Haymarket Theatre is a little uneven in quality and style, but Ralph Richardson as Sir Peter Teazle is entirely winning, Laurence Naismith as Sir Oliver Surface is endearing and Margaret Rutherford, for all her inveterate and veteran mugging, is very funny. However one may cavil at details in this production, the play emerges in smiling triumph.

For standard professionalism, nothing can excel Peter Ustinov's *Photo Finish*—an enormous box-office success. Ustinov himself takes the central role (he is also codirector of the production) and plays it with consummate skill. No doubt about it, Ustinov is an exceedingly clever man—highly endowed in every theatrical respect.

The play, which is called "an adventure in biography," presents an octogenarian novelist (Ustinov) who, in the course of writing his life story, recalls his person at various stages from infancy to adolescence, to youth, to middle age. All these ages are embodied in different actors who converse together, challenge, mock and commiserate with one another. The novelist's father—impeccably impersonated by Paul Rogers—younger at the time of his death than the octogenarian son who addresses him, is also an important figure in the Ustinov gallery.

All this, you can well imagine, is most ingenious and might lead to something like psychoanalytic perception. What it does lead to in this case is a certain amount of fun and a grudging or a fulsome admiration for the author's inventiveness. The writing is slick, salon-witty and safe; it is empty of real content. Admirably cast throughout (Diana Wynyard acting the novelist's wife at various ages is also first-rate) the play is a tour de force of showmanship—at least half an hour too long, and finally tiresome.

Seeing *Photo Finish* and the double bill of Peter Shaffer's two new one-act plays, *The Private Ear* and *The Public Eye,* I thought, "How much smoother talent is than genius." For Shaffer, like Ustinov and so many other accomplished craftsmen, can fashion handsome, civilized gadgets of entertainment which make intelligent pastimes without drawing blood—that is, without in any way arousing us from the comfort of convention, without changing us. Shaffer, who earlier wrote *Five Finger Exercise,* probably aspires to be something more than a latter-day Pinero, but at present he reaches only as far as Terence Rattigan. His message is benevolence, a plea for tolerance, an exchange of sympathy among fellowmen.

Shaffer is still a novice—albeit one of unmistakable assurance—and no judgment about his evolution and future contribution should be undertaken at this point. The sentiment which animates his work might conceivably lead to creation. But up to now he has written as one who demonstrates his thesis cleverly for stage purposes rather than as one intimate with those for whom he begs our compassion.

There is an oblique confession of this in the second of the two plays mentioned: *The Public Eye.* The public eye is the author's. A young and, for unstated reasons, confirmed bachelor, acting as a private detective, plays Puck or fairy godfather to a nice, near-beatnik woman of indeterminate origin and the businessman she has married—decent, informed, slightly stuffy. Their marriage is due for disaster because she seeks the romantic excitement of constant discovery, whereas he wants her to settle down to the role of understanding helpmate.

The play is wittily written, a very agreeable confection, deftly acted by the three members of its cast—but it touches reality with its finger tips only. Its connection with the truth of marital relations is largely conversational—the wisdom of the glib acquaintance who drops in on a family quarrel and gives apt yet irrelevant advice.

Where reality is approached somewhat more directly in *The Private Ear*, the content is, oddly enough, closer to the trite. A young man of the working class is as sensitive as he is unworldly. He left school at an early age and the proof of his sensibility is his addiction to music from Bach and Britten to Puccini and to the painting of Botticelli. He invites to his digs an even more abysmally uneducated girl he has met by chance at a concert, assuming that she too is one of those lonely, underprivileged souls who take solace in music. He prepares dinner for her with the aid of a more "experienced" (coarse) friend. The upshot is that the girl— as common a cockney lass as can be—is attracted to the fast boy and is only momentarily melted by a recorded love duet from *Madame Butterfly*. She slaps the face of her hapless host when he makes a tentative and tender pass. Scarred in spirit, disillusioned, the boy smashes the record with which he had sought to hold the girl.

This should be touching—several of my friends professed themselves moved—but it struck me only as "effective." For, apart from the ordinariness of the play's scheme, one finds the author manipulating his material for comedy gags on the one hand (malapropisms and presumably hilarious variations on the types to be found in the proletarian plays of the new British drama) and for tear-jerking pity for the unfavored on the other. We are made to feel benign without the least scratch of conscience.

The Private Ear is extremely well acted by Maggie Smith, one of the best younger players here, who in certain of her traits resembles both Julie Harris and Kim Stanley. The pantomime of petting which accompanies Puccini's music is most expertly managed by Peter Wood, a director who knows his business.

The Alchemist and King Lear, 1963

In the production of old plays theatre folk are almost always concerned with the question of how to make their texts appear fresh. Are we to gather from this that they have grown stale? Hardly. What the producers want is a way to make'the classics live as *plays*, plays to stir new audiences with the sense that the masterpieces are truly relevant to their particular and ever-changing state of mind. The goal is not to resuscitate (the material is not dead) but to create.

This has been effectively done by Tyrone Guthrie with Ben Jonson's *The Alchemist* at the Old Vic and by Peter Brook with the Royal Shakespeare Company production of *King Lear*. Each play alternates with others on the respective institution's programs and each is a massive box-office hit.

Ben Jonson's bawdy farce is admired for its construction by students of the Elizabethan drama, and its theme is perennially apt: greed and the gullibility of the money minded. A pair of petty racketeers, assisted by their moll, set out to fleece a variety of characters by pretending that they possess the knowledge to turn base metal into gold.

What has kept Jonson's play alive all these years, besides the enduring contemporaneity of its motivations and the juicy roles it offers the actors, is its writing—full of meat, blood, guts, waste matter and vinegar, capped by Latin learning and Elizabethan double-talk—a Gargantuan dish.

Guthrie produces the play in modern dress and has translated the characters into presently familiar prototypes. Certain purists may quarrel with this procedure but this leads to futile debate. Guthrie's direction is comically resourceful, full of brio and high jinks—cold and crazy as the play itself. The byplay is incessant and the pace hectic. All this would be capital were it not for the fact that one's eyes are so wholly engaged in following the stage business that the only words one is sure one recognizes are such solecisms as "travelers' checks," "Lyons" (a London restaurant), "Buchmanism," "Einstein," "Haldane" and "Airwick"—words that Guthrie has introduced to make the play's allusions conform to

the new framework. I caught only as much of Jonson's dialogue—
by no means easy in itself—as I do language at the opera.

Cocteau once asked Sergei Diaghilev, his mentor, what that
great impresario expected of him. "Astonish me," Diaghilev answered. Stagecraft cannot find a more brilliant summation. If
Peter Brook's *Lear* could claim no further distinction, it would
still be memorable because it astonishes. It astonishes by a
magisterial simplification. It eschews all pageantry and, to a large
extent, pathos. As Lear is stripped of all his goods and honor, so
the production is stripped of pomp. It is a naked production.

The stage is bare. The lights are white. Apart from a minimum
of coarse wooden props, two large brown squares of canvas stand
isolated on either side of the stage. The backdrop is a chalky
gray. In the storm scenes on the heath, squares of black material
are lowered from the flies. There is no curtain. The actors enter
while the houselights are still on, and these dim only as the action
gets under way. At the end of each act, the playing continues for
awhile after the houselights have come up. Costumes look like
leather, rough and brown. They are wholly appropriate in the
impression they make of a barbaric plainness. The battle in the
fifth act is indicated by the clangor of rattling shields: no con-
testant is seen fighting.

The actors speak with notable distinction. Every word strikes
home so that the literal meaning is unmistakable: we know what
Shakespeare wrote. The voices are strong; no one rants. Even
"Blow, winds, and crack your cheeks! rage! blow," spoken loudly
enough to be heard over the not-excessive din, is projected with a
certain degree of sobriety.

Paul Scofield plays Lear with a stern, tight, thoughtful impassivity. He looks rather like the wood carving of a hard, peasant
forester (slightly Russian!). He might be compared to a somewhat withered but still sturdy tree. When he dies, he simply
ceases to be; he subsides rather than expires. His passing is a
period. His speech is deliberate, ringingly precise rather than
sonorous or histrionically eloquent. There is no tearing of passion.
The only one who cries heartbrokenly is Gloucester as he listens
to his king berating humanity.

When Lear is reunited with Cordelia in that wonderful passage
beginning "Come, let's away to prison. We two alone will sing
like birds i' th' cage. When thou dost ask me blessing, I'll kneel

down, And ask thee forgiveness. So we'll live, And pray, and sing, and tell old tales, and laugh as gilded butterflies . . .," Scofield is dignified, poised and explanatory, like a teacher soothing a possibly unnerved child.

All through Shakespeare's text Lear says such things as "I will not be mad" or "O that way madness lies, let me shun that"—and of course he goes mad. Repeatedly Lear also says the equivalent of "Let not woman's weapon, water-drops, stain my man's cheeks," or "You think I'll weep! No, I'll not weep." But we never feel in this production that Lear is ever in danger of either going mad or weeping. He is much too resolute and contained for such frailty or unseemliness.

It would be too easy to say that this refusal of sentiment bespeaks the influence of Brecht, though without Brecht such a presentation might never have come into being. We would rather say that this thoroughly coherent production is in tune with the intellectual and moral climate of our day. It is a reduction of *King Lear* to our size.

Shakespeare's *Lear* is one of the fiercest of all plays: a wild outcry against the human condition and the folly of all our posturing and self-importance. (The play is *not* about the wickedness of ungrateful children!) "Is man no more than this . . . such a poor, bare, forked animal?" Even the Book of Job hardly expresses more bitterness. "As flies to wanton boys, are we to th' gods: they kill us for their sport." "When we are born, we cry out that we are come to this great stage of fools."

All this we understand, as does Peter Brook. For our time is one in which, with no commanding faith, sensitive souls have begun to spew venom, to mock themselves as the dupes of creation, or to immolate themselves either in inanition or in sadism—for all of which artists have been unable to find any word other than "absurd."

The calm irony of Brecht is not intended as negation but as a purification of the spirit which might lead to the understanding required for sane action. But Shakespeare is not Brecht—nor calm. I do not believe *King Lear* was composed solely as a curse upon all the houses of the Renaissance (or modern) world. *King Lear* is Shakespeare's tortured espousal of the virtue of Love in a civilization given over and abasing itself to the idol of Power. Yes, he seems to be saying, life is cruelly hard and ". . . Men must endure/Their going hence even as their coming hither," but "*Ripeness is all.*" "Ripeness," maturity, manhood, demand a brave acceptance, yea-saying fortitude—not collapse, not a gnashing of teeth nor black despair. Hope is not merely the looking forward to "better things"; it is the motion of life itself, suffered and enjoyed for its own sake.

But should my view of *King Lear* be mistaken it would not alter my interpretation of the new London production. The point is that Shakespeare's immense force, his overwhelming lyric might, the volcanic life that fires his every scene and speech are not to be conveyed in the reasoned, shriveled and bleached terms of Peter Brook's staging—impressive though they be. This "Beckett-like" *Lear* (the production and the play have been compared to *Endgame*) takes place in a realm too blank and airless even for the gesture of suicide. The world of Shakespeare's *Lear* is so rich in substance that one would be glad to dwell in it; we are rewarded for its agony by the fullness of its matter. Such a world may be full of horror; it is not *absurd*. And then, one does not attempt to describe the monumentality of the Himalayas by likening them to the Catskills!

Paul Scofield is a truly fine actor and his performance is consonant with his endowments, as it is altogether loyal to his director's plan. Irene Worth as Goneril and Alan Webb as Gloucester are vivid and individual in a cast almost no part of which is bad. After one has left the theatre one wishes to see the production again—a rare occurrence. Peter Brook is to be congratulated on a *Lear* made to the measure of our day and the circumstances of the modern theatre. For in its own right *King Lear*, as Charles Lamb said, "cannot be acted: the play is beyond all art." Still, in 1935 I saw it in Moscow in a production which Gordon Craig pronounced the best Shakespeare he had ever seen. So Charles Lamb may have been wrong after all.

Plays from the Continent, 1963

Is there any significance in the fact that the most noted dramatists writing in German today are Swiss? Switzerland, hemmed in on all sides by countries frequently engaged in and always tending toward war, no longer feels itself safe within its Alps. An innocent bystander, it may prove as vulnerable as any other "peace-loving" domain. For this reason, perhaps, its two most prominent playwrights—Friedrich Dürrenmatt and Max Frisch—serve as Geiger counters to Europe. Being themselves without offensive arms, the Swiss are in a position to moralize as well as shudder. Dürrenmatt and Frisch tremble and preach, while their colleagues in the neighbor countries either squeal or despair.

Frisch is prophetic and composes parables; Dürrenmatt, suffering at his ease, grimaces and indulges in gallows humor. Dürrenmatt is theatrically the more deft and the more sophisticated. At a time without fresh dramatic impulse both are outstanding.

The Physicists, the latest Dürrenmatt play, is a Continental success. Directed by Peter Brook, it alternates with *King Lear* under the auspices of the enterprising Royal Shakespeare Company and is almost as much of a hit as the great tragedy.

More topical than any of Dürrenmatt's other plays (one remembers *The Visit*), *The Physicists* is singularly striking. It is essentially an entertainment, but it has an importance—one which under present theatrical and social circumstances may reasonably be exaggerated.

Technically, the play is a comedy melodrama; it amuses and excites. It provides effective roles for its actors, and Peter Brook has directed it with unfailing skill. The company—particularly Cyril Cusak, Michael Hordern and Irene Worth, who plays a "Teutonic" monster in the guise of a psychiatrist—demonstrates the kind of compelling professionalism in the manner of a superior detective story which is always set down as "real theatre."

The play begins with the race of the major powers to obtain scientific supremacy for military purposes. Then the physicists decide to renounce forever their battle of wits which they know can only end in the annihilation of civilization. But, says Dürrenmatt through one of his physicists, "What is taught cannot be untaught." Those who have learned how to use the new instruments of destruction will not refrain from doing so. The power-crazed will take over; we are doomed.

This is the warning, the lesson. We may shiver; we ought to groan. We should take action. But what we do is applaud a good show. Dürrenmatt is devilishly capable; his play will be a hit everywhere. It will not resolve the issue either in our minds or in our hearts. It is not that kind of play. It is less pessimistic than cynical. The highest compliment one can pay it is to surmise that Shaw might have liked it. It should be seen.

Also worth attention is the production of Bertolt Brecht's first play, *Baal*, acted by the new English star of stage and screen Peter O'Toole.

The play was written when Brecht was only twenty-three, and it is now more dramatic curiosity than event. It reveals the confusion and anguish from which Brecht grew. In the light of the author's development from *Baal* to *Mother Courage, Galileo* and the others, we see an artist surmounting vertigo and stupefaction to attain clarity, a passage from romantic floundering to classic authority.

In *Baal* Brecht seems to wallow in the mental and moral muck characteristic of Germany immediately after the First World War. Through his central figure, the poet Baal, Brecht indulges in that "disordering of the senses" which Rimbaud once announced as his aim. In fact, there is a certain imitation of the tortured Rimbaud-Verlaine affair in this play.

Rimbaud ceased writing poetry when he was nineteen; Brecht's poet never publishes at all. In the satirical first, and perhaps best, scene of the play Baal is feted at a dinner party given by would-be patrons, dilettantes and *avant-garde* critics who have heard him recite some of his bizarre verses to guitar accompaniment—verses which the guests compare to Homer, the great decadents and finally agree to call "promising!" But Baal, ragged and filthy, only wolfs his food, asks for a donation of clean shirts and makes flagrant passes at his host's wife.

From this point on Baal (his appearance never less than epically repellent) moves on to a rampage of seduction and near-rape among girls and women who are unable or unwilling to resist the fascination of his priapic confidence. From poetized homosexual adventures and complete besottedness to total depravity and crime, Baal is finally seen crawling like a diseased animal to his death in the open fields.

At one point the poet, thinking back on his wretched odyssey, murmurs, "Everything was beautiful." In this one line Brecht characterizes the climate of an era, a state of being which led either to the "reforms" of Hitlerism or to an unconsummated effort to find saner solutions.

Despite its star and a few respectful notices, the play is not a success. Nevertheless, I suspect that, for all its romantic distortion, it satisfies a need in that part of the younger generation which wonders whether immersion in the mud may not bring it closer to salvation than squatting in the shallows of a stagnant respectability. For many the point of crisis has not yet been reached.

Baal might not have been produced at this juncture—and certainly not in the West End—had it not been for the representative and forceful actor Peter O'Toole, who seems attracted to those parts which represent "outcasts from life's feast" or, to put it another way, parts which bespeak the chaos that breeds anger.

Satire in the English Theatre, 1963

The English theatre is enjoying a seizure of satire. It all began with *Look Back in Anger*. That play was rhetorically enraged for reasons barely explicit but nonetheless sensible to its audience. There followed a series of "proletarian" plays—more troubled than affirmative—and to these too an important public was responsive. Then came the intimate revues, notably *Beyond the Fringe* and *The Establishment*, so that even the West End was glad to listen to the wistful lament and mockery of *Stop the World—I Want To Get Off*.

The American tomfoolery of *The Premise* and various editions of *From the Second City* sustained the motion. The drama of Beckett, Ionesco and company also helped to relax theatrical restraints and broaden the perspectives of the permissible.

The English, thoroughly disciplined to decorum, have always found an escape in bouts of eccentricity, low comedy and goofy humor. Now the theatre has begun to run wild in all these directions. There is an air of self-congratulation on this score.

The most generally advanced of the new satirical shows is the "musical entertainment" *Oh What a Lovely War*, the authorship of which is now in legal dispute but which has unquestionably been written and improvised under the supervision of Joan Littlewood, founder of the Theatre Workshop and director of such excellent productions as *A Taste of Honey* and *The Hostage*.

The company in *Oh What a Lovely War* is dressed in Pierrot costumes—as in *Stop the World*. A circus sideshow environment provides the permanent setting. Moving electric tapes flash messages about the accumulation of casualties and futile engagements of the First ("lovely") World War. This device is borrowed from Brecht and Piscator.

Onstage are enacted a series of burlesque episodes parodying bayonet drill, meetings of high officials and military personnel in the war zone and in London high society. The bayonet drill, under the screaming sergeant who instructs his men in the techniques and manners of murder by cold steel, is as grotesquely funny as it has always been. There are other such caricatures— equally laughable without being a bit more novel. Mingled with these are such old-time tunes as Ivor Novello's *Keep the Home Fires Burning*, and these are the only good songs of the evening.

Everyone is "crazy" about this show. Why? The performances on the whole are crude, and one is not convinced that the satire bears a direct relation to any present situation. The specific butt appears to be General Haig, who has been under blistering attack since 1918 for his bullheadedness in sending thousands to certain death in senseless "advances" which advanced nothing.

Though it rarely does any harm to scorn the military mind, I suggest that the satire here lacks point. It would not be entirely apposite in terms of the Second World War—except that that war might have been avoided if, for example, Churchill and not Chamberlain had been Prime Minister between 1937–1939. And certainly the prospect of a Third World War has to be treated in quite a different manner. Yet *Oh What a Lovely War* strikes the English as vitally relevant because it emphasizes what the young here cannot repeat too often: that the Establishment was, is and, by inference, always will be irremediably callous and stupid. Even those English who might agree that the show is not strictly applicable to contemporary affairs find in it the pleasure of nostalgia. It recalls a time of innocence when England, the most powerful nation on earth, shed its blood and drained itself of strength in a euphoria of self-confident, heroic befuddlement. At that memory—and in this the old songs are eminently helpful— strong men literally weep.

Whatever our reaction, it is certain that *Oh What a Lovely*

War is the most accomplished of recent satires. From this there is a decline to a kind of harum-scarum jamboree of ribaldry and self-abandonment. Some of this is talented and very funny, as in *The Bed Sitting Room*. Its coauthor is Spike Milligan, an endearing and original comic. Here we see England shortly after the bomb has been dropped. The war itself was of brief duration—a minute and twenty-three seconds. Heaven knows who won it—possibly the Russians—though it does not matter; it is clear that it was not England. Macmillan has turned into a parrot (the resemblance is striking), and a certain Lord into a bed-sitting-room!

There is very little politics after this; and there need not be. Everything has been cut loose from its normal moorings; the ensuing action makes the extravagances of surrealism and Ionesco look sober. The authors have achieved what they intended: to make us laugh at an utterly loony world in which the folk formerly most respected are now the daffiest because they are the least endowed with humor and a sense of their own screwiness.

Even this is probably saying too much, for there is no indication that any other world or social order (which Labour might provide, for instance) would prove any less ridiculous. Spike Milligan and his associates may personally support the cause of nuclear disarmament, and their show may represent a gesture on behalf of their convictions, but what is chiefly communicated is a shoot-the-works rapture—anarchist rather than radical.

While this, the prevailing mood, may have its healthy aspect, I cannot help but regard it with some suspicion. For when you revel in turning everything topsy-turvy, jeer at everything and affirm nothing, you may well end by standing still, evading responsibility, sizzling smugly or disconsolately in the same stew as the neighbor you appear to scorn.

The tendency to take these shows not at their face value but as signs of advanced social consciousness and superior theatrical skill is complemented by the enthusiasm for spineless dramaturgy couched in literate double-talk, as exemplified in such blather as *Next Time I'll Sing to You*, which contains little but the backwash of Pirandello. One critic has called it "the best play in London."

Am I mistaken in noticing a recent falling off in the development of English (and French) dramatic writing? John Osborne's plays, since his first three, have not revealed any remarkable progress. Pinter is not following upon *The Caretaker* with anything of wider scope. Wesker has turned to other tasks. And how much longer can Beckett, Ionesco and others of kindred temper continue voicing a view of the world which by its very nature has no issue?[*]

This waning of impetus may prove only momentary. But it occurs to me that the low blood pressure may result from a social and moral apathy induced by the fact that nearly all of us fear the future and cannot in good conscience accept the present. However, that is a realm of speculation which leads far beyond, though it lies all around, the confines of the theatre.

Britain's National Theatre, 1964

The British had to wait till 1963 to establish a national theatre for which the first concrete suggestion was made in 1848. Now that it has been set up we see that it is good. Since its opening, ten plays have been presented. Of these I have seen seven. All of them, despite the reservations I shall make, are good. I shall not speak of *Saint Joan,* transferred from the repertory of the theatre in Chichester (a sort of summer annex of the main enterprise), nor of *Hamlet,* Frisch's *Andorra* and a double bill of Sophocles' *Philoctetes* and Beckett's *Play,* which, failing to attract a sufficient audience, have been dropped.

The first play I saw—the company's latest—was *The Master Builder.* The critical response to this production has been negative. The play was held to be "dated" and fault was found with the casting of Maggie Smith as Hilde Wangel. I thought the play fascinating and Maggie Smith, one of England's best actresses, though certainly not a conventional choice for the part, quite interesting. I am exasperated when a play like *The Master Builder* is called "dated" because certain of its characters refer to trolls and Hilde speaks of hearing "harps in the air." It was as normal for Norwegians in 1892 to speak of "trolls" as for us to talk of "traumas." A trauma is no more material than a troll! And for an enthusiastic young girl of the time to speak of hearing "harps

[*] These are hasty generalizations.—H. C.

in the air" is no more odd than for a girl today to say that listening to Thelonius Monk "sends her."

The theme of Ibsen's play remains vital. It concerns the fear and frustration which often agitate the aging artist (or anyone of signal achievement) that he may be superseded by a rising generation and be found "dated"! The temptation of such a man is to suppress or deny the new voices clamoring to be heard; frequently he harbors a sense of defeat, the suspicion that he has not accomplished all that he might have done or dreamed of doing.

The Master Builder is Ibsen's confession, an avowal of the contrary pulls of his nature. The protagonist, the architect Solness, began his career by building churches, but made his reputation by putting up ordinary homes for well-to-do families. Ibsen aimed at creating great epic drama—*Brand, Peer Gynt, Emperor and Galilean*—but the world came to honor him for *A Doll's House, The Wild Duck, Hedda Gabler.* Ibsen foresaw the time when his "middle-class" art (his realism) would no longer serve our needs. He denounced the old "ideals"—the God or gods of his fathers—but felt a deep hunger for some inspirational force with which to replace them.

The dialectic of the generations, with its concomitant psychological tensions, is real enough and constant. What brings all this to life in *The Master Builder* is Hilde Wangel, a character who, for all the nineteenth-century and Scandinavian innocence of her vocabulary, is as vivid, sharp, contradictory, virtuous and amoral as any impatient young girl anywhere today. To this aspect of the role—the bubbling will to mount to the heights—Maggie Smith, with her irrepressible humor, adds a tangy contemporary touch that emphasizes what is enduring in the play.

Michael Redgrave may be a little soft for the ruthless, egocentric Solness (though "soft" men—particularly artists—in such circumstances are often unconscionably tough, even petty), but he has a certain grandeur, he is thoughtful and he knows very well what the part is all about.

The result is a production—all of it well cast—very much to the point. What is missing is *mood;* the spiritual atmosphere which must inform a play's structure. This fault, as we shall later note, is perhaps symptomatic of something in the artistic makeup of the National Theatre company.

Next I saw Farquhar's *The Recruiting Officer* (1706), in which love intrigues typical of eighteenth-century English comedy are combined with a shrewd commentary on the army's ugly devices of recruiting. The play is richly written, utterly beguiling in its characters, as well as delightfully funny in its scenes.

With a perfect cast, the production is in every way successful. Once again Maggie Smith holds the stage with a wise gleam in her eye, benevolently feminine mischief in her heart, laughter in her spirit and an attractiveness that stems more from the whole composition of her qualities than from her physical person. In the cast, too, Laurence Olivier (artistic director to this company of fifty-one actors) plays a small part in a manner so absolutely right and original that it lingers emblematically as the obtuse, mendacious, boastful, good-natured, thoroughly self-satisfied (satisfied with the fun of cheating, fighting, guzzling, wenching) petty officer who is as much at ease in the army as a pig in a trough. This characterization, which should be set beside Olivier's unforgettable Shallow and his fop in Sheridan's *The Critic,* is a masterpiece.

The Recruiting Officer was followed on my schedule by Harold Brighouse's *Hobson's Choice,* a play first produced in 1916, though it mirrors the Salford (Lancashire) of 1880. The play foreshadows the breakdown of class snobbery in England; it also proves that a "corny" comedy can be art and that social reflection may be fun. The story is of a masterful lady of thirty, threatened with spinsterhood by her plainness and by her father's exploitation, who chooses a semiliterate cobbler as her husband and sets out to stiffen his backbone and give him the semblance of an education. In doing so, she shatters the paternal fortress. *Hobson's Choice* is an utterly charming stage piece—all smiles, sound sentiment and good sense.

Joan Plowright, with her spunk and dark, determined, glistening eyes, her speech that sounds sweetly of Midland streets (the accent is usually accounted ugly, but on Miss Plowright's lips it acquires a wonderful savor) makes Maggie Hobson a girl to treasure, the salt of womankind and of British moral will.

No less effective is Frank Finlay, an actor who plays bluff working-class characters with archetypal truthfulness and lends them a warmth one might not guess they possessed. He is the darling boob of whom Maggie makes a man. Michael Redgrave has been accused (partly because of the enormous beard which frames his face) of turning Hobson into a musty King Lear. It seems to me, however, that his performance was "saved" by that beard! There are actors who require a mask—a strong external characterization—to set their imagination free. Redgrave is such an actor. His Hobson, formidable in girth as well as in height, red-nosed, cunning and stupid, blustering and weak, embattled and pathetic, is both funny and forgivable. He provides the production with a strong anchor.

Chekhov's *Uncle Vanya*, with Redgrave in the name part, Olivier as Astrov, Plowright as Sonya and Rosemary Harris as the professor's wife, was given a thoroughly understanding production. The last two acts are especially moving. Redgrave is brilliant in the scene where he bursts out against his selfish pedant of a brother-in-law, and in his final grief, inconsolable by the broken-hearted encouragement of Plowright's Sonya, he reduces us to tears.

Still, for all its excellence, the production reveals something of the company's shortcomings. Mannerism often takes the place of mood. ("Mood" results from a confluence of the actor's being with the total environment or soul of the dramatist's creation.) In this production one recognizes a company of meticulous actors who have gone reverently to work. But for Chekhov, sound craftsmanship, even dramatic intelligence, are not enough. This *Uncle Vanya* lacks, not entirely, but enough to leave me a little dissatisfied, the true core of the play—that palpable *idealism* which is at the heart of Chekhov's writing and generally of the Russian character, even in some of its negative aspects.

Thus Rosemary Harris, exquisite as the beauty gone to waste, seems more like an affected bluestocking than a richly endowed woman in whom the sap of life is slowly evaporating. The effect is unintentionally comic, but not comic in Chekhov's way, which is never the least brittle or even faintly depreciatory.

Redgrave's Vanya, on the other hand, might assume more comic meaning in the correct sense if he were less the stifled intellectual at the outset (less "romantic" looking as well) and more the flustered, slightly disheveled, self-neglecting dreamer going to seed.

The visual sign of what I have indicated is the stylized plain wood setting, which is an abstraction of nothing. It suggests hardly any place either actual or symbolic—only a kind of literal dead end, wholly juiceless. The loneliness and ennui of Chekhov's world may be stultifying, but they are never dry.

The climax and sensation of the National Theatre's season is *Othello*. With *Macbeth*, *Othello* is the most closely knit, the most tightly constructed of Shakespeare's plays. Here poetry and action are perfectly wed.

As Othello, Olivier—and this production is all Olivier, though Maggie Smith is an appealing Desdemona—builds the part with crafty logic. But what is most remarkable about Olivier's performance is not the line of its dramatic evolution or the kind of common-sense realism he brings to the opening scenes, but the bravery, the tempestuous scenic courage with which he depicts the moments of Othello's agony. Here there is such an explosion of searing sound, of groans, of gasps, of wild and broken outcries such as few English-speaking actors would attempt. Such display of histrionic temperament—in this instance the savage orchestration of the emotion of jealousy—is, despite Hamlet's admonition against overacting, the proper style for the interpretation of Shakespearean tragedy.

The killing of Desdemona and Othello's suicide are staged with fierce imagination: Othello holds Desdemona in his arms all through the speech which precedes the moment when he stabs himself with a thin blade concealed in a leather band around his wrist. This, and the elaborate murder of Desdemona, exemplify the kind of red-blooded theatre which we long to see because, while it is supposed to be "traditional," it is rarely found on our "serious" stages today.

Audiences and critics, too, have been much impressed with Olivier's Othello as a *Negro* characterization: the special gait (a slight swagger on bare feet), the resonant low-keyed voice, the somewhat weighted tone and stress of speech, the sensuous mouth, the black man's particular smile and laugh. All this is notably well done, but my mind refused to acknowledge it because I could not help thinking that all this paraphernalia might be unnecessary if a Negro were acting the part.

Everything that consummate skill, splendid vocal and physical equipment, intelligence, observation, theatrical flair can accomplish, Olivier achieves. And yet—I am almost tempted to apologize for saying it—the substance of genuine feeling, which Olivier indicates magnificently, is not actually present. I am excited; I am

not touched. I shake with the impact and daring of the performance. But I am not convinced of the authenticity of the play's
emotion, nor am I entirely informed as to its meaning.

Olivier knows all about what happens to a man suffering the
anguish of jealousy, but he can only imitate—not live it—on the
stage. Something in this marvelous actor's nature is perpetually
withdrawn. There is always a captivating mystery in Olivier's
performances of tragic roles, but also a strange stoppage of personal feeling at their center. The inner sources of emotion—the
"floodgates"—are unaccountably closed. Though he has a superb
faculty for forcing their release, his secret and most intimate sentiments seldom emerge. That is why I am obliged to consider his
acting in comedy or character roles more complete than his performances in tragedy.

Two more things must be said. The production is not especially
euphonious. The reasonable realism of the approach makes most
of the lines clear but rarely gratifying to the ear. This may also be
due to Frank Finlay's utter unsuitability for the role of Iago. He
was chosen on the ground that Othello would never be taken in
by Iago if he were a "spectacular" character, one whose "honesty"
was not of a blunt unvarnished nature. This is mere rationalization, a trick to heighten the effect of an effulgent Othello by a
dun Iago. It has little to do with Shakespeare, whose realism is
never commonplace but always heroic.

A far more important consideration is the fact that although
Olivier is intuitively right in trying to make his "Negroid" characterization a means to reveal the crucial element of sensuality in
Othello—the play is a "history of lust"—he brings to this aspect of
the part a charm, a sort of subtle, leading-man sex appeal which
is not precisely what the play demands. *Othello* is a tragedy of
desire. There is more appetite than love in the "noble" Moor.
Iago's machinations are, so to speak, only a function of Othello's
concupiscence. His sensual passion is the cause of his torment,
the true reason for his downfall. It should have a torrential force,
a volcanic heat. When Olivier suffers the throes of jealousy he is
human, all too human, which may endear him to us, but that very
fact diminishes Othello's Shakespearean stature.

If I have seemed unduly crabbed about a week of playgoing,
which at all times afforded me true pleasure and with a company
I hold in high esteem, it is because I have chosen to regard the

work of the British National Theatre in the light of art, rather than as a series of "great shows" that may serve to give a kick to our spare time. One does not gush over art; one contemplates or ponders it as an event in one's life.

"Swinging Town," 1965

Something about Paris—was it the traffic-choked streets, the political apathy, parts of the exposition of twentieth-century sculpture at the Rodin museum?—made me say, "I disapprove of most things nowadays while I enjoy almost everything." This quip ought to be borne in mind in much that follows.

I loved Paris all over again, not because of any plays or pictures I saw there but because it reeks of life. Its wounds as much as its charms are immediately revealed to the eye. Its theatre at the moment is poor but the city itself is theatre.

London now is Europe's most "swinging" town. I went to the theatre six times in seven days. Though I cannot say that I "liked" what I saw, I found everything more than casually interesting. Something is going on in England and I was glad to observe a little of it in the theatre-mirror.

The National Theatre and the Royal Shakespeare Company (the latter appears both at Stratford-on-Avon and at the Aldwych in London) command the finest acting troupes of the English-speaking world. The cast of Harold Pinter's latest play, *The Homecoming*, offers no "stars," but is so thoroughly right that it gives the impression of being the play itself. Acting everywhere in London today generally displays remarkable competence and at times brilliance. One often suspects, however, that roles are being played for recordings rather than for the stage: so much of the effect is verbal and vocal. One hears almost too well.

The plays piqued me in a peculiar way. Each of them seemed to have been conceived in one family and inspired by a single motive. Nearly all were bitter comedies with grins bespeaking self-pity and mockery. My first guess was that the British were now in the grip of an obsession, part of that sexual revolution one hears so much about these days. But I soon realized that this was a mistake. It was not the warmth of sex that emanated from the plays I saw but the chill of a vengeful frustration. Sex provided no solace, tenderness, sensual gratification, entertainment or progeny. It was closer to suicide.

It would be easy to conjecture that having frivolously defied Victorian prudery in the twenties, the British are now grimly battering away at its Puritan residue. But in the plays I refer to, sex appears to cause greater frustration than the original inhibitions ever did. The laughter provoked by these plays is rarely ribald or lewd; it is the laughter of a man jeering at his own impotence.

The ambivalence immanent in the new dramatic cycle may be discerned in the recurrence of the homosexual strain. Homosexuality may hold a special fascination for the British theatregoer because mention of its very existence was hitherto banned from the stage. The taboo has now been exorcized. Still, the presentation of homosexuality does not occur in plays which are really about homosexuality. It is made an adjunct to a play's central theme.

The three characters in Frank Marcus' *The Killing of Sister George*, a spoof on British television, are all Lesbians. In John Osborne's *A Patriot for Me*, exposing hypocrisy in aristocratic Establishments (an allusion to the Profumo case), the protagonist is a homosexual officer in the old Austro-Hungarian Empire whose betrayal of his country under pressure of blackmail is covered up by recourse to anti-Semitism. Nevertheless, scene after scene is either comically or melodramatically given to displays of homosexual misbehavior—actually irrelevant to the play's subject. If there is any pornography in these plays it is pornography of the intellect. Muddy thinking and the turbid sentimentality of chattering minds are the end results.

If it is all sex in the head, if the sexual emphasis is artistically marginal, one wonders what, apart from its theatrical effect, is its true purpose or significance. What is really being exposed is rage, the curse sparked by an inability to feel.

There is a positive aspect to this: these plays are not just smartly shocking. Despite faults as drama, they reflect a reality. We can neither dismiss nor forget them. They are almost all well written in the rhetoric of vituperation for which Osborne's *Look*

Back in Anger set the tone, and of which he is still the prime master.

The psychological condition of which the new plays are oblique signs has a social cause of great significance.

Because Britain is freer than it has ever been, its people more alert, they shake the old Establishment without seeming to move ahead to anything wholly fresh and liberating. We witness this in the virtual impasse of their politics. The conservative stagnates, the Left feels stymied. Though there surely have been "improvements" since the war, the progress made does not appear to have altered matters enough to act as an inspiring force. There is little mass enthusiasm except for "Beatles," the escape into infantilism. How then can there be any animating purpose? Where action is not sustained by confidence in concrete social consequence, the individual, unless he be a true artist, a revolutionary or a saint, lapses into depression, lethargy, cynicism, psychosis or crime. Sex becomes a substitute for the release sought, but sex by itself cannot satisfy the greater hunger or carry the burden of humanity's broader needs. Hence the sadistic sentiments it induces.

The plays themselves do not sufficiently project an awareness of this cause and are thus more symptomatic than interpretive. They strike me as being, for all their hooting and growling, fundamentally complacent. There is little sign that their authors would like to change anything or harbor some notion as to the course through which a change might take place. They appear pleased to enjoy the fruits of their displeasure—personal acclaim with the additional advantage of being definitely "in."

One of the clues to the poverty of these plays is their peculiar length. Once stated, a primary situation is repeated again and again. Nothing specific develops. The often coruscating talk is prolonged from one jibe to another, as if to illustrate the art of insult and making customers. Two plays employ soliloquies, stream-of-consciousness verbiage, semi-fantasy and, in one case, the denuding of the central character. Typical too is the use of various women as foils upon which the central male personage may play off his moral disarray and hate. The characters are not made more understandable or sympathetic as the action proceeds; they diminish with verbal extension. They are neither pathetic nor tragic: they are, at best, wretched with jokes which to the audience's delight are frequently obscene.

In David Mercer's *Ride a Cock Horse,* a one-shot novelist out of the coal pits of the North, a man who manages to render his wife and two mistresses thoroughly miserable, speaks of himself as "harassed by insight but incapable of meaningful action." Insights there may be, but not the kind which lead to new paths. That is why they harass.

What is missing in so many of the new plays is the substance of experience. Beckett's shudder is aesthetically admirable in its concise passion. Pinter's *The Homecoming* is a collage abstracted from real elements pithily picturing a society indifferent to or ignorant of any values. Osborne forages in ever new areas but always returns with the same bag of disaffection. John Arden, none of whose new plays were on during my visit, has greater scope and feeling but is not always master of his material. But generally speaking, I find that too many of the new plays, as so much else in contemporary expression, eliminate the world itself, the vessels, bones and structure, even the geography of daily life, so that we find ourselves on a constant excursion in the air, winging over everything without being permitted to land and *see* anything.

My recent theatregoing in London produced the effect—no doubt exaggerated by its intensity—of making me grateful for the romantic rattle and youthful splash of *Cyrano de Bergerac,* which I had just seen in Paris. Rostand wrote in that play, as in most of his others, an exuberant dramatization or glorification of inadequacy. If we are to suffer defeat, let us at least do so with a suggestion of splendor. And though I do not find Pirandello especially profound in *Tonight We Improvise,* which I also saw in Paris, he at least offers us the excitement of his game.

Let me add by way of exemplary paradox that my London theatregoing converted me to Socialist Realism! I have never seen a play in this style that I thought really good, but what is suggested by that dismal epithet is something to which I declare myself partial. It is the encompassing of the phenomena of existence informed by a positive ideal, an affirmation of some activating conviction in the face of enduring hardship of life. All the rest is smirking, hissing or puling surrender.

Edinburgh

~~~~~~~~~~

The 1963 Drama Conference

AMONG THE events at the Edinburgh Festival in 1962, an International Writers Conference on the Novel was a notable item. Shortly after their arrival, the guests at this year's Conference on the Drama heard that the novelists' affair had literally become a howling success. A Scottish author publicly confessed that he had been a drug addict, only to be followed by a Hindu writer who topped this avowal by proclaiming, "I am a homosexual as well as a drug addict."

I cannot say that the report of this incident set the tone for the drama conference, but it must have cast a spell. There were no equivalent revelations—not officially, at any rate—but some of the guests must have felt a certain pressure to say and do things which would be sufficiently sensational to make headlines.

After each day's session—there were six—the organizers and a number of conferees waited anxiously to learn what the press, radio and television had to say about the day's proceedings. The prevailing atmosphere was that of a theatrical company waiting for opening-night notices. When the first day's meeting was received as dull, the sponsors virtually instructed the "delegates" to whoop it up the next day. It became clear to everyone that what was involved was not a serious discussion but a show.

Kenneth Tynan, the conference's general chairman, should be held blameless in this. It is hardly possible for some fifty people to communicate with one another congenially before an audience of at least 1,500 paying persons. The sight of that throng—the best "houses" that some of them had had for a long time—froze rather than encouraged the less frivolous speakers. Some good conversations took place among them between sessions, but there could be little value for them in the open meetings.

When the third day's attendance diminished conspicuously the managers fairly panicked; the conference was expected to pay for itself. "It's all because of that first session," one of the organizers said, referring to the unfavorable press. He forgot to take into account the much more cordial "reviews" of the second day.

In his opening remarks, Arthur Kopit of *Oh Dad, Poor Dad . . .* fame wondered what the conference was all about. "Why are we here?" (Oh, these candid Americans!) Harold Pinter, most generally admired of young English playwrights, asked the same question. He ventured a simple answer, "We are here because we must all be hoping to become film stars."

The conference was chiefly a spectacle. In that light, the most enjoyable moments were those some might consider shameful or ludicrous. How clever of the Soviet guests to remain silent throughout except for actor-director Zavadsky's formal greeting and somewhat propagandistic expression of good will. The Polish contingent also remained publicly uncommunicative. "What fools these Westerners be" must have been in the minds of both these delegations.

So we yearned for "scandals." The first of these was provided by Bernard Levin, London drama critic, political commentator and one of the "features" of the highly popular satiric television show "That Was the Week That Was." His speech opening the second day's meeting was to be concerned with "What are the principal trends in contemporary drama?" According to the sponsors' bias, the choice was between the theatre of social or political "commitment" and the Theatre of the Absurd; in other words, between Brecht and Beckett. Only Harold Hobson, drama critic of the *Sunday Times,* pointed out that there might be other alternatives. Levin flatly pronounced Brecht bad and the Absurd dramatists absurd. He was clear about what Brecht meant, and he did not like it; while most of the others, he asserted, wrote plays we, the audience, didn't know "what the hell [they] were about." This, despite widespread disagreement, might have passed muster without too acrimonious a reaction if Levin had not also attempted to justify the British Government's refusal to admit into the country members of the Berliner Ensemble, who had been invited to the conference.

What offended many on the platform and a good part of the audience was not so much Levin's opinions as his coolly supercilious manner. Levin is a virtuoso of the microphone; he has an agile mind, his delivery and language are smooth and shrewd, his purpose is invidious. He looks like the youngest and smartest boy in the class, mock innocent and maddeningly plausible. His audience is usually divided among those who wish to laugh with him, to boo him or simply to paste him one on his calm nose.

After a polite interjection by Tynan and some applause and heckling from the house, Wolf Mankowitz, the playwright-producer, intervened hysterically with an assortment of outcries, among which I could only distinguish such expressions as: "Fascist! Parasite! He sucks our blood!" Levin, as usual, remained unperturbed. He had accomplished his provocative mission.

Another highlight was the rude interruption of Joan Littlewood's second speech by James Fitzgerald, the Irish director. When that talented lady described a utopian future in which every man and woman would be a genius and entire communities and groups of individuals would freely make theatre at will, Fitzgerald shouted, "What bloody nonsense!" When Fitzgerald was asked to join Miss Littlewood at the microphone and develop his objections beyond the expletive, he was torn between a desire to apologize and the need to expand on what he had called the Littlewood speech.

This was a setback for Fitzgerald, who had made a hit with the audience on the day censorship had been under discussion by reeling off a series of unmentionable four-letter words, then addressing the public as "You f - - - s!" and finally blurting out, "My God, I'm still drunk!"

The high point of the conference—if its organizers were in earnest about creating a commotion—was the Happening devised by Kenneth Dewey of San Francisco. This was an improvisation ostensibly designed to illustrate one of the possibilities in the Theatre of the Future. The Happening in question began to happen before anyone realized what was happening. First, Arthur Kopit introduced a resolution to hold a handicap contest for all playwrights: Ionesco plus ten, Rattigan minus four, and so forth. Kopit was followed by Charles Marowitz, an American director-critic residing in England, who proposed something equally goofy. He was interrupted by someone in the audience (a conferee incognito) who rose and raged, expostulating madly while Marowitz continued to hold forth.

This went on while, in the organ loft above and behind the speakers' rostrum, a nude girl was slowly wheeled on a dolly from one side of the auditorium to the other. A moment later, some of us could discern a man standing in transparent shorts (tropical kilts, so to speak) while bagpipes began playing merrily. During all this, Carroll Baker, a pretty sight in skintight gold lamé pants, moved bewitchingly over the auditorium benches as if in quest of a man, while a woman with a child crying "Daddy" mounted the podium and pointed out the presumably fleeing father. Pandemonium and laughter!

What followed seemed to me more idiotic than the Happening itself. A good (or silly) joke reminiscent of Dada antics in the twenties was denounced as a menace to the theatre, a sign of what the *avant-garde* was coming to, an example of American light-headedness, a symptom of the "totalitarian" mentality, etc.

Whatever one's reaction, the Happening was surely more telling in its pointlessness than Laurence Olivier's contribution on the first day. The audience greeted him like a god, and he spoke like one—in double-talk. On the same day, Judith Anderson averred that she loved the theatre (hear! hear!), and Agnes Moorehead, after the conference had been in session for half an hour, declared that it was an inspiring occasion, a sentiment shared by no other conferee.

Still, it would be altogether wrong to suggest that the conference was entirely on these levels of high-minded or low-grade confusion. In the final moments of the fifth day's windy talks on Naturalism in the Theatre, a significant debate took place. It was set off when an Indian playwright intoned a native chant. Someone complimented him on this charming example of Indian folk art. Wole Soyinka, a Nigerian playwright, in admirably articulate wrath, decried our regard for "local color." The exotic, which always seems to enchant the Occidental, had little merit, he said. Our delight in racial "strangeness" is condescending and cheap.

The English conferees generally spoke modestly and to the point. The most emotionally forceful yet coherent statement was made by John Arden, one of England's vital new dramatists. In appearance he corresponds to the traditional "square" notion of what an artist looks like—long-haired, unshaven, unkempt and possibly ill-washed. Puffing a prohibited cigarette, Arden spoke of the theatre as a life-enhancing "utensil of enjoyment" in a manner which did not make one blush, as Joan Littlewood's effusions did. What was embarrassing about her utterances was not that they were mistaken or pretentious, but that they had no real relation to her actual problems, situation, technique or to those of anyone else.

Arnold Wesker, author of *Chips With Everything*, a definitely "committed" playwright (a term which Americans might translate as left-wing), made remarks which did not particularly please some of his colleagues but which struck me as sincere, intelligent and appropriately personal. The same may be said of occasional comments made by Peter Shaffer, author of *Five Finger Exercise*, and by the amiable Bamber Gascoigne, the drama critic who has taken over Kenneth Tynan's post on the *Observer*. Tynan himself, unequivocally committed to socialism in politics (no sin in England) and to a philosophy of rationalistic humanism, as contrasted with the numerous antirationalists present, conducted himself with restraint and spoke sense. Peter Brook was eminently serious.

Little benefit was to be reaped from such virtues at a conference where the announcement of the imminent arrival of a beauteous film star (who made several appearances in as many sumptuous furs) was repeated over and over again. The quiet simplicity of Joan Plowright and Dorothy Tutin must have gone unobserved in these surroundings.

Among the Germans, the critic Friedrich Luft and the interesting playwright Martin Walser were correct, informative and urbane, very usefully speaking up for better translations of foreign plays. Martin Esslin, a British subject of German origin and author of books on both Brecht and on the Theatre of the Absurd, proved knowledgeable in three languages. An eager Austrian gentleman wanted to rectify all the other speakers' errors, which kept him asking for the floor at all times.

The easiest and wittiest speakers, Ned Sherrin, producer of TWTWTW, and David Frost, emcee of the show, did not bring to their allocutions some of the polished rhetoric of the French, whose most prominent representative was Robbe-Grillet, novelist and scenarist of *Last Year at Marienbad*. He found himself attracted, he said—in what is merely a seeming paradox—to the nonrealism or artifice of the film medium, but he also hoped to write plays.

What was striking in his speech, and in those of his compatriots, was that they were all rather indifferent to political commitment in the arts and that they found Brecht a definitely "conservative" influence in respect to aesthetic experiment and new forms of discovery in Existentialism. On the whole, the French, through disdain or discretion, were unusually reticent. The only exception was the Russian-born Arthur Adamov, "renegade" playwright of the Absurd, now emphatically leftist. Adamov, looking like a bedeviled monk, rose several times to praise Brecht (and O'Casey), with an occasional antagonistic reference to General de Gaulle.

The Americans were generally shy of considered thought or positive convictions. Jack Gelber, Arthur Kopit and the perpetrators of the Happening pleased the audience with a certain playful nonchalance, an easygoing anarchism. Alan Schneider's determined straightforwardness was no counterforce to this impression, nor could Edward Albee's platform reserve convince anyone that he was not entirely of an intuitional rather than of an intellectual disposition. Lillian Hellman effaced herself completely, proving how indomitable she is.

The conference adopted a resolution against all censorship and declared itself in favor of subsidized theatre. It also voted approval of Max Frisch's motion that the Rockefeller Foundation establish a bureau of qualified play translators.

The conference proved that under certain circumstances a large number of gifted and intelligent people can resemble a carload of fools. The intellectual import of the conference was nil, the social increment slight, the entertainment value considerable. The public saw a lot of well-known and presumably glamorous show folk at far less than their best (which probably consoled it), while I personally had a good time and tried to acquire a play from a playwright whom, as a critic, I had previously panned.

Paris

~~~~~~~~~~~~~~~~~~~~~~~~

Brecht in Paris, 1960

During my visit here, there were, as usual, several interesting plays written with that degree of sophistication which makes the French play, no matter what its real value, seem "superior" to most American and British plays. There was also (just about to close) Jean-Paul Sartre's three-and-a-half-hour brain buster *The Prisoners of Altona*, which, apart from Jean Genet's *The Blacks* (which had already closed), was the most impressive play of the year (page 172).

The great event of my latest theatrical expedition was the four productions of Bertolt Brecht's plays given at the Théâtre des Nations in its international theatre season—a splendid annual spring feature in Paris. The Brecht works were presented by his own Berliner Ensemble, which most critics today regard as the finest theatre company on the Continent, perhaps the finest in the world.

Much—too much—has already been written on Brecht's theories. In Europe, at least, they have already exercised noticeable influence and stimulated almost as much talk as the Method has with us. What struck me most sharply on seeing the Berliner Ensemble this time was the pointlessness of most of this talk in view of the actual performances.

The didactic element, the stylization, the detachment—all these have been repeatedly emphasized almost to the exclusion of the sheer facts of the production in their effect and meaning. In this respect the earnest thinkers in the theatre are almost as misleading as the ordinary folk of show business. Both stress what is most superficially striking: the "knockout" aspects of cleverness, laughs, excitement; and, in the case of Brecht, the scenic novelty.

The first thing we recognize in the Brecht productions is their *reality*: an utterly engrossing reality. We feel we are looking directly at the core and substance of what the plays are about. We do not sense any element of staginess, arty ornament or eye-deceiving illusion. At the same time, we are not only at ease—the ordinary naturalistic production always seems a little strenuous by comparison—but thoroughly absorbed. We are at once in the theatre—with all its sense of festival and fun—and soberly in the midst of life. We do not sweat with anxiety or often split our sides with laughter; yet we are stirred by what is serious and refreshed by what is humorous.

The didacticism of a Brecht play is always telling—unless one is intent on resistance—because the message seems to radiate from every element of the performance. The very props seem to tell a tale, convey some fundamental significance. Everything in these productions is so integrated that when an actor stops what might pass for an intensely dramatic scene (there is hardly any screaming and shouting except for purposes of caricature) to speak a bit of verse or to sing-recite a song, one hardly notices the break. The prose dialogue and the lyric interval are both phases of the same essence.

The Berliner Ensemble represents the truest theatre of our day in a very special sense. I do not yet know exactly in what esteem I hold the Brecht plays as literature, though as sheer writing they are superb. I am not at all sure that the company contains any great actors—a number are clearly mediocre—and I cannot say whether any other company in the same sets and costumes might not make the stage design appear dull. I do know that we perceive all as a single phenomenon. We are confronted with a living thing which is full of meaning and has immeasurably greater impact than anything I have witnessed in years. And *this* is theatre.

When one reads a play by Brecht—before or even after having seen it—one is astonished to find that for all the purity, simplicity and, with the plainness, the subtle elevation of its style, one thinks of it not so much as a complete play, but rather as a libretto for the opera of which it is a part, or as a film script in respect to the picture which is to be made of it. That is one reason why Brecht's plays may prove disappointing in productions not created by the Brecht company under the conditions which the Berliner Ensemble has been enabled to foster for itself.

The secret of the total power these plays impart in the productions which the playwright or his colleagues have directed is that everything in them emanates from a sense of life, a conviction, a will, a seed-sentiment transmitted in every moment, movement, color, gesture and thought, shared by everyone concerned in the performance. Not only one consciousness, but a single breath, seems to have given it life. The productions are not so much a collective triumph as they are the body of one spirit. Brecht's word has become flesh; his ideas have taken on visible form. The productions are literally a revelation; that is why—antinaturalistic, anti-"emotional" and (save the mark!) anti-"Method"—they are so unmistakably forceful, so wholly real, so inescapably immediate, so compelling and—for all the infinite care and craftsmanship involved in their making—so unaffected.

But what do Brecht's plays reveal? What, apart from their too easily captioned propaganda, do they express?

The Brecht plays I saw here were *The Resistible Rise of Arturo Ui* (page 64), written in exile in 1941 and first presented in Berlin (after Brecht's death) in 1959; *The Mother* (written in 1932), an adaptation of Maxim Gorky's novel; *Galileo Galilei*, written in exile in 1939 and presented posthumously in Berlin in 1957; and finally, *Mother Courage and Her Children* (page 61), also written in exile and first presented by the Berliner Ensemble in 1949.

Arturo Ui is an epic caricature of the rise of Adolf Hitler and his gang. The word is used advisedly: Brecht has set his play in a mythical American city and Ui is the head of a band of petty crooks in the cauliflower racket. All the events and personalities connected with Hitler's rise to power—Hindenburg, Göring, Goebbels, Roehm, Dollfuss, the Reichstag fire and trial, the occupation of Austria—have their absurd counterparts in this panoramic farce.

Though the parallels between the episodes of the play and their historical sources are quite obvious, Brecht has the factual political items which he wishes us to recall projected on a screen at the beginning of each scene. Since the play was revived after the war, Brecht's last commentary is appended after the final curtain: "You are learning to see instead of merely watching stupidly. Act instead of gossiping. See what almost dominated the world. The people finally won. But none should proclaim victory too readily. The womb from which the vile monster issued is still fertile."

The "lesson" of the play is made explosively graphic and vastly comic in Brecht's treatment, and more particularly in the brilliant production directed by two of Brecht's disciples. Of incalculable value is the virtuoso performance by one of the company's younger actors, Ekkehard Schall, who plays Ui-Hitler as a maniacal neurotic, a trembling hysteric obsessed by fear of his own inferiority and an even more violent revulsion against this fear. From a spastic stammer to mad eloquence, the creature Schall projects with an energy which at times mounts to sheer acrobatics is unforgettably convulsive. One scene, especially, in which Hitler is coached by a ham actor on how to pose and speak, is deliciously funny.

I shocked my critic friends here by saying that in a certain sense the production of *The Mother* was even a more remarkable feat than that of *Arturo Ui*. They were shocked because *Arturo Ui* is, if nothing else, tremendous entertainment, full of invention and scenic ingenuity. What I meant was that *The Mother*, which is rather primitive Communist propaganda telling the simple tale of the transformation of an illiterate Russian woman of the working class to a heroic figure of the revolutionary movement from 1905 to 1917, is presented with such muted power, such quiet humor, such fine songs rendered inspiringly brave by Hanns Eisler's music and such grave conviction, communicated not only in the acting of Helene Weigel (Brecht's widow and the head of the Ensemble), but also in the stark staging. The staging, for all its bareness, manages to attain a sculptural and pictorial distinction which conveys in its very shape, color and composition something of the earthy strength of which the play is a poem of praise and an example.

I need not dwell on *Mother Courage*—I wrote about it when I first saw it in Berlin in 1957 and elsewhere (page 61)—except to say that it impressed me even more this time. It is probably the finest of Brecht's achievements, a masterpiece of modern stagecraft in all its aspects.

The play and production which most strongly stamped on my mind a sense of Brecht's great stature as an artist of the theatre was *Galileo*, for which Erich Engel is credited with the direction. I believe, however, the first steps were undertaken by Brecht himself, who died in 1956 while the play was still in the early stage of study.

I had seen *Galileo* in the 1947 Hollywood-New York production with Charles Laughton in the leading role and, though Brecht had supervised it (Joe Losey was the director), that production gave only the faintest notion of its possibilities as a stage piece. Whether due to lack of means or to a misunderstanding of Brechtian aesthetics, which recommend a certain asceticism, it looked almost shabby. But a careful reading of the play (which takes place in Florence, Venice and Rome in the seventeenth century) shows that its physical presentation calls for opulence within that asceticism. This is fully realized in Casper Neher's all-bronze setting—a stroke of genius by this master designer—where scenes of poverty and of pomp, interiors and exteriors are all equally at home.

Galileo is the story of the struggle of reason against superstition and the forces which maintain superstition in order to hold the reins of social power. On the surface, both the thesis and the play's points appear too simple. But Brecht's simplicity is artful. He presents the case for the hierarchy, cannily aware of the dangers of Galileo's proof of the Copernican "heresy"—that the earth moves around the sun and not vice versa—with skill and something like sympathy. Indeed, when the court philosopher asks Galileo, "Are such stars that Galileo has just discovered really necessary?" the audience here seemed to turn against Brecht, for many laughed and applauded, thinking, no doubt, of our recent lunar expeditions and the fear they somehow inspire in many of us.

Galileo is entirely contemporary in view of the events of our atomic age and in relation to certain problems of conscience. When Galileo, in fear of torture by the Inquisition, retracts his theories, his most devoted pupil in an admirable scene cries out, "Unhappy the country which has no heroes!" to which Galileo retorts, "No. Unhappy is the country which needs a hero!"

But this is not Brecht's last word. At another point, Galileo admits that he ought not be forgiven his betrayal; his fear of pain is no excuse. Is the search for the truth, then, everything? Science, he says, must be concerned not only with its own findings, but with their consequences. There are thus two battles or fields of struggle. The play ends with the admonition "Protect the flame of knowledge, use but do not abuse it lest one day a whirlwind of fire consume us all."

This was not Brecht's first ending and there is evidence throughout the play that Brecht kept revising it to keep abreast of the various mutations of his thought and conscience (in one version, Galileo's defection was more or less rationalized.) Here then is a play by an intellectual which is subtle, lucid, full of meat yet easily digested by a wide audience, a play which eschews "excitement" and yet remains dramatic.

There are two supreme moments of staging in this production which exemplify what I have previously written about the Berliner Ensemble. One is a scene, largely pantomimic, in which the rabble in the square and passing priests around a street procession reveal the popular effect of Galileo's inquiries. It is a comic scene—pure theatre—but its message of how the ferment of ideas manifests itself in ordinary social behavior is made indelibly picturesque. Another is the scene in which the Inquisitor attempts to persuade the Pope to put Galileo on the rack. The Pope is being dressed. When the scene begins, he is in his underwear: he is the "naked" man—honest and forebearing. But as the talk proceeds and ever more of his ecclesiastical robes are dropped on the Pope's body, he becomes increasingly "institutional" until, at the final moment, he stands in princely glory and orders that Galileo be "shown the instruments."

The quiet familiarity of Ernst Busch's Galileo typifies Brecht's manner and content, as does Helen Weigel's two "Mothers." Brecht is a poet of classic character. He wished his work to have the authority of an objective statement which needs no stress beyond a simple grace of speech, no "art" beyond the most engaging directness, no "passion" greater than that which the truth will elicit. His technique is a reasonableness which arises when a smiling skepticism sets out in quest of a small area of certainty. This, he hopes, will prove charmingly self-evident. Not wholly in vain did Brecht claim the Chinese and Japanese among his artistic ancestors.

What does Brecht ultimately say? Trust what your senses experience, what your mind has weighed and what your most fundamental human instincts dictate. Act with your fellowmen in the name of what you have all tested and found to be needful to your life in common. Seek always, do not allow yourself to grow rigid at any point and let your goal be the peaceful enjoyment of the goods of life.

From all the contradictions of Brecht's nature, his irony and his radicalism, his homely earthiness and his "peasant" cunning, his culture and folksy common sense, there emerges something that may very well be that ineffable quality: manly virtue.

Ebb Tide, 1963

The aesthetically alert Parisian today more often finds excitement in the latest film than in the most recent play. One is inclined to laugh when one hears the clever conversationalists discuss not only Orson Welles' new film *The Trial*, but even a Hollywood job, in a manner that resembles Harold Rosenberg explaining the latest modernism.

The French theatre at the moment is not conducive to such sport; it is now at ebb tide. Not that there is little to see in the way of acceptable entertainment—there is simply a lack of conspicuous originality. Apart from the programs of the three national theatres devoted to drama, more than forty plays occupy the boards. Among them are productions of Brecht's *In the Jungle of the Cities*, Chekhov's *Ivanov*, Fry's *The Dark Is Light Enough*, revivals of plays by Claudel and Max Frisch. There is also Lillian Hellman's *The Little Foxes*, a success despite poor notices because of the presence in the cast of Simone Signoret and Suzanne Flon. One also notes with some astonishment that Anita Loos' *Gentlemen Prefer Blondes* (without music), Hecht and MacArthur's *Front Page* and Norman Krasna's *Sunday in New York*, a failure in New York but doing well here with a popular star, are also part of the general scene.

The most highly regarded production of the season is a play that was first presented by Antonin Artaud in 1928: Roger Vitrac's surrealist *Victor or All Power to the Children*. Originally a failure—it was too "far out"—*Victor* is now an outstanding success. Very French in its allusions to the period before the First World War (1908), this *drame bourgeois*, as its author calls it, is bitterly funny.

The surrealist element may be recognized in its mixture of naturalism with fantasy, comic obscenity with lyric eloquence, caricature with grotesque symbolism. Victor, a boy of nine, is seven feet tall and, as he says again and again, "terribly intelligent." He and his six-year-old girl friend are the only "normal" (or rational) people in their families. These are composed of middle-class folk, described in terms the surrealists and most of the present young generation apply to the pillars of the Third Republic. They are without exception thick-headed, indecent, ridiculous. Everyone mouths pompous catchwords while living in falsehood and filth. A strange female apparition wanders into the household, a woman who is thought to be hilariously funny by everyone except the kids. This unholy ghost of the milieu, and the symbol of death, has a dismaying affliction: she constantly breaks wind. We are ready to set the play down as macabre farce when Victor, on the night of his birthday party, suddenly falls ill and dies. The maid, entering at the final curtain, cries out, "But this is a tragedy!"

The success of this play, which antedates the so-called Theatre of the Absurd, was facilitated not alone by works of that temper but by the mood engendered through the whole history of France since 1928. Vitrac's play is also more brilliantly written and more sincerely felt—its loathing and agony more genuine—than is the case with many of the more recent examples of "absurd" inclination.

What struck me most was the horrible aptness of the domestic scenes. This is particularly true of one between Victor's father and mother as they are about to retire for the night—a night in which their insomnia, hysteria, sense of guilt, violent recriminations, miserable attempts at amatory reconciliation, self-asphyxiating venom mount to a torrent that would be bound to cripple—even if it did not kill—the child witness upon whom it all pours. I have rarely seen anything more dreadful or, for all the vaudeville extravagance of Vitrac's treatment, more true in any realistic play. The play's curtain line, the maid's outcry, is fully justified.

I shall not linger on Friedrich Dürrenmatt's *Frank V*, though it has been enthusiastically reviewed by the press. I have been assured that it is a good play but that its Paris production is not faithful to the original script. As I saw it, *Frank V* is a stale dilution of *The Threepenny Opera* in which a great bank is run by a long family line of gangsters. The conclusion—emblematic of a futilely cynical anticapitalism—is that the hypocrisy, depredation and crimes of the older money racketeers will henceforth become coefficient with legalized state business. Worse than the text is the production; it is sloppy and callously indifferent in a way not uncommon in the French theatre today. One feels that the actors do not give a damn about the play, the audience or themselves.

It is a great relief, therefore, to see *Hedda Gabler* played by Ingrid Bergman, Claude Dauphin and a carefully selected cast in a magnificently designed (and constructed) set by Lila de Nobili. The director, Raymond Rouleau, is one of the rare men in Paris (apart from Vilar and Barrault) who work as meticulous craftsmen. The scrupulous attention to detail, the precision of execution—not so exceptional in New York or London—tempted me to overestimate the event as a whole. On reflection, I realize that, though Ingrid Bergman does not make the mistake of playing Hedda as a freak, her Hedda is an honestly literal reading rather than a creation of any kind. The same is finally true of Rouleau's direction; it is correct and secure in the articulation of each separate segment of the play's action, but it is not inspired by any individual conception of the play as a whole: it lacks vital content. The production, then, adds up to what the Germans call a good "court theatre performance"—solidly emphatic professionalism without flair. Still it is *Hedda Gabler!*

The real novelty of the season is the latest Ionesco play, *The King Dies*. Its one act lasts an hour and a half—more than it should. It is the author's ode to death.

As in all of Ionesco's plays, the tone alternates between a tongue-in-cheek humor and a more or less real anguish. Most people who have commented on this play are more impressed by the author's growing seriousness (even more marked here than in *Rhinoceros*) than by his "wackiness" and for that reason prefer it to most of Ionesco's earlier work. I am not sure that they are right.

The king who is dying in the new play is you and I or Every-ordinary-Man. His domain is shrinking, his estate impoverished, his servant personnel diminished, his army depleted, his perquisites paltry. But he is delighted with himself, confident that he is supreme. His two wives—one embodying the harsh voice of reason, the other all-protective tenderness—though differently motivated, cling to him with equal fervor. But his doctor diagnoses a fatal illness. "At the end of the show," the sibylline wife announces, "the king will die."

The king scoffs at this. He feels fine. Slowly, very slowly, he begins to sense his infirmity and recognizes that he may die, indeed, that he is going to die. "But," he cries out, "I don't want to die. Why wasn't I warned? I am not prepared." Nothing can convince him that death is anything but rank treason!

The parable is absurd and poignant: absurd in the reiterated commonplace of its predicament and theme, poignant in the ghastly "surprise" which life springs on its all-too-human "king." Ionesco manages to ring changes on his material which are both witty and eloquent. This is not only due to the play's finely written passages, but to Ionesco's basic attitude: he seems to face death as do most of us today with the horrified innocence of a child being taken to the doctor for the first time.

On the one hand, Ionesco is telling us that death proves life to be an awful hoax, abysmal nonsense, a dirty trick that should not happen to a dog. This is in his role as "existential philosopher." At the same time, he is saying that life, despite everything, is marvelous in its every aspect! This is in the role of the ordinary man—a guise in which we are glad to have Ionesco appear.

I await the publication of the text before I estimate its stature. (The play's final and very long speech was obscured for me because the actress playing the horrendously dispassionate wife lisped badly and had a disturbing nasality of delivery.) Still, seeing the play, I found myself sympathetic to a certain auctorial self-exposure. Ionesco, the shrewdly grimacing sophisticate, a worthy of the contemporary nonenlightenment, suddenly stands before us and cries like a little baby. We want to console him with a "There! there! We're glad to find you're really not so very complex after all and hardly a bit Superior!" I came from the performance with a sense of liking Ionesco as a person rather more than I ever have before.

It may be noticed that most of the "better" things of the theatre today are what Anouilh has called "black" plays—plays of despair. It is the prevalent cliché. On the eve of my departure from Paris I heard an internationally famous producer of *avant-garde* films say with undisguised glee: "There is nothing to hope for nowadays. Hope is absurd!"

MOSCOW

~~~~~~~~~~~~~~~~~~~

The Soviet Realism, 1963

ANYONE WHO goes to Moscow to see theatre solely as theatre is a fool. To a certain extent this applies to theatregoing everywhere, but it holds particularly in Russia. A
convenient and agreeable entry into the Soviet world is through
the theatre lobby.

The Soviet theatre is truly popular; it attracts the widest possible audience, as Broadway and the Paris boulevards signally fail
to do. Everyone attends plays in every part of the Soviet Union.
The young people who clamor for tickets at the recently established Sovremenik (Contemporary) are much less enthusiastic
about the Moscow Art or the Maly—the more traditional or "classic" Soviet stages—but a blood tie, a family resemblance, links all
these establishments.

I saw thirteen productions in two weeks, and that, considering
what the stage has to offer in Moscow alone, is virtually a neglect
of the theatre. That city supports thirty-seven companies, all of
them offering an average of four different plays a week. These
four plays, however, represent only a small portion of the active
repertory in any of these theatres. The Moscow Art, which operates two houses, has thirty-six plays on its yearly program. (There
are 150 actors in its company.) The Vachtangov Theatre presents
almost as many. Several months of nightly playgoing would be
insufficient for seeing half the worthwhile productions.

At the thirteen performances I managed to take in there was
scarcely ever an empty seat. The theatre (including ballet and
opera) is the undisputed nub of Moscow's artistic life. Citizens
complain that tickets are hard to obtain. An orchestra seat costs

the equivalent of $1.80, and most Muscovites seem to go to the theatre all the time!

This was my third Moscow visit, the first two being in 1934 and 1935. My first reaction on the present trip was disappointment. There were no productions as brilliantly original as those of the Meyerhold in 1934–35. Toward the end of my brief stay I asked Boris Alpers, an excellent drama critic and a professor at the State Institute of the Theatre (Moscow's Central School of the Theatre), if the Soviet theatre had not been more interesting in the early thirties.

Alpers replied: "The theatre at that time astonished by its unusual production of classic plays: *Romeo and Juliet, King Lear, The Inspector General,* Ostrovsky's *Forest.* Our theatre now concentrates on new Soviet plays. While these cannot be as impressive to you, they are very important for us." It was a sensible as well as a tactful answer. Yet I insisted—in order to get a more direct response—that he name one really outstanding contemporary dramatist; "let us say," I suggested, "of Gorky's stature." Alpers laughed, as did another critic, P. A. Markov, who took part in the conversation. "Or Shaw or Chekhov?!" Alpers interjected almost before I had finished speaking. "The day of the super-dramatist is over," he said. "I hope not," I rejoined without catching the drift of his thought. "And it is perhaps better so," he added. Making a virtue of necessity, Alpers meant that the cult of personality—dramatists representing "personality"—was not altogether an asset in the collective art which is the theatre.

Both critics agreed that the leading playwright of the moment is A. Arbusov. (Another critic I spoke to mentioned Leonov.) I saw two of Arbusov's plays: *The Irkutsk Story* at the Vachtangov Theatre (first produced almost four years ago) and *They Are Waiting For Us Somewhere* at the Mayakovsky Theatre, the premiere of which I attended. Whether these two plays are better or worse than others presently to be seen I am in no position to judge, but they are typical.

In *The Irkutsk Story* (Irkutsk is the largest city in Siberia) two young men who work in an electric plant are rivals for the attentions of a somewhat flighty shop girl. One of them makes a pass at her but is unwilling to marry her. His friend and companion marries the girl. The couple have twins. Shortly after this the husband drowns in an effort to save their two youngsters, who

have gone in for a swim in the river. The work gang with which
the drowned man was employed decides to contribute part of
its earnings to support his widow. Her once-rejected suitor is
opposed to her accepting the offer. She ought to go to work, he
says. She takes a job among the men at the plant, and finds
happiness in doing so. The man who encouraged her to go to
work is now eager to marry her, but she is not at all sure she
wants him; she has become an independent woman.

They Are Waiting For Us Somewhere has broader implications. By suggesting some of the play's various thematic strands I
can perhaps convey more specifically what I had in mind in my
opening sentences.

In a small town at some distance from Moscow a conflict has
arisen between the older generation (the men of fifty) and the
young folk. "We thought they would be better than us but they
are worse," says one of the town's leaders. But he is not presented
as a sympathetic character: he is a "reactionary," that is to say, in
local parlance, a Stalinist. It is significant in this connection that
at the end of the play he weeps; he cannot understand his son,
who turns from him and rejects his views. Addressing the audience, the father cries out, "But I am not as black as the author has
painted me." The audience applauds. There are many such in the
audience and they feel that something more is to be said on their
behalf.

There is a scene in which a young man who still believes in
God is invited to debate the religious question. The playwright
treats him sympathetically. He is a good man, and cordial to the
play's atheist heroine. On hearing the fine choral singing of the
town's religious sect, she murmurs, "They have created some
beautiful things."

This motif ties in with another of the play's themes: the craving
for "lyricism." (Read: the cultivation of the arts.) The author
suggests that it may constitute an even greater need than the
advance of science.

The play centers on the importance of relieving the dullness
and stagnation of small towns. The kids there all hanker for
Gorky Street (Moscow's main thoroughfare); they want to leave
their village. (Shades of *The Three Sisters!*) The religious be-
liever says of the town, "Everyone here is either indifferent or
intolerant."

The play's heroine is the newly appointed head of the town's cultural center. She organizes a dramatic society, preaches love of the theatre, encourages the young folk to learn to play musical instruments, to improve their vocabulary by reading good books, to publish their own newspaper. In brief, she stirs the town with fresh life, so that at the end of the play the once dissatisfied youngsters are no longer eager to leave. But she has aroused the displeasure of the chairman of the town's governing board—the aforementioned "reactionary"—who dismisses her.

She is not discouraged. She feels that the impulse she has set in motion can no longer be quelled by officialdom. She will move on to other places where similar work is needed.

One other facet of the play is worth listing. At the approach of its final curtain we learn that the heroine is a former actress who during the war entertained the troops at the front, and that she is married to a man of note—a physicist, rather vain and something of a lady-killer. He begs his wife to return to Moscow with him. Very gently she says, "I know you are a great man. But it is not enough for me to be the wife of a great man. I have things of my own to do."

All this, the reader may well exclaim, is primary stuff, "wholesome" to the point of simple-mindedness. But apart from the mature and often superb theatrical skill with which these plays are staged—and more of that later—there is undoubtedly something robust and genuine in their sentiment; something which the look and "feel" of their audiences confirm and justify.

It is the audience of a new society—less than fifty years old—a society which has only recently become literate. It is beside the point to say that the Russian past produced such writers as Turgenev, Tolstoy, Dostoevsky, Chekhov. Before 1924, 85 per cent of the population could not read them. (Our own serious native drama may be said to have developed only since 1915.) The present Soviet audience is a new audience—new to the theatre and to the life outside the theatre that it is leading.

As many Russian critics have pointed out, a certain calculated optimism has been imposed on Soviet literature and drama. But there was always a definite moralizing strain, a stress on what might be called humanistic didacticism or uplift, in the older Russian literature of which much Soviet writing, particularly in the theatre, is the simplified and popular descendant. To overlook this is to be historically and artistically obtuse. Do we expect this new society to produce plays in the manner of *Waiting for Godot, The Balcony* or *Who's Afraid of Virginia Woolf?*

On a warm May evening most Russian males come to the theatre in their shirt-sleeves and without ties. Women come in the kind of dresses American lower-middle-class housewives usually wear for shopping at the neighborhood grocery. When there are musicians in the pit, they are also in shirt-sleeves, except for the conductor. To the Western eye the effect is startling, particularly when such an audience throngs the corridors, buffet and auditorium of the regal Bolshoi Theatre, whose settings and costumes are overwhelmingly sumptuous.

It is an extremely attentive audience, fervid in its applause, devoted to its artists. It is said to demand realism. Most of the new plays dismay the foreign visitor by their literal interpretation of traditional moral premises—the age-old verities. In one case a young Russian who accompanied me said of the play we had just seen, "It's too primary."

These plays mirror the dignified innocence of the audience. The contradiction within the theatrical situation here may be inferred from a conversation I had with another young man: "The trouble is we don't have enough good playwrights. Still," he hastened to add, "the plays reflect the concerns of the people." "Too simply," I prodded. He caught the look in my eye. "No, it isn't official pressure which is the source of the difficulty. These plays are what the people understand, what they are like."

I thought I would press my point humorously. Referring to the hydroelectric worker "hero" of *The Irkutsk Story,* who at the age of twenty-five has never kissed a girl, I said, "A man of that age who has never kissed a girl is not pure; he is sick." My companion laughed. Then he went on to assure me, "But many workers in our small towns are just like that." (He meant that they are chaste.) I am convinced that it is so.

The realism of the Soviet theatre is not at all like ours. To begin with, the new plays are produced with a scenic freedom, a sophistication of means, which bespeaks an advanced stage technique. Years of experiment in many departures from late nineteenth-century representationalism have furnished Russian directors and designers with an extremely rich stage palette. (There is no worry over costs.) From the vast storehouse of theatrical inventions, the new directors have learned to choose tastefully—that is, without artiness or what the Russians call "formalism"—to create effects with direct audience appeal and of great service to the content of their plays.

Most theatres are equipped with one or more revolving stages. This is of no particular advantage when stages are shallow, but most Moscow stages are extensive in all dimensions. (Broadway stages are rarely more than thirty feet deep.) The principal characters in *The Irkutsk Story* make their first entrance down a ramp which runs some sixty feet from the rear down to the stage level—and plenty of playing space remains in the foreground. The effect is magical. The revolving stage also makes the dances in the wedding scene most exhilarating. The Russians love music in the theatre and employ it generously.

In other words, while the plays themselves are usually characterized by a simple topicality of subject matter, these texts are projected with such sweep and richness that the term "realism," as we understand it, cannot properly be applied. Economically and technically, our theatre lacks the facilities commonly put at the service of extremely meager Soviet scripts.

Many Russian critics and directors profess admiration for American acting. They like its forthrightness. This surprised me— if stage rather than film acting was meant. For I found much of the acting in the Soviet theatre even simpler than ours and, what is more remarkable, less intense. What Soviet actors for the most part now seem to be after is clarity. This aim may also have a sociopsychological cause.

The American actor (under forty-five) today often goes through an agony of effort to give his acting emotional substance. In its extreme form this becomes a sweating sincerity. It would seem that the life the American actor leads and the world around him afford him little opportunity for any but casual or mechanical responses. Through his acting he seeks to compensate for a lack he feels in his environment and consequently in himself. The Soviet actor takes feeling for granted. It is always present; he does not need to strain himself to achieve it. The Russian player's concentration is bent on the most basic truth of physical action— of look, movement and relation to immediate circumstances. One is amazed by the quietness and repose of most Soviet acting. Only the comedies or highly stylized satires (as in Mayakovsky's *The Bug*) are boisterous and colorfully complex.

These impressions were strongly reinforced by the performance of a new play called *Before Supper* that I saw at the Central Children's Theatre. This large theatre in the center of town is devoted to plays for children performed by a company of seventy-three admirably trained adult actors. It has four directors and there are twenty-five plays in its present repertory.

Before Supper, I was informed, is a play for children of high-school age and for grown-ups. What struck me here was the subdued realism of the acting, combined with themes typical of the public's present temper. One might describe the acting as *healthy*. Except for rare moments of agitation, no one raises his voice beyond a conversational tone; yet the dialogue is not only comfortably audible, but is rendered dramatically clear and interesting. Thoughts become visible without stress. The inner life of the character is externally realized without the aid of physical exertion or the heavy fumes of emotionalism. The acting is lucid rather than "deep," direct without being dry. In this limpid stream that flows with an almost classic ease, both children and their parents may behold their own ideal image. Here, rather than at the Moscow Art Theatre or at the Sovremenik (Contemporary) Theatre, its youthful offshoot (now playing Gibson's *Two for the Seesaw*), the latest fruits of Stanislavsky's teaching are to be studied.

As for the play's content, its emphasis is on the "new way of life." In the first act the theme is lightly limned in a comedy scene between two seventeen-year-olds. The boy has just received a letter from a French youth whom he has never met, but with whom he has begun a correspondence. The Russian boy answers the letter with one in French which someone has told him contains nine errors in grammar. His girl friend says, "You shouldn't have made those mistakes. It gives the Soviet Union a bad name abroad." "You're a Stalinist," the boy jokingly retorts.

In the second act a man of the older generation offhandedly remarks about a French ornament done in abstract style that he notices in the room: "See how far the Westerners have gone from realism." Then he proceeds to boast that he has never crossed the Soviet border and has never spoken a word of any foreign language. This leads to a bitter dispute related to the play's plot. In the cross fire of argument, the man cries out, "You wait. He'll come back." (It is understood that "he" stands for "Stalin.") To which the reply is, "He can't be brought back. He is nothing but ashes now."

At the end of this scene the quarrelsome man notices a dicta-phone in the room—an instrument that the seventeen-year-old boy of the family uses as a diary. The old man turns pale; he fears he has been spied on! He tries to destroy the machine. The boy grabs the dictaphone speaker, holds it up to the older man's mouth and shouts, "Continue! Keep talking!" implying that under the new regime one may speak without fear.

It would be easy to dismiss this as Boy Scout dramaturgy. I shall not do so. What we have here is a kind of morality play. The atmosphere of the theatre, from stage to auditorium, is clean.

Apart from the Children's Theatre itself, almost every other theatre presents matinees for children at 11 A.M. At these, a won-derfully eager and well-behaved audience of children from the ages of five to ten see many different kinds of plays. At the Moscow Art Theatre I saw Maeterlinck's *The Blue Bird* (a Stanis-lavsky production dating back to 1908) and a Soviet play for children, *Three Fat Men*, about rebellion against a triumverate of fat rulers dressed in gold; it was done with delightful pyrotechni-cal adroitness. But the Moscow Art Theatre's latest success is the staged version of the Bernard Shaw-Mrs. Patrick Campbell corre-spondence, *Dear Liar*. The Moscow Art's repertory also includes dramatizations of *The Brothers Karamazov* and *Anna Karenina* and such old standbys as Gorky's *Lower Depths* and Tolstoy's *The Fruits of Enlightenment*.

Another great new success is the Brecht-Weill *The Threepenny Opera* (Brecht is respected but not altogether favored here) at the Stanislavsky Theatre—which is not the same as the Moscow Art Theatre. This was the last show I attended in Moscow, and I shall speak of it in connection with my visit to Warsaw. The Polish theatre—quite different from the Soviet—is highly rated by Russian theatre professionals, some of whom believe that the greatest progress in their part of the world is being made in Prague and Warsaw.

Warsaw

༺ຆ຺຺຺ຆຆຆຆຆຆຆ༻

Highlights, 1963

M Y FIRST impression of the rebuilt Warsaw—I had visited
the city before the war—was that it was like a West European city. "It strikes you that way," a Polish lady said to me,
"because you have just come from Moscow. If you had come here
directly from Paris you would think it East European."

Specific contrasts revealed themselves at my first conversation.
The same lady introduced me to a well-known scene designer at a
café where I had pastry and coffee. (The Poles of Warsaw are
addicted to pastry, coffee and ice cream—as a sort of *apéritif*,
which they consume in honorable proportion to the amount of
vodka they drink.) Said the designer, "You have just arrived from
Moscow? And what theatre did you see there?" I mentioned the
production of *The Threepenny Opera* which I had applauded
the night before. My two table companions arched their eye-
brows in surprise. "That is progress," they agreed.

I was even more surprised when the gentleman inquired if the
saxophone were among the instruments used—and whether the
jazz elements of the score had been retained. "Certainly," I answered. "They even did the twist in the prologue." This was
hailed as glad tidings. The saxophone, symbol of jazz decadence,
had for some time been anathema in serious musical circles in the
Soviet Union.

Warsaw, with a population of a million, has twenty-five theatres. Their repertory is of broader scope than that on the Soviet
stage. Examining the photographs at the first theatre I went to—a
smallish house with a seating capacity of 400—I noted that plays
by Beckett, Pinter, Wilder, Anouilh, O'Casey, Brecht, Graham

Greene and the *avant-garde* French dramatist Schehadé had all
been produced during the past two or three seasons. Many of
these plays are still unacceptable in the Soviet Union.

I attended a remarkably original production of *The Three Sisters*, directed by Erwin Axer, the guiding spirit of the Contemporary Theatre's widely representative repertory.

The two most striking elements in this presentation were the
unit setting and the subdued tone of the acting. The setting,
covered by beige cloth with delicate leaflike patterns sewn on its
surface, conveyed the feeling of a handsome lace decoration.
Even the fourth-act exterior with its birch trees is so rendered.
As for the acting, it sought no climaxes or excitement.

The production as a whole composed a tapestry of human
relationships marked chiefly by the manner in which the characters *listened* and *looked* at one another. No single person appeared central to the play's development; all were woven into a
single fabric of sentiment and meaning clearly legible through
what we beheld in the characters' eyes. Presumably minor personages like Solony became as vivid and crucial to the whole as
any of the others. It was a marriage of Stanislavsky "psychology"
(old style!) with Brechtian objectivity.

The scene of Doctor Czebutykin's (Polish spelling) despair—
when he confesses his ignorance and the medical impotence
which led to his patients' deaths—usually done as a tour de force
of emotional acting, was so casually (almost humorously) presented that without a knowledge of Polish one might suspect that
it had been omitted. Yet it moved the audience, as did the entire
production, as much as performances elsewhere in which the
scene is played with passion.

The most colorful performance was that of Tadeusz Lomnicki,
one of Warsaw's best actors, as Solony. In this interpretation,
Solony is seen as a suppressed thug, a venomously enamored pig
hiding his sick soul behind a mask of eau de Cologne, scented
lozenges and "Byronic" verse.

The two old servants, Anfisa and Ferapont (small parts), were
brilliantly real; I was told later that the actors who played them
are "stars." A very young Tuzenbach was admirable in his refinement and sensibility, though the comic inadequacy of the man
was overlooked. Among the sisters, only Masha was notable;
Kuligin was far more pallid and fragilely Polish than densely

Russian, but was still touching; the Vershinin was barely adequate. The love scenes were featherweight in their discretion, the pathos of the play a shadow. The world of Chekhov had become a memory of the melancholy past, still beautifully poignant as it fades.

I admired, rather than warmed to, this reading of the play, but I shall not forget it.

Brecht's *The Resistible Rise of Arturo Ui* is another Axer production, which he is now repeating in Leningrad. I had seen the play (a "history" of Hitler's rise to power allegorically told as the story of a "Chicago" gangster) given by the Berliner Ensemble (page 64) in a style of grotesque comedy. In Warsaw it was a brutal, Kafka-like nightmare, its setting all lead and steel.

Lomnicki, the Solony of *The Three Sisters*, was now Ui-Hitler. He played it with a savagely stylized harshness, more terrifying than funny. When Ui makes his final speech in a paroxysm of blistering energy, the actor rising to extreme heights of vocal virtuosity, I thought the effect deliberately farcical; but no one, to my initial consternation, laughed. Then I realized the reason: Hitler was never a joke to the Poles. He was a hideous reality, the recollection of which could not be anything but horrifying. During the Nazi occupation of Poland anyone found with a book in English or heard playing Chopin was immediately put to death.

At the People's Theatre (all Polish theatres are state-owned) I saw Racine's *Britanicus*, which I feared might prove a bore. I found the performance more interesting than it had been at the Comédie Française. The setting, a scenic adaptation of *tachiste* painting technique, was barbarously regal and physically stirring; the costumes as well as the makeups in gold, orange and dark brown had a sinister glamour.

Irina Eichlerowna (Warsaw's "Mother Courage") played Agrippina. Poland's outstanding actress, she possesses formidable authority and commands an arrestingly resonant voice which she controls with utmost ease. Around her, the young actors—Nero, Britanicus, Narcissus—were handsome, fervid and fluent. The play was no Racine recital or museum piece; it took on its proper stature as a timeless statement of the conflict between will (or politics) and desire.

My only disappointment in Warsaw was the production at the Contemporary Theatre of Ionesco's *The King Dies*, which I saw at its final dress rehearsal. The setting and costumes were extremely stylish—and entirely misconceived with respect to the play's requirements. (Such a setting and costumes might earn its designer rave notices in New York.) The acting, too, was without point or quality—the fault of the director rather than the cast.

I must add that the original Ionesco text, which I read here for the first time, contains its author's finest writing, both witty and touching. The play is not, as I had supposed, an ode to death, but a hymn to life emerging from the troubled depths of existentialist anguish.

Tokyo

~~~~~~~~~~~~~~~~~~~~~~

The Old and the New, 1963

SEVERAL NEW lines in the Tokyo subway system are being
built. The streets are now often little but metal or plank
surfaces over hollow space. There are gaping trenches where the
initial digging is still in progress.

This, I was. told, was why I had the impression that the city
looked as if it is still being constructed. But what I had said was
that it was not simply the streets which were being refashioned,
but the minds and hearts of the people.

In that fascinating and significant novel Yukio Mishima's *The
Temple of the Golden Pavillion* we read, "Although I was still
young, I was conscious . . . that the world of death which my
father ruled and the world of life occupied by young people were
being brought together by the mediation of war." The old, "the
tempting concept of beauty which makes people powerless to
act," as Mishima puts it, is at present under the constant assault
of headlong action. The transformation of Japan is so rapid that
the condition of the country has drastically altered, even in the
past five years.

The results are not pretty, but they are highly exciting. Tokyo
looks like a junk heap of modern mercantile and industrial con-
trivance. Pompous banks, Hilton-type hotels, bombastic office
buildings, shrill movie houses seem to be tumbling from the
heavens or being thrust up from hell amid decrepit alley shops
run by struggling artisans of another era. New York is almost
pastoral in comparison. Where elegant new Japanese-style
(wooden) houses are put up, they are occupied, as in a typical
development I visited, by such folk as a television producer, a

baseball star and an American university professor. There is inflation, and though wages increase they do not catch up with the
cost of living.

Japan, about as large as California, has ninety million in-
habitants, and one's first impression of Tokyo is that all of them
have taken to the streets at the same time. At night, when the
neon lights blaze in colors more variegated and in patterns more
eccentric than anything we can imagine outside of an action
painting, one has the sensation of being spirited away into a
monstrous fun fair on New Year's Eve. The Ginza, the so-called
Broadway of Tokyo, which is a section rather than a single avenue, is one of the numerous entertainment areas aflame in various
parts of the city, all of them covering many square blocks and
all of them "jumping."

I remarked to a Japanese acquaintance that if I were permitted
to see the new China I would regret not having been able to
catch a glimpse of the old, but on seeing Tokyo now I could see
both the old and the new Japan at the same time. He agreed. For
in the midst of the bedizened megalopolitan chaos, there are
considerable vestiges of the ancient civilization, and because of
the surrounding upheaval they are the more striking.

In a city where in the center of the downtown quarter an
edifice houses the nude "girlie" show *Tokyo Temptations,* as well
as an all-girl revue and a lavish movie emporium, there also
stands, a short distance away, the Kabuki Theatre, where all the
actors kneel in obeisance at the door of the leading player's dress-
ing room every time they are to go onstage, and once again when
they have completed their performance. The city where the Turk-
ish bath—advertised as a kind of carnival—is known as a substitute for an (illegal) house of assignation is also the city where, to
make themselves more desirable as brides, young ladies spend
years in perfecting themselves in the stylized gestures of the Tea
Ceremony, which has been called "an extension of philosophy to
the sphere of social meetings."

Certain aspects of Zen Buddhism are now employed, not only
as psychoanalysis serves in the West, but as an aid in the achievement of business success. There are Cadillacs and Bentleys on the
same streets where one can occasionally spy a man-drawn rick-
shaw in poor repair in which a geisha on her way to a beauty
parlor is seductively secreted behind a soiled drape. While devo-

tees with "libretti" of the linguistically unintelligible Noh plays sit as subscribers to that hieratic art, the leading young novelist of the moment has been compared to Gide and Genet.

Kyoto, Japan's ancient capital, still preserves much of its pristine loveliness and the new world does not jostle the old there, but all Japan is pushing its way to Tokyo. One is therefore justified in using Tokyo as the image for what is going on in the land.

Tokyo is not a theatre town unless Tokyo itself be considered theatre. True, I attended several Kabuki performances, one Noh play, one "Temptation," some modern plays—European and Japanese—as well as several charming and meaningful puppet plays. I also saw a stage and film actress who impressed me as an outstanding artist, one whom I took to be emblematic of the essence of Japanese art. Still, while I found the ritualized forms of the theatre instructive, these seemed to me less immediately cogent than the polish and sophistication of some recent novels and films. But all assumed greater interest for me because of the place and atmosphere of their setting: Japan itself.

I shall nevertheless begin with remarks about the actress Isuzu Yamada. Americans who saw Kurosawa's version of Gorky's *Lower Depths* may remember her as the volcanic virago of that film. The afternoon I saw her on the stage she was costarring in a seventeenth-century comedy in which the male star was Matsumato Koshiro, one of three brothers, all of whom are distinguished representatives of the Kabuki hierarchy.

The play itself struck me as a much adulterated piece. It is customary in Japan, as elsewhere, to present lighter fare during the summer months. I was growing bored with the spectacle—Koshiro had cast himself in a part in which at least for the first two hours he had no opportunity to shine—when a magic instant transfigured the mediocre show into a memorable experience.

Yamada, who appears to be fifty, is a powerfully built woman of unmistakable sexual potency. On this occasion, she played an artful minx who has learned to give herself the airs of a *grande dame*. A man who is trying to extract some crucial business information from her begins to bribe her with flattering words and intriguing promises. She retains an imperturbable composure. He then produces both money and a precious jewel. A barely perceptible smile modifies the line of her lips; there is a suspicion of a glint in her eye. She instructs a handmaiden to gather up the money and the jewel as if it were trash. She rises, and with the web-footed tread affected by the great ladies of the seventeenth century (adopted by Kabuki actors), she moves with stately pride toward the threshold of the room. Just as she is about to disappear, she deftly and majestically whisks the booty from the servant's care to her own. Her exit has the same poise.

Here was the cream of Kabuki humor. (By introducing women into his company, Koshiro has broken with tradition.) What I have described was so delicately accomplished that it hardly seemed to have occurred. Yet the effect, though miniscule, was electrifying. Apart from the walk—and even this partook of an illusion—there seemed to be no movement at all. Nothing was "happening," except that the apparent immobility of the scene was in itself wonderful. A certain phase of Japanese art consists of a repose which moves! One witnessed this scene—it was a second isolated in time—as if one's attention had been transfixed by the radiant node of some brilliant gem. An extreme intensity was contained in the person of the actress, whose impassive demeanor had hardly changed at all, though all had changed.

What was most extraordinary—and specifically Japanese—in this is that the actress' gait, abstractly judged by Occidental standards, might be called ungainly, unnatural, even ugly. Yet through some transubstantiation, this distortion had become exquisite. I do not mean sensuous or ornamental, but hard, clean, unemphatic and perfectly expressive of irony, cunning, nobility. Japanese art can translate the misshapen into grace. Whereas Western art seeks symmetry, the Japanese tends to make assymmetry beautiful.

It is an art of contraries. Even the forty-three-foot-high Buddha at Kamakura, in its overwhelming quietness, becomes dramatic as one gazes at it, awesome to the point of anguish. The static takes on mobility; what is almost hideous induces detachment and calm.

On visiting the stages of a film studio where a melodrama (based on the plot of *Carmen*) about traffic in drugs was being shot, I saw a starlet whom Hollywood might publicize as a sex knockout. Such faces—not at all uncommon in Japan—are favored by the Japanese movie moguls, and the roving eye of the tourist fixes on them avidly. But the most beautiful woman I encountered in Japan, the actor Koshiro's wife, had an altogether different kind of "good looks." This is the insinuating femininity one discovers in Japanese prints, a mixture of sensuality and refinement, a peculiarly enticing modesty which is sensed rather than seen.

"It was quite natural," Mishima writes, "that wars and unrest, piles of corpses and copious blood should enrich the beauty of the Golden Temple. . . . The uncoordinated design of its three stories, in which the art historian could only see a blend of styles, had surely been evolved naturally from the search of a style that could crystallize all the surrounding unrest. If instead it had been built in one fixed style, the Golden Temple would have been unable to embrace the unrest and would certainly have been collapsed long since."

Life in Japan today may be viewed as a sort of melodrama, a conflict, not between the "good guys" and the "bad guys," but between the old and the new. Though the upstart new has the clear advantage, the suspense is considerable. As in all instances where a civilization is in rapid transition, there is resistance. Those who fear or resent the passing of the old maintain that change is more apparent than real. It is easier in Japan than elsewhere to take this position, since Japan has always been able to assimilate features of other cultures and to transform them into something peculiarly its own.

Youngsters assure me that the Noh and Kabuki theatrical forms—issue of the fifteenth and seventeenth centuries respectively—are doomed. Their language is archaic and their pace, particularly that of Noh, intolerably slow. These were aristocratic modes and are said to have little relation to present needs.

But though the government does not subsidize the theatre in the European fashion, the state financed the Kabuki's American tour; the Puppet Theatre, developed in the sixteenth century, had its career renewed by a grant from the national treasury. These are taken as signs that the old theatre will not become extinct. Yet I found sold-out houses only at contemporary plays. There was greater attendance at the Kabuki than at the Noh, and while the Noh audience was predominantly elderly and the Kabuki audience middle-aged, the audience for the modern plays was conspicuously young.

A learned devotee of the old theatre made an observation which struck me as especially significant: while the present players of Noh and Kabuki are proficient in the required movement and intonations, most of them lack the "inside feeling" which must animate these forms. Actors in modern plays, it was quickly added, have much more "inside feeling." This says more than any comparative statistics on the two kinds of theatre.

The Japanese film industry, affluent some years ago, is now suffering a decline as sharp as that of Hollywood's. This is supposedly due to earlier overproduction and to the poor quality of many recent films, most of which are hackneyed as our old "B" movies. The deterioration, according to one gentleman committed to the maintenance of the traditional arts, is turning the interest of the young back to the theatre. But, he added with an enigmatic smile, none of the arts could really attract them because their bent is toward baseball, golf and country outings!

It struck me later that this remark dovetailed with another, by a university student, that the Japanese, "so clever with their fingers," were now reluctant to become skilled workers tied down to permanent jobs. They desire freedom to wander, to have a good time. With employment everywhere at hand, the young are always able to find new jobs. But labor is poorly paid and most workers live in rather squalid dwellings; that is why, someone else explained, so many people crowd the streets, where their eager pursuit of fun gives Tokyo its hectic complexion.

The attempt to resolve the tension between the traditional and the contemporary is most strikingly illustrated in the better films. One has only to think of *Rashomon* and some of Kurosawa's "Westerns" (Samurai adventure stories) to observe how detachment and skepticism allow the modern Japanese artist to celebrate certain perennially admirable virtues while subtly undermining their premises.

Masaki Kobayashi's *Harakiri* is a recent example of the interplay between new and old. Laid in the period of feudalism's decadence, its plot denounces the brutality and futility of that society's codes of honor. By thematic extension the story also casts doubt on adherence to many still prevalent and respected disciplines.

It is beautifully made and superlatively acted, with something of the chastened luxury of ancient Japanese art. Still, one recognizes that a good deal of the pleasure of *Harakiri* lies in its cruelty and the gory extravagance of its sword play and fight scenes. It offers pity and terror but little tragic purge because its values are somewhat uncertain.

Other representative new films are Kurosawa's treatment of a murderous kidnaping (a new crime for Japan) and Ozu's homey *Oyaho* ("Hello"), which centers on two little boys' desire to possess a television set. That instrument is the hero-image of the film.

The Actors' Theatre—organization and building—was founded some twenty years ago by the actor-director Korea Senda, who learned much from his studies in Berlin in pre-Hitler days. The theatre's auditorium seats 480; it is comfortable, modestly attractive, up-to-date. An orchestra seat costs less than a dollar.

Senda told me that The Actors' Theatre could not count on more than five thousand spectators for any of its productions in Tokyo. The most successful of them—*The Threepenny Opera*—had to move to a larger house to accommodate the seventy thousand people who were expected to see it. How, in view of these limited numbers, was it possible to build so fine a theatre? The actors themselves had contributed as much as 70 per cent of their earnings from television and movies.

"What idealism!" I exclaimed. "Since the theatre has been in existence for twenty years, one must conclude that there is a certain amount of realism involved as well," said the director. "Has the theatre become profitable?" I asked. "No," he answered, "but the actors now contribute only 20 per cent of their earnings."

There is a numerically unimpressive but steady demand for modern plays—as persistent as the political radicalism which is both a force, particularly in the trade unions, and not a force! As a French journalist long resident in Japan put it, there is little "spirit of protest" in the country. The present (democratic) government assumes in the eyes of the people a power as transcendental as the almost religious eminence of the Emperor in bygone days.

There is a theatre school, but I judged the actors insufficiently trained for the modern stage. I inquired if there was any knowledge among them of the Stanislavsky system. Indeed there is, I was told, but there is greater interest in Brecht's methods because "they are closer to the Japanese temperament." This is understandable when one remembers the antinaturalistic bias of the Brechtian canon, with its emphasis on objective detachment. I associated the reference to Japanese temperament with something I read in the program of the Noh theatre. In the Noh play only the main personage (apart from the men who play women's roles) wears a mask—because the tradition has it that *"the mask is more expressive than the human face."*

A conviction grew in me as I was about to leave the country that within these theatrical pronouncements lay hidden some principle or clue which might unify the multiple data of my Tokyo stay. Despite the howlers inherent in headlong generalization, I decided to make a "tableau" of my variegated impressions.

The essential Japanese approach to life is aesthetic. Japanese ethics are aesthetics. Japanese morality is more a matter of balancing courtesies than an effusion or a formalization of sentiments. What we call "heart" is a virtue rarely emphasized.

In an aesthetic world view both good and evil can be made splendid through artistic and intellectual mastery. Ugliness itself needs only discipline to be made elegant. This is pagan, "liberal" and permissive. The Japanese are an ironic people. Irony is a way of checking clashing impulses; it is a step toward balance. To be truly comprehended, life must be contemplated as a lofty spectacle which like all play has a tendency to collapse in farce. The unseemly is often considered more comic than shocking. But a fascination with blood is also clearly marked in Japanese art. Blood is the most specific emblem of life's drama, and the shedding of it (one's own or another's) serves to release the aggressive instincts which must perforce lie beneath a constantly controlled, in this case an aesthetically formalized, existence. The Japanese, polite to the point of courtliness, are prone to sudden fits of nervous rage and hysteria. Where the aggressive instinct does not find physical expression it takes on the guise of another sort of "irony" which is difficult to differentiate from malice.

The Japanese are sometimes accused of hypocrisy, a charge inevitable with the use of the mask which the formalized control of relations entails. The Japanese are eye-minded rather than ear-minded, and the eye is less "soulful" than the ear!

The democracy of the machine is now releasing new forces with tremendous speed and energy. Advanced capitalism is a great leveler. Women, once the glorified slaves and adornment of Japan, are changing their status. Many believe that women are the only ones to have unequivocally improved their condition in the new society, but the women themselves feel that their lot has not been sufficiently ameliorated.

Though homosexuality is still regarded with serene impartiality —the pagan smilingly admits every appetite—the demands of modern efficiency lead to a certain "Puritanism." Did not the Japanese Supreme Court punish the publication of *Lady Chatterley's Lover?* Yet at the same time, one finds extreme samples of popular erotica in many bookstalls. And Tokyo streets steam with sensuality.

The Japanese intellectual is convinced that in America the artist and the highly cultivated carry far greater weight and are more respected than in his country, where now only the big banker and the monopoly industrialist matter—though they were presumed to have been exorcised during the American occupation. Japan is prosperous, but everyone asks, "Will it last?"

With Music

March of the Musicals

~~~~~~~~~~~~~~~~~~

A Survey, 1962

MUSICAL COMEDY is nothing to argue about: it is to be enjoyed. Yet if you should stop to think about it, you may
discover some fascinating and perhaps fruitful opportunities for
dispute. It is said, for example, that the American theatre has become a musical-comedy theatre. Some say it mournfully, others
with pride and glee. And there are those who deny it fiercely.

The facts favor the ayes. Recent statistics inform us that eleven
musicals were produced during the 1960–61 season, fourteen last
season, and fourteen musicals, in addition to four revues, have
been announced for 1962–63. There are ten musicals occupying
the boards at the moment, and only seven plays without musical
benefit. As the number of theatrical productions each year diminishes, the near dominance of musical comedy on our stage becomes increasingly evident. As an astonishing corroboration of
what one might call the automatic popularity of musical comedy,
there is the news item (not mere publicity) that the Lindsay-
Crouse-Berlin show *Mr. President* boasts an advance sale before
its New York opening of over two million dollars.

Facts, however, are dumb things: they do not reveal the whole
truth. The theatre is a place where art, social pattern and economics are inextricably commingled. So if musical comedy is to
be discussed apart from its fun, it must be examined in all these
lights.

The hastiest and most superficial consideration makes the
reason for the box-office potency of the musical quite obvious.
Musicals are designed to please practically everyone with the
minimum of effort on anyone's part. All possibility of offense is

237

avoided. Every ingredient is scrupulously aimed at ease, comfort, titillation—as with a holiday resort. The musical is a large-scale entertainment package. Won't the man who invites his out-of-town client-friend on a business and pleasure jaunt to New York feel safer in reserving tickets for a splendid musical jamboree rather than for *Heartbreak House* or *Long Day's Journey Into Night?*

Even the weakest musical promises at least two or three good jokes, a talented performer, a bit of rhythm, one or two pretty ladies, a tune one might hum and several nice dresses—or undresses. Musicals are show business' best bet because everyone nowadays seeks relief from real or pretended pressures. A drama might require some strain of nerve or brain muscle. The most resolute theatregoer will vow, in moments of exasperated impatience, that he would rather see a good musical several times than many supposedly earnest plays once.

Though scholarly gentlemen often point out that musical comedy has its antecedents in such European models as operetta and *opéra bouffe,* as well as in certain indigenous entertainments like the minstrel show and burlesque, the bare statement that musical comedy today is the one theatrical form in which America excels seems incontrovertible.

Enthusiasts learnedly explain, furthermore, that musical comedy as we now practice it, is a special and virtually new kind of show, of which Rodgers' and Hammerstein's *Oklahoma!* is often cited as a prime example. This claim of originality for the new musical smacks of hysterical complacency. Whatever fine distinctions are made between the musicals after the great Rodgers and Hammerstein hit and those of Irving Berlin, Jerome Kern, George Gershwin, Cole Porter and Vincent Youmans, as well as those of Rodgers himself (in collaboration with Larry Hart) in the twenties and thirties, it is certain that the work of those early days was of the same nature as, and of equal (if not superior) value to, that of our more "integrated" musicals today.

To be impressive, one might refer even further back to George M. Cohan, Victor Herbert and Ivan Caryll's 1911 *Pink Lady.* The point is that there always seems to have been a vital and flourishing theatre of light comic character in America. If there is any fixed tradition in our theatre, this is it. The reason is social and historical. The story of America, by and large, has been one of energy, invention, adaptability, youthfulness, buoyancy, optimism, physical well-being and prosperity. No matter what troubles beset us, we try to remain sanguine. ("Pack up your troubles in your old kit bag—and smile, smile, smile!") Despite another strain of American creativity from Hawthorne and Melville to Faulkner and O'Neill, tragedy has been rather alien to us.

Still, there is a correspondence between our so-called serious drama and our lighter musical stage. For all theatre is one: It always reflects—in comedy as well as in tragedy—various aspects of the human landscape. Just as there was almost no important native drama at the time of *The Black Crook* (1866) and precious little during the Floradora days (1900), the sophistication of our musical shows increases as we approach the late teens and early twenties.

It is surely not a matter of chance that our musical theatre burst into effulgent bloom just as our more sober theatre produced its first crop of notable playwrights: Eugene O'Neill, George Kelly, Elmer Rice, Maxwell Anderson, Sidney Howard, S. N. Behrman, Robert Sherwood, Philip Barry. And just before the launching of the Group Theatre we had *Of Thee I Sing*. When we come to observe what is happening to our present musicals, we shall have to judge the situation in the broader context of our theatre as a whole.

There are those who maintain that while our musical-comedy theatre constitutes a masterpiece in the aggregate, very few—if any—of our musicals have achieved the artistic integrity or the staying power of the best in Gilbert and Sullivan, Offenbach or the Weill and Brecht of *The Threepenny Opera*. (Of course, none of these are, strictly speaking, musical comedy, any more than is Gershwin's *Porgy and Bess*.) Yet, despite such demurs, our attachment to the musical-comedy form is not only understandable but aesthetically justified. For musical comedy is that "mythical" phenomenon—true theatre.

What is true theatre? When still a young man, Bernard Shaw wrote, "The theatre was born of old from the union of two tendencies: the desire to have a dance and the desire to hear a story. The dance became a rout, the story became a situation."

True theatre is the telling of a story or the presentation of a situation through every physical means by which men and women, together in the presence of their community, are capable of rousing its interest and pleasure. Theatre bespeaks human action—movement and speech—raised to an intense degree of eloquence through dance, song, color, spectacle. From ghost stories and tall tales told around a campfire to the austere magnificence of Greek drama, this impulse has always shaped the theatre's essence. It is there in the performance of the Japanese Noh plays, as well as in Shakespeare. We find it in Brecht (at the Berliner Ensemble) as well as in *Pal Joey*. It was what O'Neill always dreamed of achieving.

Where on our stage today is there so much of this true theatre as in our musical comedies? Ballet, which has heightened its appeal for us enormously since the thirties, lacks speech; drama lacks song and (too often) color; opera usually misses acting. The straight play (what a terrible term) often contains ideas. But musicals may possess these as well. At times musicals would appear to be almost the only place in the theatre where ideas may take final refuge!

As we hark back to the past of our musical and nonmusical stages, we fondly recall the personalities which graced both. In the twenties our theatre—the two kinds—was illuminated by splendid constellations of players whose very presence cast a halo of magic over every occasion. In the thirties the stars began to move westward. Now they are mainly to be found on the musical horizon. How many shining bodies have we on the dramatic stage today compared with those we admire in the musicals?

The comparison may be invidious and unfair, but can you, reader, make a list of "legitimate" actors and actresses to set down beside Ethel Merman, Ray Bolger, Mary Martin, Judy Holliday, Julie Andrews, Gwen Verdon, Zero Mostel, Nancy Walker and Phil Silvers—and perhaps Tammy Grimes, Robert Morse, Barbra Streisand and Barbara Harris tomorrow? (And, oh, if she were only in the theatre—Judy Garland!) What brilliant additions to our stagecraft—not to speak of our satisfaction—have been made by such choreographers as George Balanchine, Agnes de Mille, Jerome Robbins, Michael Kidd, Bob Fosse, Herbert Ross and Gower Champion.

But halt! Some of those named have transferred or will transfer from the nonmusical to the musical theatre as others may take the opposite direction. Everything in our theatre today is in a process of flux and change—some warn of dissolution—and the musicals

mirror the alteration perhaps even more strikingly than our
drama.

Long ago—for convenience sake, let us say before 1930—what
was most important to the musical-comedy audience was beautiful girls (hail Ziegfeld!), comedians (those dear old Ed Wynn
days) and, crucially, *music*—real tunes suggesting all the wonderful things the often paltry books of the time could not say.
(Think of the *Show Boat* score—one which is most likely to
survive.) It did not matter much if you interrupted the story to
bring on the girls or to vamp into a bright, consoling melody.

The new musical strives toward "legitimacy." The book, or,
more properly, the show's subject matter, must possess a little
substance, relate somehow to our normal concerns, edge closer to
the contemporaneous and the topical. Due in large measure to
the refinement of our taste through the influence of our ballet
companies, dancing has developed into a cardinal factor.

Above all, there is now an insistence on "integration"—of
which *Guys and Dolls, My Fair Lady, West Side Story* and
Gypsy supply outstanding examples. Integration demands that all
the elements in a musical be thoroughly "cemented." The story,
lyrics, music, acting and dancing must not only fit together, but
extend or complete each other. The line or fabric of the whole
must never appear to break: one part must carry on where the
other leaves off so as to compose a closely woven continuity.

This explains, incidentally, why the girls in musicals today are
seldom as dazzlingly attractive as they formerly were. All the
advantages and talents—the ability to sing, dance, act and to look
beautiful—do not often dwell in one person.

The new musical is designed to create a unified impression, a
coherent tone, an all-pervasive atmosphere. At times this aim
appears to be attained at the expense of melody. The scores of
our recent musicals seem to have more utility than inspiration.
They have become a means rather than an end. There are signal
exceptions to this, as for example the score—which seems to improve with age—of *Kiss Me, Kate*. Still, one might point out that
such a stylistic relic as *Kismet* was successful mainly because it
was sustained by delightful—albeit borrowed—music.

What strikes many listeners as musical anemia in many recent
shows may be explained in another way. It has been widely
agreed that our theatre, in general, has become markedly less

animated since 1956–57. Certainly there have been good things of various sorts since then, but there has been a definite shrinkage, not only in the volume of productions (and profits) but in every sense in which the word *abundance* may be construed. Our dramatic theatre has thinned out—foreign plays of quality, for example, preponderated last season—and something peculiar has happened to our musical theatre as well.

Serious drama has always encountered a certain resistance in our theatre—more particularly since theatre tickets have become so expensive. Such drama can exist and thrive only when it is fired by sufficient passion and conviction to make it thoroughly arresting. For the past decade, at least, we have been living in a state of spiritual confusion. Issues are not clear-cut: there has been inner, but hardly articulated, disquiet. Boldness is not feared so much as it is baffled by lack of social support and subjective assurance. We have grown publicly mute on serious matters, for we do not know exactly what there is to be said. We cover up and are not even sure what we are suppressing. Hence the repeated, but rather vague, outcry against conformism.

Yet we do want to express *something* about what lurks in our minds. We do not like to say anything which might be deemed heavy, humorless or offensive—we do not want to rock the boat—so we kid and joke. We mask our misgivings in gags.

The social themes of the thirties and early forties begin to emerge anew as grins and grimaces in the musicals of the late fifties and early sixties. After the war, we appeased our jarred souls with sweet, smiling images of the past (or of remote places): *Oklahoma!*, *Bloomer Girl*, *Carousel*, *Up in Central Park* and *Brigadoon*. With *Finian's Rainbow* we began pushing the present, while *South Pacific*, despite its touch of exoticism, hovered around a controversial subject. Then our present begins to engage us pleasantly with *The Pajama Game*, a "labor" musical without contention, to be followed later by *Fiorello!*, a "political" show without rancor.

The contemporary keynote is struck in *How to Succeed in Business Without Really Trying*, which indicates by its very title the point we have reached. (To begin with, think of the number of musicals which are basically success stories, such as *The Unsinkable Molly Brown*.) We are unsure of our values—at least for purposes of theatrical presentation—so we are both obsessed by the idea of success (and by status or money, which is its goal), and a little ashamed of the obsession. It is no accident that *Do Re Mi, Bye Bye Birdie, I Can Get It For You Wholesale* and even, to some extent, *No Strings,* are variations on the themes of success, status push and money fixation. These are now what might be called our "social plays." They all deplore our addiction to the success-status-money fetish—but not too emphatically.

Love creeps into these shows, as it were, by the back door. They are only half-heartedly romantic. They suggest that love must ride a rough road in our competitive mechanized world. As a result, the embodiment of glamour, warmth, carefreeness and a poised enjoyment of wealth becomes strained. For shows deficient in these ingredients, it is no easy matter to write free-flowing tunes—melodies with a lift. One might as well try to put double-entry bookkeeping to music.

In *Musical Comedy in America,* one of the best books on the subject, Cecil Smith, clearly a devotee, ends by asserting that while musicals have moved "into an increasingly high plane of craftsmanship and literacy," they are still only entertainments, "and if they are art at all, they are only incidentally so." Though the distinction may be useful, one should be wary of it; it insinuates that art is that which does not entertain!

One might correct a misunderstanding here by remarking that present-day musicals are too often founded on a sort of industrial calculation, sales gimmicks barely related to true individual or personal impulse. The musical, in other words, far too frequently nowadays is conceived on a mass-production basis as corporate efforts by canny and capable showmen with an eye to profitable enterprise on the Main Stem supermarket. Art rarely springs from such sources. A musical play like the Offenbach and Halévy *La Vie Parisienne,* for instance, was a collaboration of two men who were as much imbued with a feeling—both satiric and gay— about the Second Empire as any artist of their time.

Whatever one's estimate of their separate merits, our musicals at present are as typical of the extraordinary accomplishment and the grave defects as are all the other manifestations of our native theatre. They, too—and perhaps even more at the moment than most other "attractions" our playhouses have to offer—are "the brief chronicles of the time." Indeed, certain knowledgeable folk tell us that the hope of the *Midtown* theatres lies in our musicals.

It may well be so, since they, up to very recently, have proved commercially the most advantageous as well as the most popular of our productions.

Still, the high cost of producing and operating our super-lavish musicals forces them to court disaster. During the past two seasons there have been many more well-liked and lauded musicals which have lost money than we suspect. The relatively small cast and scenic modesty of *A Funny Thing Happened on the Way to the Forum* may be a portent. Should the fate of musicals be threatened by the economic hazards that menace the life of our dramatic theatre, the institution or concept known as Broadway may collapse. This, however, does not mean that the Theatre in our country would die.

One good way to keep musicals lively, at any rate, is to avoid making too sharp a distinction between merit in one category of the theatre and another. A musical must be appreciated according to standards of freshness, imaginativeness and emotional authenticity similar to those we apply to other stage forms. Such criteria may, in fact, serve as a leaven for our theatre generally.

Some of the Shows

~~~~~~~~~~~~~~

The Cradle Will Rock, 1960

IF YOU WERE thirty and inclined toward radicalism in the days of the Federal Theatre Project, you are likely to call Marc Blitzstein's *The Cradle Will Rock* "dated." If, in the meantime, your radicalism has been transformed into that form of retirement that passes as aestheticism, you are prone to speak of the American piece as an inferior *Threepenny Opera*.

If, however, you are thirty today—or if the good old rebel time of which *The Cradle Will Rock* was a landmark passed by without your noticing it as anything more special than a period of bad business—you will probably enjoy the Blitzstein opera as a good show with a quality all its own.

The subject matter and plot of *The Cradle*—though crudely cartoonlike—is no more dated than the libretto of *La Bohème*. One is sentimental about "workers," the other about "artists." The charm of neither is specifically related to its surface story. And while it is true that without Brecht and Weill there would never have been a *Cradle*, Blitzstein has given the *Cradle* its very particular quality.

What it typifies is a certain permanent American big-city young-man cockiness, a derisive unwillingness to take any guff—political, social or casual—from anybody. It is the boy in the candy store, the man at the bar, the alert laborer refusing to be hoaxed by any pretension. It is the poor man's perpetual Bronx cheer against complacency that we hear on any city street not yet razed by traffic or the police. The music alternates between a note of vulgar guying and sweet, heartbroken yearning. Blitzstein is

245

less sophisticated than his German models; more acid in anger, more tearful in hurt.

The new production—staged by Howard da Silva with sets by David Hays—is excellent in every respect, though Blitzstein's orchestration—otherwise very effective—seemed too meager at the end to be as rousing as intended.

How To Succeed in Business
Without Really Trying, 1961

How To Succeed in Business Without Really Trying, with a book by Abe Burrows, Jack Weinstock and Willie Gilbert (based on a novel by Shepperd Mead) illustrates its title. It is a brilliantly organized musical completely integrated in its style. It is admirably cast in every role: Robert Morse and Rudy Vallee are particularly effective and they receive first-rate assistance from Charles Reilly, Bonnie Scott, Virginia Martin, Paul Reed, Ray Mason. The musical staging by Bob Fosse and the choreography by Hugh Lambert, as well as the scenery by Robert Randolph, are all stylized with steely linear sharpness exactly illustrative of the show's theme: the useless functionalism of the corporate manufacture and sale of absurd commodities—in this case "wickets."

There are clever numbers about the sacred ritual of the Coffee Break, the Brotherhood of Man (company style) and Labor's End: "Been a Long Day." There are funny lines; Abe Burrows knows how to write them, since his talent lies in the direction of a determined disengagement from practically everything but success. In brief, though it lacks the juiciness and raffish afflatus of *Guys and Dolls* (by more or less the same authors), *How To Succeed* is approximately as good a musical as you can expect nowadays on Broadway—expert and gifted. Its most lingering impression is created by Robert Morse, who resembles an uncorrupted Mickey Rooney. Because of Morse's physiognomy and manner I thought another title for the show might be Huckleberry Finn Up Business Creek.

Still, when I left the theatre I had forgotten a great deal of what I had seen. The reason? This satire merely kids. It is impelled by no gripe, scorn or actual dislike of its target. Its motivations are not so very different from what is presumably being ridiculed. Its jokes are palliatives.

Stop the World—I Want to Get Off, 1962

If during the intermission of *Stop the World—I Want to Get Off* I had yielded to the pressure (which several friends put on me) to say what I thought of the show, I might have blurted something like "I find it a little dull, but I like it" or conversely "I think it interesting, but I don't like it."

Such a reply might have been even more confusing than cagey; it certainly could not have been considered an opinion. (Why must one always have an opinion? This is a pertinent question, even for a critic—or should I say especially for a critic!) But to some extent it is still the way I feel about the show.

When I saw it first in London last March and in passing mentioned it favorably in *The Nation* I was taken to task, challenged in fact, by a leading and thoroughly intelligent American director. I explained in defense that what interested me chiefly about *Stop the World* (apart from its very clever title) was its reflection of the general spiritual climate in England at present. It is not so much a pessimistic or iconoclastic state of mind as a wryly querulous one. It is dissatisfied, distrustful without true rebelliousness or firm conviction. It is essentially an expression of discomfort, and one notices in the present instance that the parts of the stage action which stand for "I want to get off" are ventriloquistically rendered in a sort of infantile puling. Still, for all the impulse to deflate and jeer, the temper of the English in this vein somehow manages to remain genial, wistful—even "nice."

Stop the World, etc., billed as a "new-style musical," with book, music and lyrics by Leslie Bricusse and Anthony Newley—who is also its director and star—is "different." Much of it is pantomime;

it has only eleven people in its cast (including the "chorus"). Its
set, by Sean Kenney, is, like the show itself, abstract; if it were
taken to represent anything, it would be a circus tent. It has no
"story." It is a sort of allegory: the life of the common man, here
designated as Littlechap.

We see him "born," see him take his first faltering and astonished steps into the world. We hear him learning his alphabet—in
song. He grows up in hardship (a boys' reformatory is referred
to), then marries a well-born typically English girl (another song)
after he has made her pregnant. He did not wish to marry so
he complains in what is virtually the theme song of the show, "I
Have Been Lumbered." His prosperous father-in-law gives him a
job in Sludgepool (any industrial town north of London) and he
expresses his will to succeed in one of the better songs, "Gonna
Build a Mountain." He accomplishes this dreary task and is pro-
moted to a post in Moscow. Anna Quayle—the principal lady—
who at first and throughout the performance plays Littlechap's
wife—now appears, in her permanent leotard (the show does not
require changes of costumes) as a "typically" Russian girl. Rather
trite jokes about the Russians follow. Littlechap has an affair with
the Russian girl, gets her with child, a little boy who expires in
pantomime. Littlechap returns to his family where the children
find it difficult to communicate with their parents. Father and
mother bicker and quarrel in accredited (discredited) middle-
class fashion. (Song title: "Nag! Nag! Nag!") Littlechap hires a
German maid—whom Miss Quayle also impersonates. She is a
Valkyrie—and her scenes are more pronouncedly anti-German
than the Russian scenes are anti-Soviet. (It is interesting to observe that this contrast was more pleasing to the London audience than it seems to be to ours.)

Littlechap's next stop is America. Miss Quayle, now an American girl who works in a nightclub, purrs and simpers like a musical comedy ingenue of 1912. On his return to England Littlechap,
increasingly successful, stands for Parliament and is elected. His
speeches are "Mumbo Jumbo." He is knighted. One of his daugh-
ters is married under the same awkward circumstances that
trapped him in matrimony. His heart begins to fail. He sentimen-
tally recalls his loyal wife, who for all her "typical" propriety, was
sweet. He dies asking himself "What Kind of a Fool Am I?"—a
song of which the first musical phrase or its delivery proves touch-

ing. Another Littlechap is "born." The circle is complete. The clown show (or circus) goes on.

Stop the World has form and style: these are genuine virtues. It has two faults: no single element of its execution is first-rate. The set functions in a drably neutral fashion. The music is pleasant but thin. Newley is certainly versatile: he does everything. Quite apart from his share of the authorship, he mimes, sings and comments on the action. But none of these things are done with any special flair. Miss Quayle is a sturdy and likable revue artiste. In a word, the fabric of the show is dilettante or amateur. Its atmosphere seems to be more suited to an intimate cabaret than to the stage of a large theatre.

The show's second fault is the basic banality of its content. Its ideology is a dilution of the Theatre of the Absurd in British middle-class terms. It is a lighter and sweeter compound of the message from the angry young men.

Yet I cannot bring myself to reject it, and not only because it departs from the norm—which is always to be welcomed. There is something modestly and warmly affecting about it, a quality almost entirely absent from our more efficient and richly endowed musicals. The possession of this warmth—like a personal friendliness—is what seemed to engage the second-night audience despite the rather poor notices the show had received that morning. The dispirited and stereotyped "meaning" of the show is not as sensible to us as its smiling forbearance, for which many are sure to prove grateful.

Hello Dolly!, 1964

Though *Hello Dolly!* is extremely lavish in sets and costumes and is put together with exemplary skill by Gower Champion, what impresses me most in this new musical is the personality of Carol Channing.

The show by Michael Stewart and Jerry Herman has been called "the best musical of the season," and that may well be since the others were *Jennie, Here's Love, The Girl Who Came to*

Supper—all of them duds—and *110 in the Shade*, pleasant enough, with Inga Swenson, a talented and lovable singing actress supported by a generally attractive cast.

Hello Dolly! is based on (the program says "suggested by") Thornton Wilder's genial and delightfully written *The Matchmaker*. Whenever the adaptation quotes its source, the dialogue takes on a marked freshness. There is no music worth mentioning in the proceedings; the hit number, "Hello Dolly!," is memorable chiefly for its brilliant staging, color and the opportunity it affords the audience to display its affection for Miss Channing.

In an extravagant mood one might describe Gower Champion as the Tyrone Guthrie of musical-comedy direction. He has humor and an unfailing sense of what will surprise, move and strike home on the stage. His choreography is not particularly original or beautiful in itself, but with limited dance means it always manages to make a telling theatrical effect. If Gower Champion were to run a nightclub it would be the most "romantic" spot in town, because he knows how to combine elements of a traditional glamour with the tension and hectic beat of metropolitan festivity. There can be no doubt that much of the success of *Hello Dolly!* is due to Champion's special gift for composition in the building of a musical show.

Still, only Carol Channing "spoke" to me. She is not an unknowing performer, but I venture to say that she is barely conscious of what gives her presence its peculiar appeal. Even her audience may not realize exactly why they like her so much.

Goggle-eyes shining, mouth agape glistening with a multitude of teeth, her voice cracking, Miss Channing makes us believe she finds this the best of possible worlds despite a never-declared but always evident heartbreak. She is the most credulous girl in the world. She puts a glad face on unhappiness. She looks as if she hopes with all her might that she's having as good a time as she's supposed to be having or even thinks she is. She's a triumph of guilelessness over the facts of life. The audience is grateful to a person so good-humored, so without malice, so openhearted in a world where intelligence alone leads to very different sentiments. Bless her goofiness, we feel like crying. She makes life positively gay because she hears no evil, she sees no evil and will speak no evil. She is a public benefactress.

Funny Girl, 1964

Broadway scuttlebutt has it that $750,000 was spent on *Funny Girl*. For all the value in the show the producers would have been well advised to permit its star, Barbra Streisand, to come out and sing some songs on the bare stage—but not the songs she now sings, none of which are any good.

Though Sydney Chaplin has greatly improved since he made his first appearance in New York, and Jean Stapleton and Kay Medford are funny in the few moments they are vouchsafed, there is really nothing to *Funny Girl* but Barbra Streisand. The book, if it exists, is phony; there is no dancing to speak of and the music is hogwash, though some of Bob Merrill's lyrics are not bad.

For those who remember Fanny Brice—the show is presumably her "story"—the connection between that great lady, a "funny girl" who at times came close to being a tragedienne, and the star of the present is a little unfortunate. I shall refrain from comparisons because I do not wish to take this occasion to write an appreciation of Fanny Brice, but only to speak of Miss Streisand, who is a young woman of unmistakable gifts.

She was brilliantly hilarious in *I Can Get It For You Wholesale*. She manifests new qualities in her present vehicle. She has rhythm—although the rhythm in her numbers now is forced because supplied by her rather than by the composer; she knows how to color the words and phrases of her songs so as to give each of them their specific emotional quality. She has a disarming directness and a simplicity. Very little is "put on," except where her playfulness is a comic comment, usually a mockery of pretension, plus an apology for having so little to be pretentious about. The nakedness, the flat plainness of the world about her, its fundamental lack of glamour and her refusal or inability to rise above it—though because she is so talented she feels it more than she shows any consciousness of doing—constitute the essence of her appeal, her pathos. What her acting (even more her singing) says is: "I am a woman; I have imagination. I have spirit, humor,

THE NAKED IMAGE252 THE NAKED IMAGE

keen common sense, a desire to live a full, vivid life; but I dwell in a place and at a time which really deny and cheapen most of these attributes. Therefore I clown, and you who applaud me so rapturously do so because you sense what I am suppressing—our mutual bereavement from beauty."

Fiddler on the Roof, 1964

After seeing *Fiddler on the Roof* (based on some Yiddish short stories; book by Joseph Stein, music by Jerry Bock, lyrics by Sheldon Harnick) numerous members of the audience confessed (or proclaimed) that they shed tears of compassion and gratitude; others have asserted that their hearts swelled in elation, while still others were convulsed with laughter. My own reception of the show was cool.

I too found it endearing—worthy of the affection the enthusiasts had manifested. Yet thinking of it in its detail, the text lacked the full savor of its sources; the music simply followed a pattern of suitable folk melodies without adding, or being equal, to them; Jerome Robbins' choreography, though correct in its method, was not—except for two instances—as brilliant as I had expected it to be. Boris Aronson's sets did not "overwhelm" me; even Zero Mostel's performance, which cements the diverse elements and gives them a core and a shape, was open to objections. Then, too, were not those critics right, in the press and the public, who maintained there was a Broadway taint in the mixture?

Yet the longer I reflected, the greater grew my regard for the show! The steadier my effort to arrive at a true appraisal of my feelings, the more clearly I realized that the general audience was justified. By a too meticulous weighing and sifting of each of the performance's components one loses sight of the whole.

The production is actually *discreet.* For a popular ($350,000) musical there is a certain modesty in its effect. The vast machinery of production—I do not refer to the physical aspects alone— which must perforce go into the making of an entertainment of this sort has by an exercise of taste been reduced to a degree of intimacy that is almost surprising.

The choreography, for example, does not attempt to electrify, though it is rather more muscular, broader and certainly less "cosy" than Jewish folk dancing tends to be, Robbins has, on the whole, successfully combined the homeliness of such dancing with cossack energy. And though Aronson's sets may remind one of Chagall, they do not really attempt to achieve Chagall-like results. (Chagall's art is always more emphatically Russian or French than anything else. Whatever their subject, his paintings possess a certain opulent flamboyance that is hardly Jewish.) Aronson, faced with the need to move his sets rapidly, as well as to give them the atmosphere of impoverishment required by the play's environment without robbing them of a certain quiet charm, has made his contribution to the proceedings relatively unobtrusive—which a Chagall stage design never is. (There is also in Aronson's pictorial scheme a nice contrast between the ramshackle drabness of the places in which the play's characters are housed and the profuse yet delicate greenery of the natural surroundings.) Considering, too, the dizzying extravagance of Mostel's histrionic quality, his performance is remarkably reserved.

None of this, however, goes to the heart of the show's significance, which must be sought in its effect on the audience. That effect comes close, within the facile laughter, the snug appreciation of an anticipated showmanship, to something religious. To understand this one must turn to the play's original material: stories by Sholom Aleichem. Sholom Aleichem (pen name for Sholom Rabinowitz, born in Russia in 1859, died in New York in 1916) was the great folk artist of Yiddish literature—an altogether unique figure who might without exaggeration be compared to Gogol. The essence of Sholom Aleichem's work is in a very special sense *moral*. It is the distillation of a humane sweetness from a context of sorrow. It represents the unforced emergence of a real joy and a true sanctification from the soil of life's workaday worries and pleasures. Although this blessed acceptance of the most commonplace facts of living—generally uncomfortable and graceless, to say the least—appears casual and unconscious in Sholom Aleichem, it is based on what, in the first and indeed the best of the play's numbers, is called "Tradition."

This tradition, which might superficially be taken to comprise little more than a set of obsolete habits, customs and pietistic prescriptions, is in fact the embodiment of profound culture. A people is not cultured primarily through the acquisition or even the making of works of art; it is cultured when values rooted in biologically and spiritually sound human impulses, having been codified, become the apparently instinctive and inevitable mode of its daily and hourly conduct. Sholom Aleichem's characters are a concentrate of man's belief in living which does not exclude his inevitable bewilderment and questioning of life's hardship and brutal confusion.

In the stories this is expressed as a kindness which does not recognize itself, as pity without self-congratulation, as familiar humor and irony without coarseness. This is beauty of content, if not of form. For the Eastern (Russian, Polish, Rumanian, Galician) Jews of yesteryear "would have been deeply puzzled," Irving Howe and Eleazer Greenberg have said in their admirable introduction to a collection of Yiddish stories, "by the idea that the aesthetic and the moral are distinct realms, for they saw beauty above all in behavior."

More of this meaning than we had a right to expect is contained in *Fiddler on the Roof*. Is it any wonder, then, that an audience, living in one of the most heartless cities of the world at a time of conformity to the mechanics of production, an audience without much relation to any tradition beyond that expressed through lip service to epithets divested of living experience, an audience progressively more deprived of the warmth of personal contact and the example of dignified companionship, should weep thankfully and laugh in acclamation at these images of a good life lived by good people? In *Fiddler on the Roof* this audience finds a sense of what "togetherness" might signify. Without the cold breath of any dogma or didactics, it gets a whiff of fellow feeling for the unfortunate and the persecuted. It is a sentiment that acts as a kind of purification.

Is there too much "show biz" in *Fiddler on the Roof?* Undoubtedly. But apart from the fact that dramaturgic and musical equivalents of Sholom Aleichem's genius are not to be had for the asking, is it conceivable that a truly organic equivalent of the original stories could be produced in our time? The makers and players of *Fiddler on the Roof* are not of Kiev, 1905 (except for Boris Aronson, who was born in Kiev in 1900), nor do they live (even in memory) a life remotely akin to that of Tevye the

Dairyman, his family and his friends, or of the author who begat them. The producers of *Fiddler on the Roof* are Broadway—as is the audience—and, in this instance, perhaps the best of it. Those who have attended some of the latter-day productions of the Yiddish stage itself will know that they too are as alien to the spirit of Sholom Aleichem as anything we see at the Imperial Theatre.

The name of Chagall has almost unavoidably come up. The nearest thing to that artist's type of imagination dwells within *Fiddler on the Roof's* leading actor. Zero Mostel has "Chagall" in his head. Mostel's clown inspiration is unpredictably fantastic—altogether beyond the known or rational. One wishes this fantasy were allowed fuller scope in the show, even as compliments for its control are in order. For Mostel too, being part of Broadway, will fleetingly lapse into adulterations inhospitable to his fabulous talent.

Variety

No Time for Comedy

~~~~~~~~~~~

1958

I DO NOT particularly concentrate on politics nowadays and I may as well confess that I read history as art and philosophy, rather than as usable knowledge, so that like the average educated American I remain an innocent in world affairs. Still, what with the headlines and an occasional skimming of articles in the daily and weekly journals, some things seep in. Sometimes they make me laugh. I am sure they oughtn't.

Several weeks ago, for example, the Administration acknowledged a recession. A day or two later an official statement assured us that there would be an upswing during the month of March. Harry Truman made some caustic remarks about the Government's bungling. Then I read a quote from President Eisenhower's speech in which he spoke—obviously referring to Truman and likeminded critics—of "men of little faith." This was followed a few days later by a Presidential statement that things would get worse before they got better. By this time I was grinning, though I know this reaction was absolutely wrong.

Remedies for the bad effects of the recession were suggested. Tax cuts, then no tax cuts, federal spending projects, then no such projects, partial disarmament, no disarmament, and so on and on to an item which announced that our Secretary of State felt there should be no halting of nuclear preparedness since this would impede the work now being done on perfecting the clean bomb. At this point I could not suppress a guffaw—which I am convinced was wicked of me.

Such wickedness never finds itself on our stage today. (There is only the wickedness of total imperviousness to these matters.)

Our theatre rarely gnashes its teeth in an indignant smile or hoots with derisive pain. This is hardly surprising; after all we are not Europeans. George Kaufman, who we should remember was coauthor of *Once in a Lifetime* and other similar plays, once remarked that on Broadway "Satire is what closes on Saturday night." Most satirical plays on our stage are of foreign origin.

There was some kidding in *The Teahouse of the August Moon,* but it gave offense to no one at all. *No Time for Sergeants* poked fun at the army brass, but this is an almost traditional joke. No one ever asks at the end of such plays, as someone asked me many years ago during a performance of *Waiting for Lefty,* "Say, do they really mean it?" A playwright told me recently, in answer to a criticism in my review of his play, that he had tried to suggest a point of view but that the audience in the out-of-town tryout froze when it began to suspect a serious intention. The plays of industrial unrest nowadays seem to be typified by *The Pajama Game.* Voltaire's *Candide* became a giant marshmallow on Broadway.

Social satire has always been rare on our stage because satire is the product of a degree of civilized sophistication which our theatre audiences—either literal-minded or frivolous—do not usually possess. (How many plays in the history of our theatre can we compare in purpose with Gogol's *Inspector General* or Beaumarchais' *Marriage of Figaro?*) Even in terms of harmless satire in a gay vein, the last successful show I can recall is the 1946 revue *Call Me Mister*—smoother and slicker than the *Pins and Needles* of 1937–39. What is worth examining, however, is why there is less satire at the present time than in the twenties—our most self-critical as well as most self-indulgent era—or in the thirties—the period of our most acute social awareness.

To create satire which goes beyond good-natured spoofing of follies and vices that are regarded as peccadilloes, you have to have a community with strong beliefs and convictions. Almost everyone today is uncertain of his beliefs and few are rash enough to harbor convictions.

But when one's beliefs have been shaken, when convictions have been undermined by events and self-questioning has taken possession of one's soul, the consequences may still bear the marks of the believing personality. The agony which results from the destruction of once firmly held beliefs may take on a dynamic quality apparently destructive but basically the expression of a passion for a renewed faith. Blasphemy is frequently a more telling expression of the religious spirit than piety.

The satire or irony inherent in the plays of many contemporary French dramatists, beginning with Camus' *Caligula* through to Genet, Ionesco and Beckett, is a manifestation of *outrage* and not, as many suppose, the result of a wholly nihilistic attitude. They are at once savage, sometimes obscene, protests against the absurdity of our existence in a world where most of the old faiths have turned to hypocrisy and a (not always conscious) cry for a new one.

These rebels without a platform (except the stage) and without a program (except that of *la farce*: French for a riotous upsetting of the official applecart) are admitted by their very detractors to express something of their country's present spirit. Most of Western Europe (particularly France) knows it is sick, caught in a web of insane contradictions. But being conscious of this and expressing it fully in a mad satire—a comic grimace is noticeable even in the most lacerating and melancholy of their plays—is a sign of vitality.

In the hysterically prosperous twenties we had the energy and wit to poke fun at ourselves and to confess our nightmares—if only as a corrective to our creeping complacency. Besides O'Neill, whose realm was the tragic (except possibly for *Marco Millions*), there were such plays, mixing the bitter with the sweet, as *What Price Glory?* by Maxwell Anderson and Laurence Stallings, *The Show-Off* by George Kelly, *The Front Page* by Hecht and MacArthur, *Beggar on Horseback* by George Kaufman and Marc Connolly. The Teapot Dome scandal provided the pivotal theme of *The Grand Street Follies* of 1922. Even *The Garrick Gaieties of 1925*—Rodgers and Hart's first success—contained a number about the Monkey Trial which had some bite. There were occasional rumblings of real dissent—often incoherent or imitative (of the German expressionist dramatists) but nonetheless aggressive.

Very little of all this dug deep because, in a predominantly confident, or at least heedless, time there seemed little need for more than a smiling degree of self-depreciation. When E. E. Cummings' play *him* was produced in 1928 in the Village, the entire press stood aghast, not recognizing either the play's lyric and satirical quality or its implied prophecy of the coming collapse.

The twenties, theatrically speaking, moved from the sly but

painless joke of the Kaufman-Gershwin *Of Thee I Sing* (1931) into the middle thirties, when our faces grew longer, and even the essentially conservative Maxwell Anderson mixed some sneers with the chuckles in *Both Your Houses,* which spoke of America's inexhaustible fund of political inertia.

The mid-thirties, as everyone knows, was the Odets period in the theatre, which, lest we forget, was marked by a wholesomely enthusiastic humor as well as the pathos and bathos of our hopes in panaceas we did not fully understand. (Satire mellowed by sentiment was always one of Odets' strong points.) But beyond the "radical," "left-wing," hortatory plays which represented the youthful singing combativeness of the New Deal days, there sprouted on our side streets little political "cabarets" somewhat reminiscent of the *boîtes* in Paris, where the pulse of the people may always be felt beating in ragtime.

The hopes of the thirties were both rebuffed and justified by the war years and their "national unity." Tennessee Williams emerged in his gentlest mood in *The Glass Menagerie.* Saroyan's early plays took the edge off their satirical outline in tender clowning and woozy or boozy kindliness. The postwar forties in the theatre were enlivened by Arthur Miller's *Death of a Salesman,* which, for all its tearfulness, contains definite elements of satire and, generally speaking, reveals a more sober and cautious continuance of the New Deal mentality of the thirties. We still produced affably liberal comedies like Thurber and Nugent's *The Male Animal,* Lindsay and Crouse's *The State of the Union* and Garson Kanin's *Born Yesterday.*

The decline of the satiric spirit begins with the fifties. Our hopes were dissipated, rebelliousness was first frowned upon and then squelched. Social criticism now seems to lack a base, and the building of positive values appears to lack support in social realities. What new affirmations are made seem to turn inward, are always on a personal level, as if to say "please mind your own business and let me mind mine—and if we are going to take a public stand it must remain within the confines of ideologies and organizations of undisputed respectability and authority." We are not so much frightened, now that McCarthy has passed away, as transfixed, stuck, spiritually immobilized.

We do not know today if we are prosperous or not or exactly what it means to be prosperous—except that to fail to be a success is shameful. We are the leaders of the Western world, but we are not sure whom we are leading or to what. We do not know if we can stop war, though we are rather hopeless of surviving it. We pray that the psychoanalysts will reassure us, since the moralists and preachers have not redeemed us. Playwrights who have tried to portray the consequences of this disarray now apologize for their perversity and promise that with some medical assistance they will become good boys. According to our critics *and* audiences it is somehow terribly wrong to be "unhealthy," so that as John Gassner has written, "Health seems to be our brand of decadence."

To be confused is not yet to be damned. An avowal of our confusion even in terms of the comic without fear of some notes of exasperation would be a sign of strength. We live in a challenging time, but we seem unable to take up the challenge. The so-called cynicism of the twenties was creative; the solemnity and some of the immature sloganizing of the thirties and forties were still creative; what is stultifying us now is a failure to recognize and cry out that somewhere along the way our line was lost; that we must go back and find out what it was, what happened to it.

Defense of the Artist
as "Neurotic"

~~~~~~~~~~~~~~~~~~~~

1958

WHEN, during the Depression, we read headlines of businessmen who flung themselves from the windows of their office buildings, we were shocked but not utterly surprised. One thing is certain: very few people felt impelled to comment that the nature of business produced madmen.

Many of us have been made uneasy of late to read statements or to hear television interviews in which an artist announced that he was undergoing psychoanalytic treatment. The fact itself is by no means objectionable; we are prepared to believe that such treatment for the artist, as for anyone else, may prove helpful. But this is a private matter. What disturbs us is that such public confessions are presumed to reveal something about the nature of artists and their work. This, I, for one, hold to be entirely false.

Two things are assumed: that art is itself the outcome of some maladjustment or neurosis and that, if the artist were to correct this, he might either function more efficiently or, a more ambiguous conclusion, he might beneficially cease being an artist altogether.In either interpretation, a supposedly normal person might emerge—the prototype of that person probably being the one who reads the confession or hears it on the air.

The reason this view is fairly popular may be set down to our secret envy of the artist who, despite all possible disabilities, is somehow regarded as a special being. The "bohemian"—usually a defective artist—often fosters the myth both as a boast and as an excuse for misconduct, which the community usually believes to be characteristic of him. It has been said that "no man is a hero to his valet," on which Goethe commented, "That is because the valet is a valet."

There may be a·more cogent reason why the notion that an artist must be a basically "sick" person is developing into a local cliché. The idea began to gain ever greater acceptance with the spread of the romantic movement in the early nineteenth century. When the artist was no longer ready to celebrate the dogmas of religious institutions or the official policies of the governing classes, his position became more and more precarious. He was regarded with increasing suspicion. He felt himself estranged from the majority—the source of social approval. This was a hard time for him not only materially but spiritually. No man naturally prefers to live an alien among his fellows.

The artist's defense was, "I am in revolt against the centers of established opinion. They have turned me into a kind of pariah. Very well, I shall be a pariah, cultivate my differences, dwell in an attic, dress and behave in a manner distinct from that of the respectable folk who scorn me and whom I shall now scorn, starve if need be. But I shall persist. If this be madness, I shall nurture my madness and glory in it."

That this summary of a long cultural process is more than a surmise is exemplified in the work of such a master as Thomas Mann, whose *Death in Venice* and other early stories dramatize the artist's inability to cope with society, his morbid sensitivity, his anomalous psychology and behavior. All of which is supposed to explain why a person becomes an artist. Whether this was Mann's last word on the subject I doubt, but, as a description of how many people see the artist, it is not only accurate but by now commonplace.

My criticism of this is first a historical one: the artists in the sturdiest periods of artistic creativity—Greece in the fifth century B.C., the Renaissance, France under Louis XIV—did not think of the artist in this way at all. (Then, and later, the artist who was a general, a senator, a diplomat, a physician, a scientist was not uncommon.) Much more crucial than this, however, is my belief that the whole concept of art as a consequence of some inner disturbance is a distortion of the creative act.

"The nature of man is to know," Aristotle said. Art is a knowing. It arises from our contact with the world outside and within. Life is a challenge from the day of our birth. It is a challenge we accept through every hazard, or we should soon give it up. We face the challenge by a constant effort to understand it, to become, so to speak, intimate with it—to bridge the gap between our individual isolation and everything outside ourselves. The sense of connection we establish through this effort is a source of deep pleasure even if what we discover and the search itself are fraught with anxiety. The most rabid pessimism in art is still an affirmation of life. If it were not, the artist would not trouble to commit his blasphemies to paper, canvas, song or stage.

It is the nature of man, then, to develop and practice the artistic faculty. In this sense, all men are born to be artists. (We observe this in children whose health is judged in the perspective of their play.) The man who is not to some degree endowed with the artistic impulse is a dull, if not a positively maimed one. It is part of the imbalance of our times that we so often view art as an extracurricular activity, marginal to the serious concerns of living, an escape from reality.

"I'm very happy that I had writing as an outlet to my reactions to experience," a playwright recently said in an interview. "Otherwise I would really have gone off my trolley." Hard-pressed in the crisscross of confusions, the modern artist says the right thing. Not to express one's self—the expression need not be professional—not to articulate in some humane fashion what one has witnessed, felt, dreamed happily or apprehensively—that, in the last count, is to be truly unhealthy.

Many artists, in defiance of the indifference or condescension that often surrounds them, may overstate their case, but I am inclined to applaud when Stanislaus Joyce reports that his brother James believed "poets are the repositories of the genuine spiritual life of their race." And if the English critic Cyril Connolly says too much when he writes, "It is the quality of an artist to be more imaginative than his fellow men," it is nonetheless true that we seek this quality in the artist to echo, enhance and extend our sense of life.

If, as I say, art is life-affirming, how to explain to the person who listens, worried or smug, to the artist as he apologizes for his sickness, and who seems thereby to take it for a fact that artists, being artists, must necessarily be sick or, at least, neurotic people?

Before entering a discussion on this phase of the subject, I must begin by voicing serious misgivings about all the terms employed when we speak of "sick" artists as a class. Though there can be no question that many artists are at least as sick as the waiter who is too distracted to remember the dishes we order or the hackie who constantly mistakes the address he is about to drive us to, none of these artists is any more mentally disturbed than the butcher, the baker, the candlestick maker whose irascibility and ineptitude are becoming increasingly evident to the most superficial observer.

Another thing to be noted before we go on to the heart of our discussion is that, with the average neurotic whose inefficiency, rudeness or misdemeanor perturbs us, there is no compensating factor. The sick artist may be a trial to his friends and family but, at worst, his occupation leads to a result which interests or instructs even when it does not produce positive pleasure.

Let us now turn to the "modern" artist, about whom a Viennese doctor, Max Nordau, wrote a book, circa 1890, called *Degeneration,* in which he tried to adduce marks of insanity in such men as the Impressionist painters, Wagner and Ibsen (this book, by the way, was brilliantly refuted in a little-known essay by Bernard Shaw called *The Sanity of Art*).

We may take an indisputably half-psychotic artist like Strindberg as an example. In the sixty-three years of his life, he wrote more than fifty plays, sixteen novels, seven autobiographies and nine other works. He conducted semiscientific experiments, founded a theatre and helped foster dramatic expressionism. Many of his plays—which exercised a considerable influence on Eugene O'Neill—are still produced and read in many parts of Europe. Though this work—all of it beautifully written—veers from the idyllic to the hysterical, from religious exaltation to intellectual rage, the amount of concentrated effort, thought, study expended in producing this work indicates an energy and a creative force far greater than those employed by all the critics who dismissed him as "sick."

Art is *the health* of the artist. Insofar as the artist engages in his art—I do not refer to those who merely hang on to the fringes of the "art world"—the artist is always healthy. Art being a central function of man's life and a prime manifestation of his humanity, the artist is sane as long as he works as an artist. Apart from this work, he shares in the lesions to which all of us are subject. If he is made to appear more damaged than the rest of us, it is because he gets more publicity; the importance of his job makes him an object of greater social concern.

There still remains the problem of those awful, torpid, sordid, morbid plays, novels, etc. These adjectives rarely mean much more than that we do not like what they describe, but to the extent that our dislike is justified, we must remind ourselves that the artist has not created the world into which he is born.

The artist "imitates" nature in a double sense: he reflects society and, through his response to it, helps create a new world—one which may in some way be affected by what he has created. Much so-called negative (pessimistic, destructive) art has a positive purpose and a salutary effect. Can anyone maintain with equanimity that the world we live in today is an entirely smiling or stable one? Show me the person who answers with an unqualified "yes," and I will show you a fool.

Where does the idea come from that a play or any other work of art to justify itself must necessarily be "happy" or "encouraging"? The province of art is the whole range of human experience. Ecclesiastes is as sound Scripture as the Song of Songs. What miserable product of our contemporary dramatists (sometimes referred to as "decadent") matches the horror of the plots of Aeschylus, Sophocles or Euripides? *King Lear,* a black play if ever there was one, is as much a part of Shakespeare's greatness as are any of his comedies.

Our revulsion at certain "morbid" plays is often an unknowing plea for antidotes and narcotics. When the appetite grows for such dramatic sleeping pills—with a generous admixture of sugar—we ourselves become denatured. A quality of sanity is the capacity to endure what is difficult. Hope and faith which shrink from the recognition of evil are merely evasion.

We have heard it whispered, in tones which range from sniggering to indignant, that many of the new actors are "nuts." For that matter, one is often asked, aren't many of the people who are attracted to the theatre crackpots—in some way or other queer? My first impulse in answer to this is "Yes, these people are crazy if they suppose there is enough work to satisfy the needs of all those who would enter the theatre's ranks."

There are two curses in the theatrical (particularly the acting) profession—enough to drive anyone off the deep end: unemployment and the lack of continuity even after merit has been demonstrated. But insofar as acting is an art—and I believe it can be—it, too, shares in art's sanity.

It is true that certain neophytes gravitate toward the stage as a relief from inner pressures, in the expectation of indulging their troubled souls in the theatre's benign masquerade. We cannot blame them for this but, if they succeed in forging a career for themselves, they will learn that the stage, being full of constraints and duties, demands not only real training but arduous discipline. If what finally happens is that they have "sublimated" their personal dilemmas through their craft, we can only agree that they are to be congratulated and the stage blessed for it.

The amateur whose main objective in going into the theatre is self-therapy may arrive but will not long remain there. For every actor who "cures" himself through psychoanalysis in order to be able to function on the stage (I repeat there is nothing wrong in this), I can show you five whose distemper has become controlled or modified because they have made themselves true professionals. One does not enduringly act, write or compose out of mental illness.

The very fact that many of us are inclined to associate the arts with disease is either a sign we know little of the history of the arts or that we live in an environment which is itself tainted. The clamor for "healthy" art in the face of some of the most creative work of our theatre and other arts is frequently a clamor for conformity of the most stuffy sort. Quite apart from the question of dignity and self-respect, the last thing the artist today need do is to apologize either for his vocation or his mental condition. The artist able to work as one is indeed fortunate to be engaged in so wholesome an occupation. Whether he is sick or not, we should all cherish him—as long as he remains an artist, that is, a creator in our society, which wobbles halfway between prayer and destruction.

Clifford Odets, In Memoriam

1963

A REFERENCE to Clifford Odets' *Waiting for Lefty* or *Awake and Sing* is now not so much theatre talk as historical evocation. It recalls the nineteen thirties. It was the era of the Depression and that effort to overcome it, the New Deal. It was the time of bread lines, the shacks the unemployed built called Hoovervilles, the closing of the banks and the spirit of "we have nothing to fear but fear itself."

In the theatre it was the period of the "proletarian" play, the borrowed slogan "art is a weapon" and acting troupes calling themselves "unions" and "collectives." Its shining figure was Clifford Odets. And thereby hangs a certain misunderstanding. The label "left-wing theatre" obscured rather than revealed the nature of the phenomenon.

Plays like *Dinner at Eight, Stage Door, The Children's Hour, The Petrified Forest, Our Town, The Philadelphia Story*—none of them political—were far greater box-office successes than any of the plays dubbed "left-wing."

Waiting for Lefty, first given at special benefit performances off Broadway and given only briefly on Broadway, was not, in the usual sense of the word, a popular play. It was the herald of a mood that dominated the country.

That mood was something more than a political reality. *Lefty* aroused many people, including most of the reviewers, to whom political radicalism of any sort was abhorrent.

The play was a protest against the lethargy induced by the fun and games of a previous prosperity, as well as against the dumbfounded bewilderment of the Wall Street crash and the widespread unemployment that followed.

270

Lefty waved a flag for a renewal of energy; it defied despair in the swinging, singing slang of our big-city streets. Its essential message and its manner were as native to us as jazz, revivalism or, for that matter, Yankee Doodle.

What did most theatregoers, who hailed Odets then, know of taxi strikes and tactics of labor unions? This poster play was not so much a call for a left turn as a summons to youth to bestir itself. Our hearts were lifted high.

In Odets' first full-length play, *Awake and Sing*, old Jacob speaks of Marx and translates him into a series of homely misquotations. Toward the end of the play we learn that Jacob had collected some Marxist literature but none of it had ever been read or even opened.

In *Lefty* Dr. Benjamin speaks of his father with tremulous affection as a man "who's read Spinoza all his life." Though Odets, whose formal education ended after two years at high school, later became a well-read man, he never studied Spinoza and knew hardly anything of Marx—just as he never read Chekhov until after his plays began to be compared to the Russian's.

Spinoza, Marx and such others stood for learning, loftiness and a concern for the underprivileged. Odets knew much more about Victor Hugo's *Les Misérables*.

Though he had a rare and thrilling gift for dialogue, he was no "literary" man. He converted a certain inarticulateness into a tenderly defiant, highly humorous American eloquence. The "comrades" he invokes in *Lefty* are more kin to Walt Whitman's "Camerados" than to Moscow's.

The bulk of Odets' work was self-portrayal. He was an impassioned romantic, what he himself called a "moral idealist." His central theme was the difficulty of attaining maturity in a world where money as a token of success and status plays so dominant a role.

This has very little to do with being a "reformer." His very flesh experienced the lure of those false gods. He struggled against their temptations all his life. He could neither wholly succumb nor yet entirely defeat them.

When little Cleo in *Rocket to the Moon* (the Odets of 1938) describes with touching innocence what she yearns for in a world not yet made, her would-be protector, Mr. Prince, murmurs,

"She's an artist." Cleo corrects him. "I'm a girl and I want to be a woman." The golden boy—Odets—wanted to become a man.

His most successful play, *Golden Boy*, is the dramatization of the Odets dilemma. It is the parable of his career and a prophecy of his fate.

Joe Bonaparte is a pugilist *and* a violinist; he is torn by conflict between the sensibility that might make him an artist and the urge to power or the glamour and clamor of public acclaim.

The fiddle and the fist! Naïve and unlikely as these alternatives seem to be in a literal context, they became pertinent and poignant in Odets' powerful idiom. Bonaparte makes himself a boxer because of his fierce determination to be somebody ("with his name in the papers," as Ralphie in *Awake and Sing* puts it).

When Bonaparte in a bout breaks his hand, the instrument of his talent, he exults in the knowledge that he no longer can meet the challenge of his lyric self. As a champion of the ring, he is reduced to a racketeers' commodity.

While I was working on my book *The Fervent Years* in Hollywood, I told Odets that in it I had written, "for Odets Hollywood is Sin." I laughed as I told him this. "What are you laughing about?" was his rebuke. "It is."

Now think of Charlie Castle and the little floozie of *The Big Knife*, written twelve years after *Golden Boy*. The girl is a confused victim of the Hollywood industry. She is both sordid and pathetic, the best written, the only wholly realized character in the play. She is Odets' female alter ego.

Castle is an inconclusively drawn figure because Odets wavers between the statement that Castle is trapped by the film world's corporate power and an admission that he really loves the lush life that has debilitated his talent.

The Country Girl is a dramatization of self-deception and a cry for help. The actor who has lost his grip and becomes an alcoholic blames his failure on his wife. Only toward the end of the play do we discover that it is she who has saved him from total destruction. What the actor, Odets implies, needs beside his wife's faith and strength is a man who can direct him, someone to keep him firmly on the path of his artistic responsibility.

Most of Odets' work was a confession. He told us of his anguish at sharing those values in our civilization that he despised. He begged for protection from the contaminations against which he always raged and which he realized infected him. Stronger than the sound of torment that rose from his clash by night was the urgency of hope, a belief in ultimate salvation, a desperately noble affirmation of what was purest in himself and the exalted ideals of his race and his country.

Here we find the source of Odets' importance. His work reflected not only his own faltering but the time and place with which he struggled. What was subjective becomes objective. His problem is ours—then and now. His is another American tragedy.

The warmth, the intimacy, the pulsation, the familiar and very personal way Odets expressed that tragedy establish his victory. They contributed to the vocabulary of our time, made our theatre genuinely part of our culture.

The work of many dissimilar playwrights who followed—Tennessee Williams and Arthur Miller, to mention only two—stems in considerable measure from the impetus given our theatre by Odets.

An Odd Hamlet

~~~~~~~~~~~~~~~~~~~~~~~~~~~~~~~~~

1964

I WALKED OUT on John Gielgud's production of *Hamlet*. I had followed it attentively for three hours and I could no more. Not that this was the worst *Hamlet* I had ever seen—far from it—but after witnessing countless productions of the play, I could not take another which, apart from commercial considerations, had so little purpose or reason for being.

Almost as taxing as seeing *Hamlet* again under such circumstances is the irritation of reading comments on its leading actor. For how is one to judge a Hamlet unless some idea is conveyed as to what the play itself is supposed to mean. Do we really know what it means?

It is many different things to different people. The "traditional" or schoolboy's *Hamlet* is the story of a man cursed because "the native hue of resolution is sicklied o'er with the pale cast of thought." While this may be generally true, it explains very little. Hamlet in the play is extraordinarily animated, rashly impulsive, even fierce. (He kills not once, but several times.) He turns on Ophelia in passionate scorn; he enters heedlessly into dueling contests, jumps into graves, terrifies his mother. Inactive? Far too active!

Hamlet is the most "interpreted" figure in literature. Among the interpretations in recent critical writing are those of Ernest Jones, Bertolt Brecht, Francis Fergusson, Lionel Abel. Gordon Craig, who directed the play for the Moscow Art Theatre in 1912, thought the play's action signified a search for the truth in a world of gaudy deception. (He covered all the characters except Hamlet in a sheath of gold.) In Moscow last spring, I saw a note

274

in Craig's hand restating the play's theme as a conflict between the material and the spiritual. Underneath it Stanislavsky had affixed *his* comment: "That is *not* the play."

Hamlet has also been called the first "existentialist" play. Hamlet's dejection, his "nausea" ("How stale, flat and unprofitable seem to me the uses of this world") precede his hearing about the murder of his father and cannot be wholly ascribed to his mother's too hasty remarriage.

One of the most startling interpretations, based on a 1956 production in Krakow, is reported by the Polish critic Jan Kott in his *Shakespeare Our Contemporary.* In the Krakow production of *Hamlet* the play was seen in the murky light of Stalin's Russia! The play became preeminently political. The keynote is "Something is rotten in the state of Denmark"—a line three times repeated. Special emphasis too was laid on "Denmark is a prison." Even the Gravedigger's speech "Now thou dost ill to say the gallows is built stronger than the Church" must be stressed in this altered context.

Everyone in *Hamlet,* Jan Kott writes, is *spying* on everyone else—even the dodo Polonius. "Behind every curtain in the Elsinore palace," he goes on to say, "someone is hiding. . . . Fear gnaws at everything: marriage, love, friendship." This may have been directly relevant to Shakespeare, the critic suggests, for the play was written when the Essex conspiracy against Queen Elizabeth was in the making. In *Hamlet,* Kott continues, everyone talks politics. There is no room for love in such an atmosphere. "When politics displaces all other concerns, it becomes a form of madness."

The various interpretations tend to overlap and merge. So the one just referred to parallels that of Francis Fergusson, who asserts that "the rottenness of Denmark" constitutes the play's central situation. This is faced by two basic postures: that of Hamlet's Renaissance skepticism, which makes him doubt the wisdom or efficacy of revenge, and that of the other prince, Fortinbras, who might be conceived either as a medieval knight or as an ultramodern man who, without metaphysical question, proceeds to get his job or duty done.

I have myself always thought of Hamlet as a passionate person capable of heroic action but "corrupted" by misgivings as to the human worth of such deeds. There is such a confusion of motives in him, because of what he beholds outside and within himself, that though brave enough to undertake anything, he cannot convince himself that any course of action is the just one.

Hamlet is far too rich a work to be wholly clear. (That is why T.S. Eliot accounted it a "failure.") Hence a safe manner to stage it is by way of sheer melodrama, as a glorious showpiece—which may well have been the Elizabethan way. It was certainly Tyrone Guthrie's way in his Minneapolis production. What must never happen with *Hamlet*, if it is to interest us in the theatre, is to produce it in a haphazard, ad-lib fashion. And that is precisely what has occurred in John Gielgud's production.

It is not a "bad" *Hamlet*, but rather no *Hamlet* at all. I was not disturbed or mystified to find the play set in a simulacrum of a New York backstage during rehearsal time, with actors in their work clothes (though the Player King, Queen and their attendants wear costumes). All this may have been intended to show that the play could do without theatrical "trappings," that it is universal. But as the play progressed, with here and there a nice reading and an occasional bright bit of business to illustrate the text—the actors' diction, be it said in commendation, was nearly always intelligible—I could not discern, apart from its plot, what the play was supposed to be about. In what way did it show, as Shakespeare tells us the theatre must, "the very age and body of the time"—except perhaps by its exposure of Broadway opportunism?

We are given little beyond a series of disparate recitations composing no consummate idea or picture. Hume Cronyn's Polonius had its witty points; Alfred Drake's Claudius, within very modest limits, made sense. But the only truly stirring moment is vouchsafed us by the Ghost of Gielgud's voice, which possesses qualities of true characterization, situation, mood and feeling, though I must also add that I detest Hamlet's father taped and sounded on a public address loudspeaker.

I could see little more in Richard Burton than his splendid personal attributes. His voice is powerful: its forte might smash a windowpane; his person is impressively robust, his speech excellent, his readings reasonable, his mask suitably troubled. Yet I could not tell to what creative end this histrionic instrument was being employed. The actor's mind, for all his effort, seemed elsewhere, distracted, as if the challenge of this stupendous role was something he could manage technically but which engaged no part of himself in any profoundly personal sense. As a result, Hamlet's agony and indignation often seemed little more than churlishness. He appeared unhappy enough but not about anything in the play.

Like so many actors today, Burton is now a mere visitor to the stage. Without discipline, without a commanding theatrical structure or institution, without a dominant director, no actor can be used as an artist to the extent of his capacities. There is something "lost," almost tragic, as Burton stands on the stage amid, but distinctly apart from, his fellow actors. He looked altogether uncertain as to whether he wanted to pursue his career as an actor any further.

The Moscow Art Theatre
in New York

~~~~~~~~~~~~~~~~

1965

WE ARE MORE than gratified by the presence at the City Center of 49 members of the 140 who comprise the acting company of the Moscow Art Theatre. But there is in America so little knowledge of the Soviet theatre that it may be useful to note a few facts before entering into any consideration of the four productions the visitors have chosen to present.

We frequently speak of the Moscow Art Theatre as if it were the only Russian troupe in existence. By our standards it is certainly a venerable institution—it was founded in 1898—but the august Maly Theatre has a longer lineage in the Russian realistic style, having first taken root in 1824. It is still sturdy.

Strictly speaking, the Moscow Art Theatre is not without cavil the most widely preferred company of the Soviet capital. Some of the younger theatregoers regard it as a kind of "academy"— highly respectable but no longer representative of the most vital impulses of the moment. When I was in Moscow two years ago I counted twenty or more major theatre organizations playing in repertory and offering three or four different plays every week. The recently formed Contemporary Theatre was favored by the youth; the Vachtangov, the Mayakovsky, the Red Army theatres also had their champions. Several Soviet critics were of the opinion that the most interesting of all Soviet theatres today was the Gorky Theatre in Leningrad. Its leading player, Cherkassov, was held to be the finest living Soviet actor.

I set these items down not to argue a point but to establish a perspective. On my first visits to Moscow in 1934 and 1935 the theatres which attracted me most were the Meyerhold and some of the small "studio" theatres. But that was before an official or state aesthetic had been proclaimed. What I found most stimulating at that time was later attacked as "formalism." In this connection, I might have echoed Jacques Copeau, "father" of the new theatre movements in France, when he said in 1923, on the occasion of the performances given in Paris by Tairov's highly stylized Chamber Theatre and the Moscow Art Theatre, "I am more attracted today to what Taïrov is trying to do than to what Stanislavsky has done, but Taïrov has not achieved perfection; Stanislavsky has." There can be no doubt that the Moscow Art Theatre occupies a central position in the Soviet and perhaps in the world theatre of our time.

The productions in New York are "traditional": they do not exemplify the most typical work of the present-day Moscow Art Theatre—as does, for example, its staging of Tolstoy's *The Fruits of Enlightenment*. (The company's repertory numbers thirty-three plays.) The dramatization of Gogol's *Dead Souls*, which was first presented in 1932, remains pretty much as Stanislavsky left it. (I saw it first in 1935; several members of that cast are acting the same roles here now.) *The Three Sisters*, directed originally in 1901 by the theatre's cofounder Nemirovich-Danchenko, was revised by a "disciple" in 1958. That is also the case with *The Cherry Orchard*. Only Nicolai Pogodin's *Kremlin Chimes* is "new"; it was first directed by Nemirovich-Danchenko during the war and was revised by others in 1956.

Though the present company is less brilliant than the original one seen here in 1923, which contained at least five actors of supreme rank, it is still superb. (The men are generally superior to the women; this was so from the beginning.) All are consummately trained, dedicated and scrupulous craftsmen, mature in fiber, commanding in experience and accomplishment. What is most immediately striking is the company's natural virility.

Yet it is a mistake at this juncture to judge them—as many are prone to do—singly. To engage in such evaluation, we should see them on their own stage in their complete repertory. Here we must view them—as their best performances bid us—as a unit.

For all its vigor, bounce and color, a certain mustiness clings to the production of *Dead Souls*. This may be due in part to the fragmentary nature of Mikhail Bulgakov's adaptation, which, while faithful (except for the ending), makes every scene take on a formal resemblance to the preceding one. This is also true of the novel, but the novel is not only sustained by its narrative line but by Gogol's pithy comments on it. They give the book an epic value, a tragicomic and satiric poetry. *Dead Souls* is not the story of a swindler but a grotesque and heartbroken panorama of Russia. Its central character is not Chichikov but the land itself, contemplated from afar (Gogol wrote the book in Italy) by a wounded member of the "family," derisive and homesick, resentful and hopelessly "hooked" on the place and people whose every idiosyncrasy, enlarged by humorous recollection and spiteful love, he knows as intimately as his own skin and pulse.

Still, the play is fun. (The production here seems to have been reduced by the technical and architectural limitations of the house.) But it is not its frolic which leaves one with the deepest impression but the sense it imparts of the terrible sadness of provincial Russia in the early nineteenth century, cradle of odd characters and inspiration of rebel genius. If the play and its playing (some of it delicious) strike us as "exaggerated" to the point of freakishness, much the same may be said of the book—except, as remarked, that the book gives us a large frame of reference which is lacking in its stage adaptation.

Russia had changed considerably by the end of the nineteenth century but not nearly enough. The educated middle class had a much broader awareness of the dreary backwardness of their country, suffered from it, despaired, often broke down in nervous apathy or wretched nihilism. But at its core there was an undying aspiration, a humanism, which being severely repressed became more thoroughly grounded, more fervent, more truly Christian than any elsewhere extant. It is from this matrix of unhappiness and yearning that Chekhov emerged.

No more telling and touching testimony of the Chekhovian legacy—still rich with generative force—may be found anywhere than in the Moscow Art Theatre production of *The Three Sisters*. In it Chekhov asks the specifically native (but still universally applicable) question "We Russians are peculiarly given to exalted ideas—but why is it we always fall so short in life?" Chekhov does not answer the question (is there an answer?), but the manner in which it is asked in *The Three Sisters* makes it a great play. For the humility, the loving observation, and the embrace of what is most precious in our lives which inform the play, give it a stature far more exalted than its apparent scope.

How quiet is the Moscow Art Theatre production, how delicately quiet. Conventionally speaking, it is "undramatic." Tragedy overtakes all the play's characters; yet it would seem that nothing special happens; everything is done as if part of a humdrum reality. We are in a provincial household with lonely, sweet, surly, silly, warmhearted people, where life runs an almost uneventful course. How dull it all could be. Yet it goes directly to the heart, stirs the soul, moves the mind, braces the spirit.

There are many ways to produce *The Three Sisters*, and there have been hot debates as to which is the right way. Even Stanislavsky and Chekhov were reputedly at odds on the subject. The production in New York is characterized above all by a certain *nobility*—this, without strain, without posturing, without "pathos." There is hardly any sentimentality; there is clearly no neurosis.

All is relaxed. There is barely a climax, a marked stress. The action flows like a slightly eddying river of understandable behavior, of which we never miss the least ripple. One notices a certain carriage or bearing in the actors which makes them immediately impressive. No one is given to eyecatching display. Truculent Solony hardly ever raises his voice. When he leaves the stage, we notice him crumble in grief for an instant and then resume his destructive bent. Vershinin's idealistic speeches are wistful ruminations, spoken conversationally and given body by the character's warmheartedness. Irina dreams with her eyes constantly fixed on some distant horizon. Olga is restrainedly staunch, truly a general's daughter. Masha is not a hysteric. Kuligin is homely, uxorious, honorable, and when affected by truly emotional circumstances he reveals sensibility and perception. He is not bright, but neither is he a fool; he is mediocre, but a man. The aged servants are not comic relief. Andrei is shy and inadequate within an unrealized strength. The doctor is crusty, gone to seed and cynicism with wasted power. Natasha is an obtuse middle-class upstart and hence something of a coquette, not a bitch or a termagant.

One does not think of "pace" in this production—so often emphasized in our journalistic animadversions on direction. If there is "slowness," one is not conscious of it. There are no pauses because the silences—long or short as the case may be—are also action as absorbingly eloquent as the unhurried speech. (There is, for example, the moment during which Masha and Vershinin gaze at each other across a room: it is a truly beautiful love scene.) The attitudes, placement and groupings of the characters are natural, but they all have meaning, tell a "story." They frequently compose pictures which fix themselves in memory as emblems of a period, of a sentiment, of a human stance. Everything is humanly justified and everything adds up to a virtually musical continuity.

Is this realism? Not as we have come to identify it on our stage. Without being larger than life, it is simple conduct so artfully selected that it becomes symbolic and, subtly, grand. Realism has ceased being casual and becomes style with all the dignity we associate with the classic theatre. The actors are people who really live on the stage—a life purified of accidental and personal dross.

If I am overlavish in my praise of the production, as some will surely maintain, what remains? Chekhov remains. Whatever one may think of this or that actor, piece of stage business or theatrical device, *The Three Sisters* at the City Center communicates what is essential: the image of good people, living an unfortunate existence, isolated in social gloom and individual failure, yet somehow bound together by the savorsome substance of their being—their delight in small pleasures, their consanguinity in play, in pain, in longing, in wonder, in the intimacy of their bereavement coupled with their inextinguishable desire for something more, something better, something greater in their lives.

Russians, even more than Americans, are given to examining and identifying themselves. In enthusiasm or rancor, often with a mingling of both, the Russians are endlessly preoccupied with their national destiny. It is a kind of agonized patriotism. This uneasy self-consciousness is symptomatic of a "new" and powerful people aware of their late development among nations. Just at the moment when Gogol was about to reveal his genius—then to be followed by a line of master novelists—the critic Belinsky (1811–48) complained, "Russia has no literature." All this self-accusation is evidence of growth; when self-congratulation sets in there is a decline.

Gogol, in *Dead Souls,* derides his country in anguished and loving laughter. Chekhov weeps softly and gently mocks the sloth of the educated middle class of a later time. Some critics have found a devastating ennui to be the main theme and target of Chekhov's work. But Tolstoy, I believe, has defined ennui as the desire for desire. In this vein I have always thought of Chekhov as the dramatist of yearning. His people long to break their bondage. Their "chains" are largely social-political, but because Chekhov thought of these impedimenta as inevitable burdens of the human condition in general, his stories and plays transcend the limitations of narrowly "sociological" writing.

In *The Three Sisters* the grief and yearnings are at their most intense. *The Cherry Orchard* (Chekhov's last play, written in 1904, three years after *The Three Sisters*) marks a progression to another stage of the Russian saga. It is more "historical" than his previous plays. In it the earlier social implications begin to take more definite shape. While the younger folk of *The Three Sisters* speak of working, in *The Cherry Orchard* one sees a man at work.

By the "historical" aspect of *The Cherry Orchard,* I mean that we see in it four generations: the senile servant Firs (old Russia), who speaks of his release from serfdom as a disaster; the masters of the estate who have developed grace, sensibility and detachment from reality through the legacy of the aristocratic forebears; the burgeoning energy of the merchant Lopakhin, of peasant origin and now of capitalist status; the seedlings of future revolutionary movements in the still fumbling student Trofimov and young Anya, whom he addresses as if he were "above love."

The motor force of the play is certainly Lopakhin. He is possibly in love with the owner of the cherry orchard, Ranevskaya, whom he regretfully but unequivocally removes. How does Chekhov feel about these people? He is understanding and affectionate. He makes us see what is fatuous about Ranevskaya and her brother Gaev but also that they are full of heart and profoundly kind. Lopakhin is bearish without malice, endowed with a coarse drive capable of killing without deliberate intention. The young are aspiring birds, not yet full-fledged, with wings weakened by the heavy air of their environment. Still, they will fly and our hope is in them. Chekhov is a seer, a tender god ready to accept whatever happens in life which, painful though it may be to individuals, is somehow "just."

In the ambiguity of the play—an ambiguity neither mystic nor opaque—lies the cause for the debates as to how it should be staged. It is said that Chekhov thought Stanislavsky had made his characters maudlin and had, indeed, "ruined" his play. Yet, reading the text, one notes how often the stage directions indicate a character weeping. In 1935, when Meyerhold produced several of Chekhov's one-act plays, he called the evening "Thirty-three Faintings." Every time a character became "emotional," he or she fell into a sort of cataleptic spell, accompanied by music with a "dying fall." But the Soviet public remained cold to Meyerhold's comment. (Chekhov had not intended his comedies to be that dispassionate.)

There can be no doubt that Stanislavsky's Chekhov was more sorrowful than certain latter-day readings considered more "advanced." I shall never forget the heartbreak—not without its humor—when Stanislavsky, as Gaev in the original production, reached ineffectually for his handkerchief, then, unable to control himself, burst into tears while bidding his sister and family home farewell. The revised Soviet production, praised by Kenneth Tynan for having blown "the cobwebs off the play," is much more straightforward. The new historical perspective dictates this. Lopakhin becomes very nearly a heroic figure—attractive, immensely forceful, almost elegant, admirable in every respect. After all, he represents the march forward in Russia's development!

The Moscow Art Theatre production at the City Center, like that of *The Three Sisters*, was effortless and infinitely scrupulous, with several excellent performances and, as usual, marked by a feeling for the effect of the whole. There is certainly no "fainting" and very few tears. Yet I suspect that the ground has been pulled from beneath the play. Some of this impression comes from the fact that the Ranevskaya of the occasion strikes one as a solid and sensible bourgeoise, not a touchingly befuddled romantic— soulful, inept and, above all, lost. This Ranevskaya should not run off, as Chekhov has her do, to take care of her moribund and rascally lover in Paris, but settle down comfortably with the reliable and eminently successful Lopakhin. Making Chekhov a thoroughly "positive" dramatist makes him a much blunter one.

Pogodin's *Kremlin Chimes*, written during the war (approximately forty years after *The Cherry Orchard*), does not convey the Russia of the twenties as much as it does the state of contemporary Soviet playwriting. I am not at all contemptuous of it, but I wonder if it is as socially salutary as Soviet authorities presumably believe it to be.

The theme is the Bolshevik attitude toward the old intelligentsia in the early days of the regime. Lenin is made the embodiment of the Soviet position. An electrical engineer, convinced that he is to be discarded by the new government, comes to realize that Lenin is not only eager to make use of, but to honor, the engineer's knowledge and collaboration. He too can help the new Russia.

There is truth in the thesis; to scoff at it is snide and mistaken. The play is encouraging and resolutely good-natured. That it is crude in construction and primitive in characterization are grave faults—faults which are perhaps inevitable under the circumstances of its writing. (Mature drama never appears full blown in any new society.) It is a good thing too that Soviet dramatists devote themselves to what actually concerns the majority of their countrymen in the task of bringing about spiritual and ideological coherence.

What disturbs me in *Kremlin Chimes,* apart from its artistic shortcomings, is that its mode and mood are not entirely the spontaneous outgrowth of a natural sentiment but the product of a prescribed plan. There is more self-criticism in the more recent Soviet plays, but it rarely extends beyond the official demand for optimism—which nearly always ends smacking of complacency. And where complacency persists rot begins.

I would not have Soviet dramatists veer to pessimism. They are not pessimistic any more than are the Soviet people, nor should they be. But a positive view of life is sound only when all that is negative is truly experienced and expressed. That is why the "sad" Chekhov and the bitter Gorky endure and in the end prove socially more invigorating than any of the Soviet plays. Wholesome Americans and staunch adherents of the Soviet system should both learn that nothing is so debilitating as an automatic optimism, good cheer turned out by rote. To be sure, a studied and entrenched pessimism is even worse. Both postures are evasions.

The settings for *Kremlin Chimes* look fatigued; the production has been determinedly trundled about from country to country, to meet routine resistance almost everywhere. The acting, which has some delightful moments in minor parts and highly efficient jobs in the more prominent ones, lacks the firm roots to be found in the other productions. Still, I found the evening engaging and the company's efforts appealing. I looked at it all, not with the eye of the theatre professional (usually removed from all considerations apart from the "art") but with fellow feeling for citizens all over our world where very little is simple enough to be facilely dismissed or innocently received.

Plays and Politics

~~~~~~~~~~

1965

To THE QUESTION "What has the American theatre to say at the present time about the state of American politics?" the answer is "very little." The question which might then more pointedly be put is "Why?" Those who ask either of these questions are usually more interested in politics than in the theatre. Still, they are good questions for people devoted to the theatre to ask themselves. The effort to answer will momentarily make them ponder politics and also induce them to think a little less superficially about the theatre itself.

In any discussion of the theatre, one of the first things to inquire about is the nature of the audience. On Broadway, where most new plays originate in America, the audience never pays less than $2.50 for the poorest seat, and often more than $6.90 for the best. One can hardly call this a representative audience, even in the era of affluence. It excludes most teachers and students, many people in the professions but not in the high income brackets, and what used to be called the "working class." It is an audience of the business community: manufacturers, buyers and moguls of the plushier trades. It demands titillation. Hence musicals and light comedies are almost the only shows which sell out. The economic setup of the New York theatre makes it extremely difficult for plays which do not sell out to return a profit. And what does not make money soon disappears. What is believed likely to disappear does not get produced.

This facile explanation tells less than half the story. To proceed beyond it leads to perilous ground. I have no statistics, but I venture to say that in the main Americans are not genuinely concerned with politics.

The ordinary American might define politics as something to do with elections and graft. He is convinced that China is a menace, that Communism is evil, that taxes are too high, that juvenile delinquency is outrageous, that while the atom bomb is dangerous it is necessary, that our way of life, being the best, must be defended. Politics is something to which one lends oneself for a few minutes a day on TV, or can be disposed of by a cursory glance at the headlines and by gossip about "personalities." Politics is a sort of sport, and no one except a politician devotes himself to it.

This view is understandable, given our history. There have been very few deeply disturbing political events since 1865. Compared to its effects on Europe, the First World War was for us a mere scratch. Such scandals as those of the Harding administration or of the Jimmy Walker regime were jokes. A mere handful of people were aware of the implications of Franco's assault on democratic Spain. To judge by the aspect of our big cities at the time, the Second World War was a happy occasion. We disapproved of fascism because of its bluster, and we heartily disliked the Nazis because they produced sickening sensations in our stomachs. The causes of the war, our own or our Allies' responsibility in its outbreak, were obscure to us.

The Depression of 1929–39 shook us up. For a time we responded politically, although when the crisis passed many of us grew impatient with Roosevelt and his reforms. But the Depression was a condition no one could overlook, and our theatre gave striking evidence of the fact.

Came Eisenhower, the new normalcy and McCarthy. The Senator scared the wits out of us before he destroyed himself, but we have not yet recovered from the infection he spread. For years now, not only political discussion but all discussion of vital issues has been timorous or feeble. Such discussion may lead to dissent. Nowadays we hardly know what to dissent from except such enormities as totalitarianism, the insults of inimical powers, narcotics and teen-age killers. Dissent usually involves criticism of our country, than which there is none better on earth. Dissent, moreover, smacks suspiciously of softness in regard to foreign ideologies. We had enough of that in the thirties.

Today the civil-rights struggle—especially in its painless forms —stirs a great many people. But when prejudice of this stamp is dealt with on the stage it is in a musical like *West Side Story* or in a sentimental play like *A Raisin in the Sun*. Nearly everybody, and especially those who are peculiarly touchy about aesthetics, shudders at the hate in LeRoi Jones' plays. I myself am frightened and mortified by it, but we occasionally need to realize its presence and to see it dramatized in full terror.

We hear that there is a new radicalism in the colleges and among the young who are exasperated by the flatness, the inexpressiveness of our lives. Though the manifestations of this trend are sometimes raw and foolish, it should be viewed as a hopeful sign if it leads to the discipline of study, thought and firmness of conviction. Nerviness is not enough.

The fighting in Vietnam troubles us and we are becoming increasingly vocal about it. The majority of our countrymen react automatically, either approving the government's policy as a matter of simple patriotism, or denouncing it without facing the central issue: whether or not the possible victory of communism in Asia is something that non-Communists are prepared to accept.

If I am only partly right in these assertions, politics as such can hardly be expected to prove a proper subject for American theatrical entertainment. But should I be thought mistaken there are still other phases of the question which the liberal mind often overlooks.

Granted that plays dealing with politics on our stage usually are reduced to such convivial dramatizations of columnist chatter as *The Best Man* or to empty melodrama like the play made from Allen Drury's *Advise and Consent*, one must also recognize that very few political plays of more than momentary value exist in dramatic literature generally. What we sometimes name political plays are plays of social significance or historical plays of broad political application.

Shaw wrote several political plays—*The Apple Cart, Geneva, On the Rocks*—but they are hardly among his best. Shakespeare's histories possess general political meaning, but they are political only by extension and analogy, as is the case with Miller's *The Crucible*, Sherwood's *Abe Lincoln in Illinois*, Kingsley's *The Patriots*. There are also social-political "allegories," written in various veins, like most of Sartre's plays or Genet's *The Balcony* and *The Screens*.

Not long ago a play about the Hiss case was produced on

Broadway but, like most such accounts of recent events, it was an inconsiderable piece. Only the Germans and French have thus far accepted a stage version of the Oppenheimer case. Even Kingsley's dramatization of Koestler's *Darkness at Noon*, cited as the Best Play of the Year 1950–51 by the New York Drama Critics' Circle, remained largely inoperative. I could name several other similar plays, like Maxwell Anderson and Harold Hickerson's *Gods of the Lightning* (about the Sacco-Vanzetti case) or John Wexley's *They Shall Not Die* (about the Scottsboro boys), which flashed by without attracting anything but the most limited attention.

Far more effective than any of these were the documentaries presented by the Federal Theatre Project at low prices—*Triple A Plowed Under* and *One-Third of a Nation*—which produced audience impact through their novel staging and immediacy. But for the popular treatment of topical subjects, the movies and television are more appropriate media. Even Odets' *Waiting for Lefty* (about the taxi drivers' strike in the thirties) proved forceful not because of its political message but because of its colorful idiom and youthful fervor. For the rest, with the exception of his anti-Nazi *Till the Day I Die*, Odets' plays are not political at all but social, akin in this respect to O'Casey's early work.

A social play stems from a particular environment which to a degree is a reflection of a political condition. Chekhov's plays and Shaw's *Heartbreak House* are examples. Osborne's *Look Back in Anger* has English social connotations though its political direction is by no means clear. Gorky's dramatic work, rightly held to be inflammatory in Czarist Russia, was not at all propaganda for a particular party or a guide to an unequivocal political solution.

Since all plays are the products of mores and attitudes common to particular sectors of society and are addressed to a public presumed to be attuned to the dramatists' state of mind, one might maintain that all plays are social. (Even the Ziegfeld *Follies*, I have often said, could be regarded as a mirror of its times.) The reason why the social basis of drama is not more often pointed out is that audiences and reviewers prefer to think of plays wholly in terms of entertainment or, betimes, of art. In this way they avoid the discomfort of dealing with troublesome matters. They want to divorce entertainment (or art) from their daily concerns. The wish is justifiable, since their concerns are often trivial, but by this amputation they frequently rob both entertainment and art of their primary value.

There is a sense in which the theatregoer who seeks relief from his workaday cares is right. The domain of the theatre is universal, nothing human is alien to it; but the most durable and hence most profoundly influential plays are those which transcend their immediate "journalistic" material. What we seek finally in the theatre is an escape—into reality.

Our ordinary activities are dross of transitory interest even to ourselves. What we truly long for is to be transported to some realm of truth, the purest consciousness. This superreality which lifts us above the ordinary traffic of existence is what the theatre (along with the other arts and, some may add, religion) aspires to, and in its greatest and blessedly rare occasions achieves.

What makes Chekhov's plays so touching is not their depiction of the unhappy middle class of Russia at a certain period, but the use he makes of this subject matter. From it he wrings the "music" of idealistic yearning, the aspiration which both torments and elevates the hearts of not particularly bright folk everywhere. What lends stature to Ibsen's *Hedda Gabler* is not so much the psychology of a lady caught between two social classes, but our recognition that we are all a little like her—unable to find any sphere which completely satisfies our innermost needs.

Plays of so-called classic breadth, from Aeschylus to Racine, attain such heights. The better realistic plays of modern times move willy-nilly toward the same goals. Patently social plays, like those of Shaw and Brecht, Büchner's *Danton's Death* or Hauptmann's *The Weavers,* are sustained by a similar afflatus. Political plays, when they are intelligent and honest (Hochhuth's *The Deputy,* page 80), are to be welcomed even when they do not qualify as art. How many plays of any sort do? Still, the annals of drama teach us that specifically political plays seldom reach the loftiest peaks—unless one calls Euripides' *Trojan Women* or Shakespeare's *Julius Caesar* "political."

Nearly all social plays of merit exercise political effect, although the degree or exact orientation of such effects are not always determinable. We may cite such old examples as Beaumarchais' *Marriage of Figaro* as relevant to the French Revolution and Gogol's *The Inspector General* as relevant to all bureaucracies. There is no doubt that the naturalistic plays of the middle and late nineteenth century exerted liberalizing persuasion, first in Germany and Russia, and later in England and France. On the other hand, a sizable portion of the Paris audience just before the Second World War applauded Shakespeare's *Coriolanus* as a reactionary play which others (Brecht, for instance) have interpreted in another sense.

We come now to what for our present purpose is the crucial problem: "How is one to account for the fact," a friend writes me, "that the more dramatic the general political situation becomes, the more intensely private and ingrown are the preoccupations of our more talented playwrights?"

The answer is that the plays referred to in this query, though hardly political, constitute our social drama! There *is* a connection between the theatre and politics. It is sometimes direct and positive, at other times indirect and negative. Today it is mostly negative. The Theatre of the Absurd, seen as a generic phenomenon without judgment as to individual talents, is, whether the writers themselves agree or not, a direct consequence of the social-political climate in most of the "free world." It represents despair and sometimes an oblique protest in regard to the societies from which the plays emerge. They are mockingly bitter outcries signifying a sense of impotence. They present our world as a frightful mess, a ridiculous fraud; a tragic farce. There is nothing left for us to do, they tell us, except to suffer and wait (for what?), jeer and try to avoid hurting anyone, or, in extreme instances, burst the bonds of decorum and reason (which have been of no avail) to find some sado-masochistic "mystical" release. America, they intimate, is smug and hypocritical. Britain's stiff upper lip has gone slack with indecision, France poses in a caricature of grandeur. The Soviet Union abides in a straitjacket; China is a threatening tyranny. According to some of these playwrights it is entirely possible that life itself is no damned good and probably never has been. So they turn their backs on all this and now and then seek repose within some no-man's-land of bleak contemplation or lunacy.

I do not speak in contempt. Today many artist-intellectuals (not to mention others) feel spiritually homeless. They believe themselves deprived of any reliable political, social, religious base. For them all the old faiths are meaningless. That is why in America they appear to take special satisfaction in patronizing

the credulous thirties. Their political posture consists of their refusal to assume any. And, one should add, no wonder. The moral
and political atmosphere of the world is confusing everywhere. It
is easier to assail these new and personally benign nihilists by
argument than to reassure them with concrete proposals. The
most "advanced" among them are trying to formulate an aesthetics of nonart.

Insofar as these impulses represent protestations against all
that is bogus in our society, and if in the process of protest new
means of expression are discovered, this anarchic tendency performs a positive function. But a persistent turning away from the
world ultimately leads to a conformism as dull and debilitating as
complete accommodation.

Very few of the new plays have any action. Indeed, hardly any
of them require it, because they deal with states of being in
which will power has become superfluous. Since most such plays
are based on the assumption that nothing is changeable, they
present characters who never bother to change anything. We
approach the dead end of drama.

To extricate himself from this dilemma the future playwright
must consent to dwell in "error." He must take a walk into the
awful world, get to know it ever more intimately and widely.
What is chiefly wrong with Soviet realism is that it is not sufficiently realistic. It is usually little more than publicity. Still, the
aims of that realism, liberated from officious supervision and Phil-
istine dogma, are healthy. They bid the dramatist make contact
with society, explore the hardships and triumphs of labor, probe
the souls of men and women in the travail of the new civilization
as it is being formed or of the old as it destroys itself. This
tradition gave Russia and the rest of us such writers as Gogol,
Turgenev, Tolstoy, Dostoevsky, Chekhov and Gorky—none of
them literalists—and has still much to offer.

As soon as they have attracted notice through early success,
American playwrights now tend to become encrusted in professional circles and thus rapidly to detach themselves from their
creative sources. They deteriorate into provincials in the sterile
ground of fashionable Broadway intellectual coteries.

When we learn to see ourselves and our neighbors truthfully
against the broadest horizons of human concern, we shall perhaps
not need to clamor for *political* plays; good ones will do.

To the Young

~~~~~~~~~~~

1961

THE GREATEST obstacle to creativity in the American theatre is the stereotyped idea that only numbers and size count, that only mass media are important. Only what is "big" matters, has influence. There are perhaps only a million regular theatre-goers in this country. Mathematically, then, the theatre with us is not a mass medium. But this does not, therefore, mean that the theatre is without social force.

I might, to begin with, adduce the argument that many plays serve as screen material or are assimilated into television shows—thus becoming part of mass entertainment. Such an argument, however, would not be only an evasion, but a falsification of my thesis.

Every valid expression of a fundamental idea relevant to human personality, to society, to objective fact has life in it which will bear fruit—no matter how special, abstruse, eccentric it may at first appear. Einstein's equations—intelligible at first to only a handful of scientists—have revolutionized the twentieth century. The strange conjectures of a Viennese doctor, Freud, have penetrated all our thinking, not only in the fields of psychology and medicine but in education, law, literature. The patterns of obscure and presumably "crazy" artists in Paris are now commonplaces of household and commercial decoration as well as of architecture—even among people who still regard those artists as phonies.

Bernard Shaw's early plays were hardly noticed when they were first presented in tiny London theatres. (One of them, in fact—*Mrs. Warren's Profession*—was suppressed by the police in its first New York production.) More recently a young English

294

actor of no outstanding histrionic ability, John Osborne, wrote a play called *Look Back in Anger* which was given at a smallish off-center theatre in London; it made a whole generation of Englishmen—in and out of the theatre—conscious of a serious change in their country's social character. The name of the play's pivotal figure—Jimmy Porter—has become a sort of byword in Britain. What is first whispered in secret may one day be shouted from the housetops.

The conventional rejoinder to this is that a play is not like a scientific formula, a philosophic doctrine or a new form in one of the other arts. A play will either please at once or expire. This was not true of Chekhov's, Ibsen's or Shaw's plays. Or, more pertinently, take the case of so well-known a play as Sartre's *No Exit*. It was successfully presented in a small theatre in Paris. (Most of Ionesco's plays are still given in small theatres.) *No Exit* was a failure on Broadway (as was another famous European play: Beckett's *Waiting for Godot*). But *No Exit* has been playing ever since in community and college theatres all over our country.

What is really in everyone's mind when people speak of success is profit. That is the crux of the matter. But even the concept of profit should be debated. Where communities support libraries, opera houses, art museums, symphony orchestras—as in most European countries—there are also theatres that produce plays many of which are recognizably unsuited to a large public. These plays are not necessarily dismissed as less significant or less valuable than the more popular ones. In fact many critics on such occasions maintain that these "off-beat" plays are frequently more useful to the community than the others and endeavor to explain the worth of these special plays in the hope that they may someday command a wider audience.

This, you may object, is a foreign instance. We are concerned with our United States. Failure in the theatre with us is viewed not as a disappointment but as a disgrace. The reason for this is that we equate excellence with success, and success with fortune. In a virtuous mood we deny this, contesting instead that we do not produce plays for our individual pleasure and edification alone. To fight this primary principle is to appear misanthropic, undemocratic and, what may be considered even more horrible, impractical!

This is a half-truth that masks our fixation on large numbers and our appetite for money. A noted playwright, when I suggested that he might invest some of his own funds in his play, exclaimed in sincere consternation, "But, Harold, I have only $250,000 in the bank!" To live as a member of the community with the "best," to feel that he need no longer suffer a social inferiority complex, to maintain the self-esteem he had finally achieved, this artist felt he had to possess a very sizable bank account. If his income or savings were to be reduced to, let us say, that of a college professor he might once again count himself an inconsequential citizen. In our theatre we are a little like Willy Loman, the sorry salesman of Arthur Miller's play: we want not only to be liked, but to be well liked.

I do not recommend as an antidote that we reject "popular appeal." The most "revolutionary" playwright wants to gain the sympathy and the plaudits of the widest possible audience. The quest for publication or production denotes a search for allies. The dramatist who denounces his fellow countrymen does so because of some faith he wants them to share. There is a positive—perhaps even a creative—purpose in plays of seemingly destructive intent. They may finally prove salutary.

The cliché that genuine creativity and popular appeal are incompatible or antagonistic concepts is debilitating. It leads not only to bad business but to artistic incompetence. Let no one tell you that it does not matter that a play is poorly written, awkwardly constructed, sloppily produced and acted as long as it has "something to say" or that its aim is artistic superiority rather than mass attractiveness. This is double-talk. On the other hand, I cannot possibly enumerate the number of plays produced every season which are intended to draw the great public but which fail to entertain or elevate—and therefore "flop."

A normal approach to the theatre may be exemplified in certain of my own experiences. In 1938 a play was submitted to me by William Saroyan, to whom I had previously written, encouraging him to turn to the stage. The play he sent me—My Heart's in the Highlands—was by no means a difficult one; if anything, it was oversimple. It was a folk tale—humorous, tender with a loosely articulated ideological point: though the artist may seem an eccentric creature, simple folk need him and will feed him, for he brings them the solace of his music. Some of my colleagues demurred at the idea of our (the Group Theatre's) producing the play because in those days young folk felt that plays had to be "dynamite"! I felt that Saroyan had a fresh talent, he sounded a heartening note in a wryly smiling manner which deserved to be heard.

I was hardheaded about the project. The play had only a wisp of a plot and though delightful might seem far too slight for Broadway. I decided that it should be very economically presented at five special performances. When the play was given, the majority press verdict was highly favorable. The Theatre Guild, which had previously refused to offer the play to its subscribers, now agreed to do so. It ran for six weeks. To me this meant that the play had been a success—though it had made no money.

I counted the play a success because it had pleased many more people than I had supposed would be pleased; it had also encouraged a new playwright, who was to write a more popular play later on; it had introduced a new director, Robert Lewis, a new composer, Paul Bowles, both of whom initiated their eventful careers with this production. In short, I thought of the play in terms of its function for its author and for our theatre. But others who admired the play bemoaned its "failure" in view of the money "lost." That money, by the way, was supplied from a portion of our profits in Odets' *Golden Boy*.

Then, in 1949, there was Carson McCullers' *A Member of the Wedding*, a play which brought acclaim to one of our finest actresses—Julie Harris. No manager wanted to rent us a house for this play; it was sure to be a dud. It had hardly any story: a twelve-year-old girl insists on accompanying her brother on his honeymoon, to become what she called "a member of the wedding." How silly! It was difficult to raise money for such a play— and at that time Broadway production was approximately half as costly as it is now. But we managed to get it on. It was a solid success.

The point in this case is not that I had any foreknowledge of the play's eventual success. (A conjur man knows as much about what will or will not succeed as any Broadway producer!) In fact, I feared a terrible fiasco. But I did believe it a lovely play— and hoped and worked hard to make it as good as it could possibly be. Had it failed I should have been very sorry indeed, but my appreciation of its quality would have remained undiminished—and I would have continued to produce more such "hazardous" plays.

Then again, in 1955, Jean Giraudoux's *There Will Be No War in Troy,* which we called *Tiger at the Gates,* was offered me for direction. The play had been produced successfully in Paris some twenty years before. It had been available in various translations to both English and American producers who professed to admire it. Their excuse for not doing the play was that it was a so-called intellectual and very "talky" play, besides being in the costume of a place and time not ordinarily associated with popular entertainment. We decided to produce the play in London first, where the audience might prove more receptive than a New York audience. The English manager assured us that the contrary was true: Londoners were more backward in regard to such plays than New Yorkers! The play was warmly received in London and most enthusiastically in New York. It ran six months in the latter city— not as long as certain other plays of lesser merit, but it did show a profit. I was not only satisfied, I was elated.

Instead of dwelling on these comparative success stories I shall speak now of an out-and-out failure: a play none of you ever heard of. In 1931 the Group Theatre chose to do a play by that name—about unemployment. It was not a very well-written play, but it dealt with a crucial problem and lent itself to a fine ensemble production. We believed it our duty to produce it. It ran for only nine performances. Brooks Atkinson of *The New York Times* opened his review of it with this statement: "Seldom has a bad play stunned an audience so completely." In his second review, the same critic added " '1931'—is sufficiently forthright in the theatre to upset a playgoer's natural complacence and to make the life of these times more intelligible and vivid."

The failure of this play was personally disheartening. But it inspired the organization of several new off-Broadway ventures whose aim was to present plays of a similar nature. It also paved the way for the cordial reception of some of Odets' later and much more successful plays. This forgotten failure exercised more influence than its brief run would indicate.

To cite a more immediate instance, I should mention what was perhaps the outstanding play of last season in New York: Jack Gelber's *The Connection*—a play about drug addicts. It was not written as a sensational piece—Hollywood fashion. The press, to begin with, dismissed it as altogether negligible. If it had been produced on Broadway it would have closed at once. But it was given in a little off-Broadway theatre by a company calling itself The Living Theatre. The reviewers for the weeklies praised it; the play ran all season and continued to run. The author was sufficiently encouraged to write another play.

The history of Bertolt Brecht's and Kurt Weill's musical play *The Threepenny Opera* is also significant. First produced on Broadway in the early thirties, it died unmourned. Produced in a small off-Broadway theatre six years ago it was acclaimed by everyone—ran for years, while one of its tunes became a leader on the Hit Parade! Later produced in larger houses on the road at necessarily higher prices, it was a failure again.

From all this we may learn that even the terms "success" and "failure" need further examination. The honest and truly devoted craftsman may succeed even in these economically uncertain times. Many of our most respected and successful theatre people have not worked with success in mind so much as with the will to create fine things. And since the theatre at its best has always been the bearer of significant tidings—whether of an emotional, psychological or social character—the theatre cannot fail to exercise considerable influence even in our so-called mass-minded civilization. He who speaks eloquently, truthfully, persistently will finally be heard.

The path is not an easy one; it never has been. What has the playwright who was the great hope of the thirties been doing since 1955? One of the most gifted dramatists since O'Neill, he has written several screenplays—none of them to be classed with the least of his stage plays. My considered opinion is that the writer I speak of has been serving Hollywood not only to make more money than he may be able to earn in the theatre but more particularly because he cannot bear the peculiar psychological embarrassment attendant on Broadway defeat. (Even though, be it noted, none of this writer's plays have ever been fiascoes.) The threat to the talented man on Broadway is not so much poverty as lack of plaudits—that esteem which produces favorable publicity and its by-products.

We are back again at the social phenomenon which is at the root of so many fears and subsequent evils: our ideals are directed toward externals, the glaring, the flashy, the noisy, the multitudinous. Money plus popularity have graduated from being conveniences to the point of conferring "moral" status. Herein lies the secret weapon of conformity.

I hope we never have a depression like that of the thirties. But the anguish of the thirties helped form the Group Theatre and Odets, it helped foster the careers of directors like Strasberg, Kazan and Lewis, and finally those of Tennessee Williams and Arthur Miller. If the theatre, the movies, radio and television were to be struck by another wave of economic hardship, they would not go under: they would shrink and become more modest with consequences which might ultimately prove beneficial. There is already evidence of this in the rise of independent movies. The growth of the off-Broadway theatre movement, the extension of community and college theatres, the development of new theatre groups in San Francisco, Washington, Texas may be harbingers of renewal.

The difficulty for the creator in the New York theatre is that production has become terribly expensive, the cost of tickets too high and nothing but smash hits—plays which fill the house immediately after the opening and for a long time afterward—can survive. In London, where tickets today cost exactly what they did before the war, a play which can only fill two-thirds of the house may prove profitable. In New York this is virtually impossible.

This condition fills everyone who works in our theatre with an agony of fear. The game is to the bold, but the boldness now in demand is the speculator's rather than the artist's—so much so that while it is greatly to the credit of the producer and the cast of Ionesco's provocative play *Rhinoceros* to have done it on Broadway, I believe it might have been wiser to have done it elsewhere. Less profits would have accrued to all concerned from such a production, but my guess is that despite a largely favorable press there will be little profit on Broadway to the producer and, in a sense, less honor, because fewer people to whom the play would mean something beyond an evening's fun will be able to see it at Broadway prices.

That is the paradox and the dilemma: if you play for the high stakes of Broadway success—in terms of money—you are limiting yourself in a cultural sense. Your audiences are likely to be less representative of the more serious public. Many of the most significant writers of our time are bad bets commercially under present economic circumstances.

Shakespeare without stars is impossible now on Broadway; so, generally speaking, are Shaw, Ibsen, Pirandello, O'Casey and most of the other classic dramatists. So are nearly most "gloomy" plays. (*The Visit*, a rather "shocking" play, was sustained by the glamour of the Lunts.) Indeed, when we speak of such plays we strike a sore spot of the American theatre.

You may have heard it said that any criticism of our country's procedures, customs, manners or morals lessens its prestige. I doubt the truth of the allegation; Europeans like us best when we do not declare ourselves superior in every way. Boastfulness, even a too resounding pride, gives the impression of complacency—particularly resented when evident in the fortunate. But it is more or less established fact in theatre history since Ibsen that plays critical of the dramatist's native culture have been the most important plays of their time. In America, many of our acknowledged best plays, beginning with Eugene O'Neill, have been "troublesome." As a young and very lucky people it is hard for us to accept what we call the "downbeat." Tragedy is associated in our minds with remote people and epochs: the Greeks, the Elizabethans, the Russians, the Scandinavians.

Despite the success (off-Broadway!) of O'Neill's *The Iceman Cometh*, of Miller's *Death of a Salesman*, of Williams' *A Streetcar Named Desire*, we want our "sad" plays nowadays to possess the sweet balm of Wilder's *Our Town*—which be it noted is situated in a rural vicinity of another era. This peculiarity of ours may not in itself be a vice—though the inability to be objective about pain and evil is not a sign of health—but it does add to our difficulty in presenting somber, bitter or controversial plays on Broadway. Such plays are not necessarily good or "artistic"; but when we shun plays simply on the grounds that they are grim (like the man who left the theatre indignantly five minutes after the curtain rose on Arthur Miller's *All My Sons* when he realized that it was not a comedy) we are perilously close to artistic inanity. The result is the prevalence today of musicals.

Some of the best plays now being written abroad and, to a certain extent, here are declarations of pain of one kind or another. For our theatre to remain vital and to exercise a broad influence it must allow room for such plays. Free speech in the theatre as elsewhere is the surest guarantee of a sane polity.

Some American playwrights have known how to combine the serious statement of major themes with something akin to our popular tradition. This might be said of Thornton Wilder's *The Skin of Our Teeth*, for instance—written with a view to our war-time situation. One of Eugene O'Neill's objectives, I believe, was to encompass the history of America's spiritual struggles in plays with simple, strong plots. Steinbeck's *Of Mice and Men* and Saroyan's *The Time of Your Life* also represent worthy attempts to speak subtly in a folk vein.

We must never abandon the task of essential creation despite all the obstacles in the way. Our very difficulties may force a solution. The problem should not resolve itself to a choice between writing down to the mass audience or shunning it. The answers lie within the conscience, tenacity, fortitude and skill of individual artists. Each man must learn what he wishes to say and work very hard to say it in the manner most compatible with his spirit, taste and inclination. But a resolute objectivity is required; if what results from one's impulse is a play which seems most suited to a small public it is foolhardy to insist that a great public embrace it. Nor, as I have tried to remind you, is the work enjoyed by a small public futile in terms of mass influence. Sooner or later in one way or another the mass will absorb it. The good popular playwright is as devoted to his work and as industrious as the esoteric playwright. Perhaps the musical *Guys and Dolls* says as much about certain phases of big-city life as certain more earnest entertainments.

The so-called masses contain many publics. The practical problem before us is how to reach the right public for each kind of play. The Federal Theatre Project sought and found new audiences all over our country. The warm welcome to Shakespeare in New York's Central Park is another significant sign. The success of plays like Williams' *Summer and Smoke*, O'Neill's *The Iceman Cometh*, Giraudoux's *Tiger at the Gates*, Eliot's *The Cocktail Party*, Fry's *The Lady's Not For Burning*, when presented under the auspices best suited to them, is also evidence that we need not think of the public as one undifferentiated mass.

Our newspaper and weekly drama critics have of recent years become more receptive to novelty and originality. Although very few critics have assumed the responsibilities of leadership—in the sense that Bernard Shaw as a critic did—some of them give evidence these days of wishing to be of service to the larger and permanent concerns of the theatre. Their hearts at least are in the right place.

Ours is not an altogether homogeneous society. It is difficult to interest everyone in precisely the same way. The only exceptions to this rule may occur at times of national crisis, such as war or a natural catastrophe which affects the whole community. Plays at such times tend to become documentary, propagandistic, overly sentimental. Motion pictures and television usually treat topical material with more immediate effect than the theatre. The theatre in relation to these other media is as verse to prose. The theatre is, so to speak, the "metaphysics" of the news. Plays like *Sunrise at Campobello* and muscials like *Fiorello!* are chromos of popular legend: they have value as reminiscence after the fashion of campfire songs.

My message to young people in the theatre today is more than ever "To thine own self be true." In a way the mass you seek to please does not exist—only people do. The "mass" has no face; it is therefore largely inhuman. Discipline yourselves to speak from your heart and from your mind, that is, from your own experience, to the people who have provided you with the ground and framework of that experience. The more scrupulous your effort to make the passage from your conscience and consciousness to theirs the more successful you will eventually be—in whatever way is most important to you. In short, every decade the childrens' call must be raised anew: "Come out! Come out! Wherever you are!"

INDEX

Clurman.

The naked image; observations
on the modern theatre.